Praise for *Game Theory and the Tr*

"Integrates social science with game [theory] for reaching optimal outcomes in settlement negotiations. With the suggested procedures, the most contentious custody issues will be easier to manage. The recommended processes remove incentives for intractable conflicts while helping attorneys and mediators arm parents with the skills and mindset to keep future differences from escalating to full-fledged disputes. A unique and creative contribution to family law."

—**Dr. Richard A. Warshak**, author of *Divorce Poison: How to Protect Your Family from Bad-mouthing and Brainwashing*; Clinical Professor, University of Texas Southwestern Medical Center

"Our system definitely has flaws. This book offers up some very interesting ideas on how to solve the problems in that system. Hard to disregard this book."

—**Ike Vanden Eykel, Esq.** Firm CEO and Managing Shareholder, KoonsFuller, P.C., Dallas, Texas

"Think settling a divorce case is easy? It might be if there are no major issues involved. Otherwise, getting two people highly emotionally involved with each other to agree on every issue from children to money requires a great deal of skill. Fortunately, for divorce lawyers, there is a field of study available to help. Unfortunately, most divorce lawyers are not aware of this field or how it can help. The field is 'game theory,' and its application to divorce negotiations is remarkable. Now, a new book by a psychologist, Kenneth H. Waldron, and a divorce lawyer, Allan R. Koritzinsky, discusses the concept of game theory and its application to divorce. This book is must reading for every lawyer involved in this field."

—**Gregg Herman, Esq.**, Certified specialist in family law by NBTA, Loeb & Herman S.C., Milwaukee, Wisconsin

"Good family lawyers are problem solvers, sometimes having to resolve complex, problematical financial and parental disputes between high conflict adversarial parties. This book is a useful tool in aiding lawyers and mediators reach optimal results leading to settlement of the parties' differences in a way that will have lifetime positive effects for all members of the family. There are no better words that a family lawyer can hear from a former client years after the divorce is final than 'Thank you. You made a difference in my life.' This book and the game theory philosophy enhance the chances for that result."

—**Leonard Karp, Esq.**, shareholder Karp & Weiss, P.C., Tucson, Arizona and co-author with psychologist wife, Dr. Cheryl L. Karp, of *Domestic Torts—Family Conflict, Violence and Spousal Abuse*

"Waldron and Koritzinsky have written a gem for anyone interested in conflict theory, family conflict, and divorce in particular. Taking a sophisticated approach to the analysis and application of game theory to divorce, they provide a powerful explanation of how divorce procedures are set up to increase conflict and how they can be altered to produce more effective, durable, and constructive outcomes. They provide a sophisticated conceptual analysis and at the same time an immensely practical approach to the overall process of divorce and to the specific issues that divorcees face. In the process, they make a significant contribution to our overall understanding of conflict and conflict intervention. I really liked the book."

—**Bernie Mayer, Ph.D.**, Professor of Dispute Resolution, The Werner Institute, Creighton University, author of *The Conflict Paradox*

"The authors have given an intriguing analysis of why today's family laws – structured to be fair and equal – actually *discourage* settlement and *encourage* litigation. They go on to explain the game-like nature of bargaining over many divorce issues, and the potential influence of the court on negotiation strategy. Lastly, they show some ways that the game of divorce negotiations may be modified and designed by the lawyers and parties to be more cooperative and effective in accomplishing both parties' interests."

—**William A. Eddy, LCSW, Esq.**, President, High Conflict Institute, co-Author, *It's All Your Fault at Work*

"*Game Theory and the Transformation of Family Law* by family law attorney Allan R. Koritzinsky and psychologist Kenneth H. Waldron is a must read for any family law attorney who is interested in assisting the client in reaching fair solutions in divorce cases. The family law attorney cannot directly say to the client, "This is a game I would like you to play with your spouse" to resolve your custody and financial issues, because the attorney will hear "this is not a game to me". However, artfully directed advice to the client, using the Game Theory techniques so well developed in this book, will defuse the anger generally present in most divorces and will help the parties and their children go separate ways successfully, instead of building mistrust and increasing conflicts. Having practiced family law for over 50 years, and having negotiated hundreds of settlements, the techniques learned from this excellent book will provide me more structure and insights regarding future settlements."

—**Daniel J. Jaffe,** Founding Partner, Jaffe and Clemens, Beverly Hills, California

"This book raises the reader's consciousness to the danger of unintended consequences arising from seemingly rational decisions. Those unintended consequences may result in hurting rather than helping the person making the decision. The authors posit a formulaic approach to decision- making in order to maximize an optimum result and avoid unintended consequences. Whether one buys into the use of formulas, matrimonial lawyers reading this book will surely broaden their thinking when considering strategic or tactical decisions and thereby better advise their clients. The book suggests a sensible big picture approach for resolving divorce cases in a problem-solving manner and contrasts that to hardball negotiations and expensive litigation where both sides are trying to gain unwarranted advantages. I recommend this book to any matrimonial lawyer."

—**Donald C. Schiller,** Senior Partner and Chairman of Schiller DuCanto & Fleck LLP, Chicago, Illinois

"Divorce is one of life's most difficult events, following closely the trauma, pain and anger experienced by people who lost a spouse or a child by death. Attorneys, therapists, the court system, and many other professionals have attempted for years to properly address the challenging negatives experienced by divorcing parties. Many cases result in permanent scars and ongoing anger, which negatively impact the divorcing parties, their children, other family members and other individuals and businesses, which are negatively impacted by the divorce process and the results of that process.

In my almost half a century of divorce practice, I and the attorneys and other professionals helping divorcing parties have been seeking ways to improve the methodology and the process. We sought to reduce the personal and financial cost to the parties and everyone else involved in divorces.

Over the years, we made modest improvements, such as requiring mediation, other court-ordered efforts to resolve the disputes, involvement of psychologists and other helpful professionals. Unfortunately, we have not been able to overcome the many harmful and costly negatives created by emotional and financial impacts of divorce.

After many years of analysis, testing and creation, the book, *Game Theory and the Transformation of Family Law*, written by attorney Allan R. Koritzinsky and psychologist Kenneth H. Waldron, has been completed and will make a dramatic positive impact to divorce cases throughout the United States and beyond.

This outstanding and creative methodology tool will enable the professionals involved in divorce and the courts to educate clients how to apply a new way of resolving the many issues involved in a divorce case. It will have a remarkable and positive impact, reversing the negatives of divorce, which have been in place for decades. The creative and simple processes create a new methodology which will dramatically and positively impact the entire divorce process. Simply stated, this outstanding creation will result in needed improvements in reaching fair agreements and will reduce dramatically the personal and financial costs incurred by divorcing parties and others negatively impacted by the divorce.

The many professionals helping in divorce cases will be educated by the new methodologies created and taught in the book. They will then teach the divorcing parties. This will enable the parties to apply the game theories to reach settlement much faster and at lower costs. It will reduce the negative costs in money, relationships, psychological impact and other negatives associated with divorce. The effect of the application of the methodologies contained in the book will dramatically improve the divorce process for all who are involved in it.

If applied correctly, *Game Theory and the Transformation of Family Law* is similar to the discovery and application of penicillin, with similar dramatic improvements to people's lives."

—Edward L. Winer, Retired Partner, Moss & Barnett, Minneapolis, Minnesota

Game Theory and the Transformation of Family Law

A New Bargaining Model
for Attorneys and Mediators
to Optimize Outcomes
for Divorcing Parties

Kenneth H. Waldron, PhD
and
Allan R. Koritzinsky, JD

UNHOOKED BOOKS
an imprint of High Conflict Institute Press
Scottsdale, Arizona
2015

Publisher's Note

This publication is designed to provide accurate and authoritative information about the subject matters covered. It is sold with the understanding that neither the authors nor publisher are rendering legal, mental health, medical, or other professional services, either directly or indirectly. If expert assistance, legal services, or counseling is needed, the services of a competent professional should be sought. Neither the authors nor the publisher shall be liable or responsible for any loss or damage allegedly arising as a consequence of your use or application of any information or suggestions in this book.

Nothing in this book is to be considered as the rendering of legal advice for specific cases, and readers are responsible for obtaining such advice from their own legal counsel. This book is intended for educational and informational purposes only.

Cover design by Gordan Blazevik
Interior layout by Jeffrey Fuller

Printed in the United States of America

Foreword

Millennia ago, one or more of our ancestors figured that there must be a better way to resolve disputes than hitting each other over the head with clubs and killing each other's brothers, sisters, spouses, children, and friends. So they invented a legal system. Elders negotiated disputes. After a while the elders became judges. I am both an elder and a judge. After spending many years as the guardian in the Cook County, Illinois, system, I became a Cook County Illinois judge and am currently on the family law bench.

In this newly evolved legal system, pretty soon litigants discovered that some of their friends were better at advocating their cause, so lawyer-type people evolved. Now, we have judges and lawyers to resolve human disputes. Was this new system an art or a science?

Medicine is both an art and science. A malignant tumor is a malignant tumor and whether it can be dealt with depends upon the nature of the malignancy and skill of the practitioner. Our justice system is neither art nor science but a microcosm of the human condition, messy and unpredictable. Laws are created by imperfect, at times avaricious human beings, to be interpreted by other human beings who may be smart, industrious, and insightful or not very smart, not very industrious, and not very insightful. These judges sift through facts which seldom are black and white but usually various hues of gray, presented by lawyers, some of whom are good, some of whom are bad, and most of whom are in between.

Despite being mired in the human condition, or perhaps because it is, the legal system does work on most occasions. However, it works best when resolving otherwise irresolvable non–family law disputes. Our jurisprudential system frequently falters when trying to sort out the emotional complexities and frequent irrationality of two people attempting to dissolve their marriage.

It is not surprising that individuals embroiled in divorce cases frequently act irrationally. They are hurt. They are angry. And they are often hurt and angry for a rational reason. Their partner is just that: a partner. Yet they have shared much more than partners who own a business, for instance. Often they have shared life's most treasured intimacies: a first kiss; a longing; a desire to be in the company of the other; an intense infatuation; a deep physical and spiritual love; sex, wild, unbridled, lustful, tender, quiet, and romantic; sometimes pregnancy; childbirth; naming this new human being; protecting and nurturing a newborn, a toddler, a child; working together to straighten out finances, to buy a car, a home. Then discord sets in, pain, arguments, dealing together with exigencies, crises. A relationship that began between two partners, companions, lovers, and parents moves toward the end with the loss of empathic compassion and the presence of hostility and contempt.

Some people going through a divorce are troubled and irrational to begin with. For years, sometimes decades, they spend enormous energy, time, and expense to "get even" with their partner. They will consciously use everything at their disposal, including children, to stick it to that man or woman. Several times a month I caution a parent that his or her behavior will cause his or her child enormous emotional turmoil and pain not only in the present, but also much more egregiously in the future. I can almost see the wheels turning in the litigant's head: "I don't care, as long as it hurts my former partner." There is very little that can be done with these people, except to try to curtail their time with their children.

Most people enduring a divorce are decent and rational individuals who, because of the circumstances, are placed under enormous stress that not infrequently causes them to act out in a most irrational manner. When I caution these individuals that their actions could be causing their children grave emotional distress, both now and in the future, they recoil. I think that I know what they are thinking: "The judge is wrong. I would never, either consciously or unconsciously, harm my child." They are sincere and would pass a lie box on the issue. But their conflict continues because they do not believe that their conduct will cause any harm. Indeed, they rationalize their conduct by believing they are actually protecting the child or children from the bad partner.

World War I caused the deaths of almost ten million human beings. Its truce led to World War II and the deaths of tens of millions more. There is much to show that World War I was the most avoidable of wars. Leaders permitted themselves to be dragged into the conflagration because of past slights and irrational allegiances and because they relied on the advice of generals whose profession encouraged war. The generals assured the leaders that a war would be short and their side would be victorious.

Divorce cases are not dissimilar. War is imminent. The parties consult with lawyers whose livelihood depends on discord. Their training is in protecting a client through the vicissitudes of battle. Lawyers presume dispute and aim at protecting their client, trying to gain as much as possible while minimizing the losses.

Dr. Kenneth Waldron, a psychologist who for over thirty years has worked in this arena, conducting research, testifying in divorce cases, providing co-parenting counseling; publishing and presenting worldwide and developing court-related parent education programs, and Allan Koritzinsky, an attorney who for over forty-five years has represented individuals in divorce cases, provided mediation and arbitration services, and published important legal works, have written an insightful book, this book.

"Enough is enough," they, in effect, write. The legal system can be better than this; it can serve vulnerable people and families better than this.

More important, these authors do much more than criticize our present system. Introducing the well-researched field of game theory, they distill principles using formulas that have been honored by Nobel prizes. They propose a system that, in many cases, could vitiate the discord and create a more rational approach to deal with an otherwise irrational human event. They provide a comprehensive approach to divorce negotiations that takes the "dispute" out of dispute resolution and achieves optimal outcomes not only for both of the litigants, but also for the children in those families. Perhaps most remarkable, they propose a system that does not require an overhaul of legislative laws, case law, or even local rules. What they propose is more dependent on a shift in the attitudes and practices of the professionals, especially the lawyers, involved.

My response to this book is, "Yes, we can do better; we can serve these people and their children better." This comprehensive book looks at all facets of divorce and provides lawyers, mediators, and the legal system with a science-based roadmap to achieving optimal outcomes for divorcing spouses and families when there are children.

— Judge Patrick Murphy
Cook County, Illinois

Mini-Review

Veteran psychologist Kenneth Waldron and long-respected divorce lawyer Allan Koritzinsky suggest nothing less than a complete paradigm shift in thinking about divorcing parents. Using academic and mathematics-based game theory principles, they write that the "system" and divorce lawyers unintentionally foment increased conflict and litigation. It is well worth the effort to read and understand how game *theory* can improve outcomes in *practice*, where attorneys and mediators can guide divorcing parents toward a long-term, goal-setting process that values the well-being of their children over other perceived personal gains.

— **Angela B. Bartell,** Bartell Dispute Services, Madison, Wisconsin, retired judge and family mediator and arbitrator

Contents

About the Authors ii

Acknowledgments and How it All Began v

Introduction 1

Chapter 1:
A Primer On Game Theory Principles 27

Chapter 2:
Game Theory Principles And The Divorce Game—General 65

Chapter 3:
Traditional Divorce Analyzed 107

Chapter 4:
Game Theory: Applied To Custody, Residential Placement
Schedules And Co-parenting 121

Chapter 5:
Game Theory: Applied To Property Division And Support 175

Chapter 6:
Game Theory: Advanced Topics 215

Chapter 7:
Game Theory: Procedures For Decision Making, Solving
Problems And Concerns, And Resolving Conflicts 271

Chapter 8: Checklists
Putting A New Way of Thinking into Practice 297
Child Planning Game 301
Financial Planning Game 304

Glossary 309

Word Index 313

About the Authors

Kenneth H. Waldron

Kenneth H. Waldron, PhD, currently works at Monona Mediation and Counseling in Monona, Wisconsin. He was trained as a child psychologist, specializing in child and adolescent psychology and adoptions. He was trained in divorce mediation in the late 1970s and began working with families in the context of the family law arena. By 1985, he had a practice devoted solely to family law work. He performed custody evaluations for several jurisdictions in California, developed a mediation practice, and also developed one of the early parent education programs. He also developed a treatment model for co-parenting counseling, which over time has expanded to include specialty treatment programs for unique problems, such as parent-child estrangement. He helped establish the parent education program in Madison, Wisconsin, and helped design and establish a group co-parenting counseling program in Illinois. He has served as an expert witness in numerous states and in Canada, both as a family evaluator and as an expert on social science research related to divorce. He has been trained in collaborative divorce as a child specialist and coach.

Dr. Waldron has presented on topics related to families with divorced/separated parents in jurisdictions around the United States to lawyers, judges, mediators, and mental health practitioners. He has regularly presented to students at the University of Wisconsin Law School. He has published in both local and nationwide journals on various topics related to children of divorce and has published books on parent education and the effects of divorce on children.

Dr. Waldron is a founding member of the Wisconsin chapter of the Association of Family and Conciliation Courts (AFCC) and is currently on the chapter's board. He has also served on the board of the Wisconsin Inter-professional Committee on Divorce. His current practice is devoted to serving as court-appointed expert, performing custody evaluations, and testifying to social science research, divorce mediation, co-parenting counseling, and specialty counseling for problems associated with divorce.

Contact information:

Kenneth H. Waldron, PhD
Monona Mediation and Counseling LLC
6320 Monona Road, Suite 314
Monona, WI 53716
Office: 608-442-3420
kenneth.waldron13@gmail.com

Allan R. Koritzinsky

Allan R. Koritzinsky, JD, is a retired partner with Foley & Lardner LLP and was a member of the General Commercial Litigation, Tax & Individual Planning and Estates & Trusts Practice Teams. He was also the chair of the law firm's Family Law Team.

As a family law attorney representing individual clients for over forty-five years, Mr. Koritzinsky focused on divorce law, alternative dispute resolution, and, with colleagues, worked in estate and business planning and real estate transactions. He also had experience in tax, valuation, and fiduciary litigation matters.

A native of Wisconsin, Mr. Koritzinsky earned his undergraduate degree in history and his law degree from the University of Wisconsin–Madison. He is admitted to practice law before the United States District Court for the Eastern and Western Districts of Wisconsin; United States Courts of Military Review and Appeals in Washington, DC; the United States Seventh Circuit Court of Appeals; and the United States Supreme Court.

Mr. Koritzinsky was active in the following professional organizations: Fellow of the American Academy of Matrimonial Lawyers (AAML) (1977–2009); Diplomat in the American College of Family Trial Lawyers (1977–2009); Member of the national AAML Board of Governors (1994–1997); former National Chair of the AAML Arbitration Committee and a Past President of the Academy's Wisconsin Chapter; former Chair of the Dane County Bar Case Mediation Program; named a Wisconsin Super Lawyer (*Law & Politics Media, Inc.*), 2005– 2008; and listed in *The Best Lawyers in America* for over twenty-five years. Mr. Koritzinsky was the 2011 recipient of the State Bar of Wisconsin Senior Lawyers Division Leonard L. Loeb Award for "important contributions . . . made to your clients and to your community through your legal expertise and personal dedication."

Mr. Koritzinsky has authored or co-authored numerous articles and books and lectured in lawyer and judicial continuing education seminars throughout his career. He was also a Lecturer/Instructor at the University of Wisconsin Law School, teaching Evidence, Civil Procedure, Alternative Dispute Resolution, and Real Estate. While in Viet Nam (1967–1968), he taught full semester courses in Comparative Law and Introduction to American Law at the University of Saigon Law School.

Mr. Koritzinsky retired from Foley & Lardner LLP (1994–2009) on February 1, 2009. Since retirement, through Allan R. Koritzinsky, LLC, he has been doing family law consulting and mediation-arbitration work, as well as working as a business and real estate consultant and acting as a co-trustee of a generation-skipping trust.

Contact Information:

Allan R. Koritzinsky, JD
Allan R. Koritzinsky, LLC
3815 Signature Drive
Middleton, WI 53562-2387
Phone: 608.770.4275
Fax: 608.828.9395
allankoritzinsky@gmail.com

Acknowledgments

How It All Began

In 1995, I was having lunch with a friend and fellow psychologist, Steve Seaman, who had excitedly reported that he read a book about John Nash, the famous mathematician and game theorist. I knew nothing about game theory. I was trained as a child psychologist, but through a series of coincidences, my practice had drifted into family law. I was trained in the late 1970s in divorce mediation, and in the 1980s became increasingly involved in performing custody evaluations for courts. By 1985, my entire practice was devoted to some aspect of working with families in which the parents were going through or had gone through a divorce, or at least a separation. (Paternity cases were not as common then as now.) I provided parent education groups for parents in conflict and co-parenting counseling for those who were having trouble working cooperatively with one another. I continued to do custody evaluations.

It was apparent to me, as it is to most professionals working in the legal arena of family law, that there is something wrong with how the dissolution of marriages is handled in the legal system. However, it was difficult to put my finger on exactly what was wrong. What I was most struck with, however, was how spouses engaged in such self-defeating behavior not only while going through the divorce but also years after the divorce was over. I realized that some spouses are simply troubled people who have difficulty with most parts of their life, so it was no surprise that they would have trouble during and after a divorce. I also saw instances in which spouses behaved constructively with one another and with their children, regardless of good legal advice to do otherwise. But there was a large group of spouses/parents who were not troubled but behaved in ways that harmed their children and even themselves. I tried to help by offering parent education classes and co-parenting counseling. Sometimes it made a difference, and sometimes people continued with their self-defeating behavior patterns. I was puzzled by this irrational behavior from otherwise rational people.

Steve Seaman showed me an example of game theory on a napkin—the "prisoner's dilemma," one of the more easily comprehended examples of a game theory principle. The example demonstrated that if a situation is set up properly, rational people behaving in their self-interest will make self-defeating choices. My mind began clicking away. It suddenly occurred to me that perhaps people who were behaving in self-defeating ways as they were going through a divorce were in fact making logical choices—meaning that their behavior could be explained.

Steve learned years later what he had set in motion with his little drawing on a napkin. I immediately obtained and read the book about John Nash, which was later made into a movie, which I also saw. I then began searching bookstores for anything I could find on game theory. I read, I studied, and I struggled to learn the complex mathematics involved. As I did, a curtain lifted and I began to understand the problematic fit between how the legal system addresses the dissolution of marriages and the spouses and families involved. When I began to incorporate game theory principles into my mediation and co-parenting counseling, my success rates dramatically improved.

The Game Theory Team Evolved

In 1997 or 1998, at another lunch with another friend, family law attorney Allan Koritzinsky, we discussed various aspects of divorce and, slightly embarrassed by my geekiness, I spoke of my hobby with game theory and a little about how I was incorporating it into my work. That set into motion the next stage leading to this book. He and I eventually teamed up with another psychologist, Michael Spierer (and later a journalist, Patricia Simms), and we developed a comprehensive system called "DivorceMapping™," which focused on a number of different aspects of divorce. My part was the application of game theory to divorce, Allan addressed the legal aspects of divorce, and Mike focused on dealing with problematic people with personality disorders. Pat assisted us with the editing. We met regularly, created a system, presented on it in several locations, and eventually posted the system on an accessible website.

Then I decided to write this book. I give this history because, although I am the principal author of this book, the ideas in it are not entirely mine. Sir Isaac Newton once said (paraphrased): although his ideas seem original, he was standing on the shoulders of men who had come before him. He captured a great truth: ideas build on one another and take shape with many influences. The ideas in this book come from many books I have read about game theory, too many to even remember who said what; from years of experience working in the family law legal arena, including the many comments of other professionals I have met, including attorneys and judges; but most of all, from the insightful interactions with my dear friend Allan. Allan not only added to the ideas, but also has a knack for asking questions that force one to think something through and clarify. His thoughtful curiosity helped crystallize the ideas that form the substance of this book. Although I wrote this book, the content is honestly the product of group think with Allan, and therefore, he is as much an author as I am, something for which I am deeply grateful.

Two people also read earlier drafts and contributed invaluable comments, Judge Patrick Murphy, who also provided a forward to the book, and Carolyn Bennett, Wisconsin Bar Association. Others were so kind as to wade through this material and offer their endorsement. To all of these good friends, we offer a deeply felt thank you.

— Ken Waldron and Allan Koritzinsky

P.S. After co-authoring this book, I now imagine a conversation, going back to 1994 when I joined Foley & Lardner LLP- a 500-lawyer law firm, to head up their national Family Law Practice Team. They asked: "Where do you want to have your office and locate your Team- on the 5th floor with the transactional lawyers or on the 4th floor with the litigators?" I responded: "That's an easy question: Of course, on the 4th floor." Now I wish I had spent those next 14 years on the 5th floor. And you will know why after you read this Book.

— Allan R. Koritzinsky

Introduction

Rational People; Irrational Behavior

I mentioned in the acknowledgments that for years I was puzzled by the seemingly irrational behavior of rational people going through a divorce, until I discovered game theory. I also mentioned in the acknowledgments the prisoner's dilemma, the example that Steve Seaman showed me on a napkin. This example is presented in many versions, but the basic idea is as follows:

The Prisoner's Dilemma Example:

Two crooks commit an armed robbery, but had masks on and would not be able to be identified, if caught. They also managed to hide the money they had stolen. However, the police caught them, with their weapons on them. Because they had criminal records, matched the general description of the robbers, and had guns on them, the police were pretty sure they were the perpetrators but needed more evidence to convict them. The police put the two suspects in separate rooms. The interrogator said the same thing to both men. He said, "We know you and your partner committed the crime. However, it is unlikely that we are going to be able to prove it. However, you are convicted felons caught with guns on you. That will get you three years of prison time. However, I am prepared to offer you a deal. If you confess and serve as a witness against your partner, we will recommend that you only serve one year and then are paroled, because of your cooperation. Your partner, who does not cooperate, will get seven years."

The astute suspects asked, "But what happens if we both confess?"

The interrogator went on, "If you both confess, we will recommend that you only serve five of the seven years."

Game theory gives us a specific approach to analyzing choices in a grid. This is an analysis of what is called a "simultaneous choice game," because each of the players has to make a choice not knowing what the other player is choosing. We will present more on this in Chapter 1.

In our grid, this is the deal that is being offered to the suspects:

Prisoner's Dilemma

	Prisoner 2 Maintain silence	Prisoner 2 Confess
Prisoner 1 Maintain silence	Prisoner 1 = 3 years Prisoner 2 = 3 years	Prisoner 1 = 7 years Prisoner 2 = 1 year
Prisoner 1 Confess	Prisoner 1 = 1 year Prisoner 2 = 7 years	Prisoner 1 = 5 years Prisoner 2 = 5 years

Examining the grid, we see that prisoner 1 gets three years if he stays silent and his partner stays silent, but he get only one year if he confesses. Thus, he does better to confess. If prisoner 2 confesses, he gets seven years if he stays silent but only five years if he confesses too. Thus, no matter what prisoner 2 does, prisoner 1 does better to confess. Prisoner 2 faces the same choices. Therefore he, too, does better to confess, no matter what prisoner 1 does. The rational choice for both prisoners, then, is to confess, but as can be seen, they would have both done better had they both remained silent. They made the rational choice, but it looks irrational because they made a self-defeating choice.

The Auction Example:

There is another famous experiment done with audiences during presentations on game theory. It is an auction. The presenter holds up a $100 bill and announces that he is auctioning it off to the highest bidder, but there is one twist in the rules. The second highest bidder also has to submit his or her bid, but does not get the $100 bill. The auction begins. Before long, the presenter has bids well over $100, sometimes close to $300. Why on earth would someone bid over

$100 for $100. That seems totally irrational. But is it? Let us explain.

What happens is that the experiment quickly becomes a bidding war between two people. On the surface, it appears that the highest rational bid is $99. However, the second highest bidder, say one who bids $98, is facing the loss of $98, or that person can submit a bid for $101 and only lose $1. However, the other bidder is now faced with losing $99 or bidding $102 and only loses $2. Suddenly, the bidding is no longer for gain; it is to reduce loss. Subjective experience enters into the contest. There is the subjective experience of loss tolerance; that is, which bidder can tolerate the most loss. Other subjective values might also come into the bidding war, such as a need to win to avoid the shame of losing. The objective goal of minimizing the loss of money and the subjective goals harbored in the hearts of the bidders make the self-defeating choice of spending $200 for a $100 bill rational.

These experiments, and many others like them, demonstrate that rational people will make rational choices which are actually against their own interests, if the context is set up a certain way. In our auction example, a rule was introduced that led to rational people behaving irrationally. In the prisoner's dilemma game, the flow of information was interrupted; the prisoners could not speak to one another. Had they been able to, they would have both stayed silent. Likewise, people will make rational choices that serve their best interests if the context is set up differently. That is the essence of this book. It is about the context in which divorce occurs and whether that context promotes choices that are in the interests of the divorcing spouses or choices that are self-defeating, but in both cases rational.

Law of Unintended Consequences

In economics, there is a concept called the "law of unintended consequences." The concept is that by taking a set of actions to achieve certain goals, we can create consequences that were unintended, often unpredictable, and potentially more aversive and costly than even the successful achievement of the target goals. A recent example is the increasing demand for corn as an alternative fuel source. I will not go into the history of corn in the United States, but suffice to say that corn has been a favored crop by the government for many years. It is no accident that most Midwest farms are dominated by the rotation of corn and soybeans. Many incentives have been created over time for the growing of corn. Thus, it has become one of the largest agricultural crops in the country.

In recent times, increasing pressure has been placed on reducing oil consumption in the United States. Some of this has been for economic, some for political, and some for environmental reasons. Since having alternatives to oil is one means of achieving this goal, an industry has grown up around this idea; specifically, the raising and refining of corn to produce ethanol. A recent push to increase ethanol production on its face appears to be a laudable goal, with no losers. A fledgling industry has increased demand and thus can become ever-more efficient. Corn growers have a market of increasing size, increasing demand, and thus increasing prices. We have an increasing amount of alternative fuel, hopefully decreasing our dependence on oil.

The unintended consequences, however, are the effects on the world supply of food. If more land is devoted to a higher yielding crop, namely corn, less land is available for the production of other foods, including rice, wheat, oats, even grasses, and other vegetables. If more land is devoted to the grade of corn that is the cheapest and most efficient for ethanol, then less land is devoted to edible corn. The economic laws of a free market system tell us that decreasing supplies creates increasing costs and even shortages. Thus, the unintended consequences of growing corn for fuel are higher food costs and food shortages for some parts of the world, especially staple foods such as rice. This leads to increased starvation and, as we have seen recently, the beginnings of social unrest associated with food problems (e.g., food riots in Egypt). In this way, the goal of decreasing dependence on oil, while maintaining a luxuriant lifestyle in the United States, has, played a role in increasing starvation and social unrest in other parts of the world. These world problems could eventually lead to substantial problems and costs to the United States. Are starvation, unrest, and perhaps a revolution in countries with starving populations a price that we are willing to pay for an increase in the production of ethanol? Does the achievement of the laudable goals balance well with the unintended consequences?

We have similar examples of unintended consequences in the family law arena. In Washington State, in about 1995, a committee advised the state to adjust the manner in which they make temporary orders when parents file a petition for divorce. The committee was comprised of well-meaning skilled professionals, including mental health professionals, who attempted to design temporary order standards that protected children and minimized the short-term impact of the parental separation. A law was passed that followed the recommendations of this committee. The basic principle was that the temporary parenting patterns following the parents' separation would, as closely as possible, resemble the parenting patterns for the year prior to the separation—what the children were used to. In other words, if the wife had been taking primary responsibility for the children during the year prior to the separation, the children would live primarily with her after the separation. The husband's participation with the children would be mirrored in residential time[1] to what had been the case for the year prior to the separation. This is consistent with social science research; that is, that children adjust best to a divorce if they are given the changes involved in small, time-spaced pieces, rather than sudden enormous changes. Continuing with established parenting patterns while the children adjusted to their parents' separation and other changes in their lives before being required to adjust to a different parenting pattern seemed a kindness to children, with the goal of minimizing the negative impact of the parental separation and reducing the children's level of distress.

What were the unintended consequences? While the courts can give lip service to having temporary orders that do not prejudice long-term orders, most attorneys will acknowledge that *status quo* carries a great deal of weight in the court system. What is temporary tends to become permanent. Therefore, residential placement schedules for children that are set at the temporary orders hearing are very likely to affect the long-term residential placement schedule orders.

We have seen this in another aspect of a separation: which parent moves out of the homestead. Prior to 1969 and the warning of *The Disposable Parent*, it was standard for the husband to leave the homestead at the time of the separation. Ninety percent of custody orders at the time awarded the children to the mother, and often included her keeping the homestead, so it made sense for the husband to move out. After 1969 and the men's movement to maintain a more active post-divorce role with children, with increasing frequency, attorneys advised the husband not to leave the homestead at the time of the

---

1. Because every jurisdiction has different terminology for physical custody of children, we will use "residential placement" or "residential time" to refer to the schedule where the children spend time with each parent.

separation. While good legal advice, this often led to increased conflict between the parties, real increases in domestic violence, and increases in fictitious claims of domestic violence in order to obtain "kick out" orders. This trend, still very strong today, developed in response to the concern about how *status quo* affects long-term orders. When men attempted to play a more significant post-divorce role in their children's lives, and attorneys advised them to stay in the residence after filing a petition, this resulted in unintended consequences, which included harming the quality of the co-parental relationship. Because the co-parenting relationship is a very important predictor of outcomes for children, a further unintended consequence might have been damage to the children in many families. But let us get back to the situation in Washington State with the temporary order law.

What happened in Washington State when temporary orders were set based on the parenting patterns pre-separation? There were two effects. First, if the husband planned to initiate a divorce and saw an attorney, he was advised to hold off filing and spend substantially more time with the children, so that he would be awarded more time with the children at the temporary orders hearing. We have some evidence of this change based on attorneys' advice to fathers wishing to file for divorce. Likewise, wives who planned to initiate a divorce and contacted an attorney first might be advised to do what she could to reduce her husband's involvement with the children and document his low level of involvement. This latter is conjecture on our part. More important, these new laws had a second effect: to substantially increase the amount of litigation at the temporary orders stage.[2] The point of dispute was the parenting patterns of the year prior to the separation. Ironically, a wife, who might have begged her husband to be more involved with the children and who became very pleased when he finally seemed willing to do so, would often find this to be adverse to her interests when six months later he filed for divorce. Increased delays and shock at the point of separation, increased deceit between separating parents, increased litigation early in the legal process, and increased animosity plaguing the co-parenting relationship were all the unintended consequences of a well-intentioned, scientifically supported law. Oddly, the final unintended consequence for the court was more ambiguity as to what the actual parenting patterns had

---

2. The estimate of one of the psychologists on the panel advising the legislature was that litigation at the temporary order hearing tripled almost immediately.

been and so the law became nearly impossible to enforce with any confidence.

Another example is a law change made in Wisconsin in about 2005. Sections of the child placement statutes were rewritten after a controversial battle occurred between various interest groups. There was a move afoot by men's advocacy groups to write into the law a legal presumption of equal residential placement time with both parents, with the burden of proof on the parent who did not want equal placement schedules. There were other add-ons to this that included such provisions as limiting or eliminating the use of guardians *ad litem* in family law cases. The overall goal of the men's advocacy groups was to level the playing field when it came to post-divorce custody and residential time with children. This clashed with the goals of other interest groups, including women's advocacy groups and the State Bar Association, both of which wanted to keep the law more open to a wider range of options. Women's groups of course had the interest of protecting mothers' roles as primary parents with children, and the bar association had the interest of preventing a legal presumption that took the issue out of their hands altogether and ignored the actual situations in individual families. The end result was a fundamental shift in the law from being child-centered to parent-centered.

I should note that all three groups had legitimate concerns for the interests of children and were not as self-serving as it might sound. The bar association had the genuine concern that if the law shifted to a one-size-fits-all cookie-cutter approach to residential placement schedules, while the interests of some children and some families might be better served, other children and families would be put at risk where the factors did not support a presumption of equal residential schedules with each parent. Fathers' groups genuinely believed in their cause— that is, that children will do best with equal involvement with their fathers and mothers. Likewise, mothers' groups genuinely believed that children will do better, when children have been raised primarily by the mother prior to the separation, that such an arrangement continues.

Through a series of negotiations and compromises, the final law that passed is seemingly benign. The key issue is that it became a legal presumption that orders will "maximize" residential placement time with both parents. In other words, and on a pragmatic level, courts were given the somewhat ambiguous instruction to "maximize" the post-separation residential placement time with fathers. This gave mothers the wiggle room to still be "primary," gave fathers a much closer step to "equal," and gave attorneys room to litigate factors that might make "maximize" equal in one case or less in another.

However, the culture of divorce in the Wisconsin legal system shifted with this new law. First, court-connected mediation services reported that they were much less successful in resolving residential placement disputes, and more cases were proceeding to custody studies, a psychologically and financially costly process that almost always included the appointment of a guardian *ad litem* (an attorney representing the "best interests of the child"). Second, custody studies, which traditionally promoted settlements, because they were in a sense a preview of what would likely be a litigation outcome, were less successful in leading to settlement than they had been in the past. In spite of an expanding number of steps designed to reduce litigation (e.g., required parent education, mediation, custody studies, co-parenting counseling), an increasing number of cases went to litigation—the unintended consequence.

Perhaps Unintended, but Not Unpredictable

Why would more cases go to litigation? Let us take a typical case and examine it. Let us assume that we have a wife who is or at least perceives herself to be entitled to primary residential placement of the children. Perhaps she has done the lion's share of the parenting to date and she holds some of the historical assumptions of the superiority of mothers with children. Let us assume that there are a few other facts to support her view (e.g., husband is impatient with the children or travels a few times per year for work). Let us assume that the husband has been or perceives himself to be a very active and involved father who, while spending less actual time with the children than their mother, believes he has a great deal of value to add to the children's lives and that he is entitled to equal residential placement time after the separation. Let us also assume that he has some additional minor facts to support his case (e.g., wife's father is an alcoholic or wife tends to be overly indulgent with the children, who tend to be better behaved with him). Let us assume that neither party has a serious determinative factor to raise in litigation (e.g., child abuse), making the outcome of litigation unpredictable.

Let us further assume that when facing an unpredictable outcome, people in general tend to be excessively optimistic (social science research supports this assumption). Given the statute in Wisconsin and a general climate in the legal arena that supports father involvement, why should the father in this case compromise to any schedule less than equal when he has a fairly good chance of achieving equal through litigation? In the reverse, why should the mother agree to equal, when she will likely do no worse than equal in trial and might do better?

Additionally, child support guidelines in Wisconsin create financial incentives for winning this dispute that compensate for the transaction costs of litigation. In other words, the father has two incentives to litigate, rather than settle: first, he perceives that he has a likely outcome of equal residential placement; second, he perceives that the savings in child support will pay for the transaction costs to litigate the placement schedule and, over time, might actually be a net financial gain. His worst-case scenario in court is to end up with a schedule of slightly less than equal, the settlement position that he could have taken without a trial, so this is not a loss. In other words, he is unlikely to do worse in a trial than if he settled for less than equal and is likely to do better. In the worst-case scenario, his only loss is the transaction cost of litigation.

His wife has similar incentives. Even if she can get a residential placement schedule of eight or nine days out of fourteen, while the father gets six or five, respectively, she might well receive child support, which pays for the litigation cost and perhaps a net gain over time. She is unlikely to do worse than equal, because that is all that the father is seeking, but she might do better. Her worst-case scenario is to lose in court, get an order for equal residential placement (which was her settlement position anyway), and have the transaction costs. This is all true, but in real life, the litigation costs, along with the transaction costs of holding/divesting assets is significant but often not understood or quantified accurately.

In a particular case, we could actually figure out the best bet for both parties. By estimating the probable transaction costs, the total child support differences between an equal schedule and the mother's desired schedule, and the likelihood of the outcome in trial (e.g., knowing the judge's tendencies, recent trends in court, the "quality" of the facts), we could approach the situation like a poker hand. An expert poker player will determine the odds of winning with particular cards and measure that against the ratio of the bet to the pot (potential winnings). If representing the father, for example, an attorney might be able to predict that the odds of being awarded equal placement, with a particular judge and given the facts, are 60 percent. The transaction cost (litigation expense) is likely to be $7,000. The savings in child support, if equal residential placement is the outcome, over the lifetime of the children, is $62,000. So, the poker player has a hand with a 60 percent chance of winning, the bet is $7,000, and the pot is worth $62,000. One can see that if on average a person wins 60 percent of the time on bets of $7,000 with a pot of $62,000, it is a great bet. Likewise, the mother's attorney has given her a 40 percent chance of winning, with a $7,000 bet and a pot worth $62,000. She, too, has a great bet.

Litigation: When Both Parties Have Good Bets

It just takes a little math to see why both parties have a good bet. Let us assume that there are ten bets. The father bets $70,000 (10 X $7,000) and wins 60 percent of the time, thus winning $372,000 (6 X $62,000). The mother bets $70,000 and wins 40 percent of the time, thus winning $248,000 (4 X $62,000). This seems counterintuitive—how can both parties be making a good bet? Surely one has to lose. *This is true because each party is only playing one time.* Just like the poker player, as expert as she is, might actually lose this hand, the expert poker player always plays scientifically; that is, plays the odds, even though in an individual hand she might lose. Only in playing ten hands like this (i.e., when she has a 60 percent or 40 percent chance of winning with a $7,000 bet and a pot of $62,000) is she likely to make a profit. Our divorcing couple will play just one hand, but if they are smart, they will still play the odds. But why? This happens because the state has made the pot so big; that is, the differences in child support with different residential placement schedules over the lifetime of the children can be a very big pot indeed. The ambiguity in the law thus promotes litigation as the rational choice.

Litigation: When It Produces Objective and Subjective Payoffs

We could make our example even more intriguing by adding a number of payoffs other than the child support dollar amount. For example, let us assume that if the mother gets the schedule she would like, and the associated child support amount, she will be able to continue to work part-time. Thus she escapes the challenge of seeking and obtaining full-time employment plus also meets her goal for the children to continue to have an after-school available parent. This is what is called a combination of important objective and subjective payoffs. It is hard to put a dollar amount on her goal of being the after-school caregiver, only working part-time, and avoiding the anxiety of seeking full-time employment, leaving her current position and workmates, and so on. However, we could assign certain values to these gains and show that she is actually making a very good bet if she wins. Let us also assume that she considers herself the superior parent, has a great deal of personal meaning in life associated with her role as mother, and fears the perceived social shame (or expectations of her family of origin) of not continuing in her role as primary parent. Now we can see that in addition to the child support money, there are numerous payoffs for her that make it a very good bet to litigate. If she loses in court, at least she does not have to explain why she voluntarily abdicated her role.

We could also assume that the father has many additional psychological and emotional payoffs that he is seeking. For example, let us assume that he feels he has been bullied into a secondary role in the children's lives by the mother and her parents and wants a chance to prove not only that he is equally capable but also that the children will be much better off with an equal residential placement schedule.

Litigation: The Unintended Consequences

Thus, when facing settlement time, all of the incentives have now moved in the direction of the father not settling for anything less than equal and the mother refusing to settle for equal. Forty years ago, this "bet" might have been a terrible one, because the father's attorney might have told him that unless he can prove very serious allegations against the mother, he is going to get every other weekend, period. One would not bet $7,000 on a $62,000 pot if one had a 1 percent chance of winning. As we can see, changing the law in Wisconsin to include the phrase "maximize time" with both parents created an ambiguous situation in which the father has a reasonably good chance of prevailing, if litigated. Wisconsin therefore created an unintended consequence of substantial increases in litigation. The unintended consequences include substantially more time and expense on the part of the court system, which funds the failed mediations, the custody studies that fail to settle the case, and the increased court time and expense. Other unintended consequences include substantial damage to the family, regardless of who prevails. Social science tells us that the residential placement schedule is a poor predictor of outcomes for children, while the co-parenting relationship is the primary predictor of outcomes. The process of custody evaluations and litigation substantially lowers the chance of a good co-parenting relationship when compared to parties who settle in mediation.

Game Theory Predicts Human Choices

Thus, while the destructive consequences of the compromise family law bill in Wisconsin were unintended, they were not unpredictable. This perspective is a *game theory* perspective; that is, we are applying principles learned in a special branch of mathematics called "game theory." Game theory uses a range of mathematic approaches to strategic relationships between people and is able to predict (fairly reliably) human choices. By applying some simple mathematics in our example above, we were able to see that the rational thing for both the father and the mother was to take a position, never budge, and litigate in court. This is because the legislature set up the game with rules that made this choice the most rational one.

Conflict between Separated Parents

Game Theory Also Predicts Strategies

The reader does not need to worry about understanding game theory—*not yet*. We will explain this later. First, we want to explore another facet of game theory, and then we will get to formal definitions. In addition to helping us predict what choices people will make (in our example above, to litigate rather than settle), game theory also helps us predict the strategies that people will use to play the game. For example, if we step back and examine what would give a poker player the best chance at winning over time, we can easily see that if a poker player always knew which cards the other players held and yet the other players never knew what our poker player held, she would likely come out ahead every time. She would quit hands when she could see that she had little or no chance of winning, would bet up hands in which she had winning cards, and so on. However, she is also aware that the other players would be in the same position if they could tell what she had and she had no idea what they had. Thus, not only are the individual bets calculated mathematically (as in our earlier example), the poker player will use strategies aimed at discovering (or making an educated guess about) what cards the other players are holding while at the same time doing everything possible to deceive the other players about the contents of her hand (e.g., wear dark glasses, have a poker face, bluff sometimes). Thus, we can predict not only choices (to stay in or fold) but also strategies (to deceive and analyze). Other games with different rules and payoffs promote other types of behavior.

In Divorce, the Parties Predictably Play "Chicken"

In divorce, we can also discover through game theory which strategies spouses are likely to use. For example, even if a spouse anticipates "folding" prior to an actual trial—that is, settling because the costs of litigation exceed the size of the savings/gain in child support—it is a better strategy to wait to settle at the last minute, in hopes that the other side will settle first. This is a game similar to "chicken." In chicken, two drivers start driving directly at one another. The first person to pull out is the loser, just like the first person to settle before a trial is the loser. It makes no sense to pull out right at the beginning in chicken before giving the other person the chance to pull out. So, the predictable behavior is that both players will drive directly at one another, hoping that the other person pulls out first. Also like litigation, if neither pulls out, a disaster can ensue.

In Divorce, Other Strategies Are Predictable

Let us look at some other predictable behaviors in litigation. If the parties plan to litigate, the best strategy is usually enhancing one's own position (i.e., looking one's best) while denigrating the other parent and his or her position (i.e., making the other person look bad). Separation typically involves months to years of this kind of thinking, and how many couples are able to say, "We're both great people, but just want to go our own ways?" If they can't do this, then the Court system is set up to exacerbate and embed this kind of thinking because traditional litigation looks to the past rather than the future. As in politics, one has to be careful to be subtle and not go overboard, but mud-throwing is the most successful strategy. This is why politicians, who at the beginning of an election race vow to keep it clean and to focus on the issues, get down and dirty as election day comes closer—

the politician who is behind literally has nothing to lose and will throw mud by the bucket. In game theory, we can actually assign values to certain types of strategies and can calculate and thereby mathematically prove that this is accurate—that mud-throwing is an effective strategy when the goal is to convince a third party (i.e., in politics, the voter; in divorce litigation, the judge) that he or she ought to prevail. In general, although the person throwing the mud loses points in the eyes of the third party, the person on whom the mud was thrown loses more points. If two people start equal and one throws mud and loses two points but the other person looks bad and loses three points, the one who threw the mud moves ahead.

Thus, we can predict that, if the goal is to have one's position prevail, the best strategy in divorce is one that increases parental conflict and also decreases the chances that the parental conflict will diminish over time. This strategy creates so much hurt, insult, deception, and distrust that the parties would be hard-pressed to try, or even to want to try, to improve communication and cooperation when all is said and done. When we add in the other factors—that there is likely a "winner" and a "loser" and that the transaction costs were so steep that both parties might feel like they lost—we have the ingredients of a moderate- to high-conflict divorce. At least politicians understand that they are just playing a game and can avoid taking it personally. Parents, whose interests and whose perceptions of their child's interests are at stake, have a very hard time not taking it personally.

In Divorce, the Current System Increases Conflict

We do not need to go into detail here on the detrimental effects of parental conflict on children, particularly if it becomes an imbedded part of family life for the rest of childhood, and after. We are all aware of this fact. In all of the social science research on how negative conflict affects children, not one study has found that it is good for children. At best, some children seem able, through personal resilience and other mitigating factors, not to be too damaged, while most suffer not only in their childhood but also throughout their adult lives. Thus, ironically, while the legal system throws numerous opportunities in the paths of separating parents to develop healthy communication and cooperation, the fundamental system itself appears to be set up to increase parental conflict. Just as the rule in our auction example that the second highest bidder also has to pay, the outcome in such a divorce is a self-defeating loss for both players.

The question that we will ask later in this book is this: Could the legal system be set up in such a way that the best strategies for separating parents are those which *increase* the chance of a good co-parental relationship and decrease the chances of a poor one? In economics, the *invisible hand* of capitalism asserts that by seeking and rewarding self-interest, the common good is served. Can self-interest in a divorce be corralled to promote effective communication and cooperation?

The Rise of Alternatives to Traditional Family Law Practice

There is a system-wide intuitive understanding that the legal system, as it deals with separating parents, seems to make matters worse. Attorneys often find themselves in the painful dilemma of having to choose a strategy that not only increases family conflict (e.g., writing the angry accusing letter) but also best serves the interests of the client, advancing the chances that the client's position will prevail.

Divorce Lawyers Have a Reputation Problem

As we have seen in the past twenty years, however, significant efforts have begun to reform the legal system. We will touch more on some of these developments in the next section. Here we want to focus solely on changes within the rank and file of family law attorneys. The reputation of family law attorneys has dropped like a lead balloon. I have co-presented with an attorney who starts her presentation by asking attorneys or, on several occasions, law students what adjectives come to mind when she says "divorce lawyer." As a psychologist, I am shocked at the words that come out of attorneys' mouths. I will not repeat those words here but will state that in recent years we increasingly hear the same adjectives from parties to a divorce. We hear this from parties in our mediation programs, many of whom refuse to hire attorneys because of their reputation, and we hear this from parents in our post-divorce co-parenting programs, whether they had attorneys or not. The criticisms, sans expletives, from divorcing spouses, attorneys, and law students fall into three basic categories.

1. **Divorce lawyers are expensive**. This is true in terms of hourly fees and in terms of total cost of the divorce. In the area in which we currently practice, hourly fees for divorce attorneys range from about $200 to $400 (though in major cities, the rates can be

substantially higher). By attorney standards, those fees might not seem high, but to the average Joe or Jane, those fees are frightening.

Beyond the hourly fee, many clients feel little control over how quickly those fees add up and multiply. One attorney writes a letter to another attorney and the meter starts ticking. Emailing can be equally expensive, due to the number of them used in a case. To put this in perspective, imagine going to a fine restaurant and when you look at the menu, there are no prices. You ask the waiter the cost of certain dinners and the waiter tells you that they charge by the ingredient and the amount of time spent by personnel on the meal. Some meals take longer than others, and it is difficult to say at the beginning how long things will take. If the customer wants to substitute an ingredient, for example, that changes the price, depending on the ingredient and the additional time added to the meal preparation. The waiter even tells you that the additional time that he took answering this question added cost to the meal. So you order something and sit there. With every minute that passes you see the price going up but are afraid to ask questions about the meal because that, too, will increase your bill. Finally the meal is delivered and you eat. You ask in passing what the cost is, but the waiter smiles and tells you that it matters how long you take to finish and how much of a mess you make at the table for the busboy to clean up. Finally, as you are ready to leave, you get the bill and it is surprisingly high. No matter how good the food, would you be happy with your experience?

2. **Divorce lawyers create unnecessary conflict**. We are amazed at how many of our mediation clients who have enough money to afford lawyers refuse to retain one, even though we recommend that they do so. Their reasoning is that if they hire attorneys, they will begin to have conflict with one another that neither spouse wishes. The lawyer's commitment to "zealous advocacy" often means that they focus on legal issues, and not on the client's goals of separating with minimal disruption to children and lifestyle and maximizing their chances of future benefits. We are usually able to talk them into at least consulting with attorneys once they have reached mediated agreements and give them the names of mediation-friendly attorneys. However, more often than we wish,

those attorneys *do* begin to unravel the agreements made and begin to position our clients for disputes. In other words, our clients are often correct when they want to avoid hiring attorneys out of fear of unnecessary conflict. We will discuss the reasons for this later.

3. **Divorce lawyers do not really care about their clients**. This will come up in odd criticisms (e.g., "I am putting my lawyer's children through college instead of my own") or flat-out negative statements. This is an interesting criticism because most family law attorneys take the representation of their clients' interests quite seriously. This seeming contradiction, however, has a logical explanation. Divorce lawyers care about their client's *objective legal interests*, but not necessarily about their *objective psychological and emotional* interests and perhaps not about their *subjective legal or personal interests*. We will explore this in more detail in later chapters. Here we want to point out that lawyers often assume that they know what is best for their clients. Lawyers divide property and time with children. They traditionally do not have the tools to prevent or mitigate loss and trauma. Contextual issues seem only relevant to the extent that they can be used to move the balance scale off 50-50. For example, in recent years attorneys have recommended to their clients not to leave the homestead during the pendency of the action. This is good legal advice because leaving the homestead often creates a legal disadvantage. It is terrible advice for the family, however, increasing the chances of more parental conflict, even domestic violence, and a household thick with tension. In one such case, the fifteen-year-old son put it this way to one of the authors: "The tension in this house is so bad, if you lit a match the whole place would explode."

In our experience, this diminished reputation of "divorce lawyers" is largely both deserved and undeserved. Most family law attorneys, for example, genuinely care about their clients and their children, will often go out of their way for their clients, sometimes undercharging for actual time. More important, spouses going through a divorce are in a system that is counterintuitive and requires special knowledge that a family law attorney possesses. To some extent, getting a divorce without attorneys is like going into the jungle without a guide. Thus, often the attorney is really looking out for the client's long-term interests in a system that the client might not understand.

Although we are going to simplify this a bit, because of this negative reputation, combined with an increasingly do-it-yourself culture with access to information via the Internet, family law attorneys have been steadily losing market share to *pro se* representation since about 1990. In discussing this with a judge friend of ours, he stated that he believes that family law attorneys have simply priced themselves out of the market. We think that this might be true in part, but that the other two elements of the divorce lawyer reputation (cost and conflict) also make a big difference. For example, people will go to a very expensive restaurant if they perceive it is worth it and they know in advance the cost. Or, they will spend huge amounts of money on a wedding or a vacation, if it is worth it. The problem with family law is that the cost is high but many people (maybe most) are less inclined to think it is worth it. In about 1994, the rate of *pro se* representation reached about 50 percent in Arizona. That trend has continued and appears to at least be nationwide. In our county in Wisconsin, for example, a 2004 study found that in only about 40 percent of cases was there at least one attorney retained and in only 17 percent of cases did both parties have attorneys. This means that about 72 percent of people going through a complicated legal process are doing so without attorneys (60 percent plus half of the additional 23 percent who did not have representation while their spouse did).

The family law system has adjusted somewhat to these changes in culture, but not nearly enough. The most significant change has been the invention and spread of collaborative divorce practice. Less substantial has been attorneys serving as divorce mediators and even less substantial has been the fledgling efforts to start a "cooperative divorce" process. This latter effort is an attempt to mimic many of the processes of collaborative divorce, but maintaining the ability of the attorneys to represent their clients in litigation if there is a failure to reach settlement. A recent study in Europe found that about 85 percent of collaborative divorce cases settled on all issues. The remaining 15 percent did not and had to start over with new attorneys. Cooperative divorce is an effort to settle in a collaborative style but also represent clients if that fails.

Finally, family law attorneys, both in collaborative divorce and not, have actively integrated social science (non-lawyer) practitioners into their work with divorcing spouses. Family law attorneys will send their clients for short-term divorce counseling, coaching, co-parenting counseling, and education groups and will often consult themselves with social scientists for guidance on legal issues involving children. In one practice in North Carolina with which we are familiar, part of the intake process in the law firm, which only does divorce law, involves meeting with an on-staff social worker who helps plan all of the "treatment" for the case and makes referrals to mental health practitioners as needed.

The legal system has often been described as the most conservative system in the United States, maintaining traditions and changing only very slowly. This recent experimentation with approaches like collaborative divorce is a testament to the loss of market share in recent times. It is wonderful that attorneys are experimenting with other "products" to offer clients. Nevertheless, family law attorneys still suffer from systemic problems from which they cannot escape. Because of this, these changes in the practice of family law, while improvements, fail to address the underlying reasons that both family law attorneys and their clients are often instinctually aware of a poor fit for families inside the legal system. There are three basic reasons for this underlying dissatisfaction.

1. **The family law system is based on a fundamental principle that undergirds why an attorney cannot work for both parties: the interests of the parties are at odds with one another**. Thus, an attorney cannot represent both parties because that would be playing both sides of two sets of interests. The legal system describes this as a "conflict of interest." Every step of the way, every legal issue is viewed through this lens. Thus, every dollar that one party gets is a dollar lost by the other party. Every day of residential placement time gained is at the expense of a day to the other party. Every advantage in a relocation case is sought. This fundamental assumption is so deeply embedded in the legal system, from law school to every day of practice, that it is nearly impossible to contemplate a different *Weltanschauung*. From the minute that the client walks through an attorney's door, both the attorney and the client begin on the assumption that the *other* attorney and party are opponents, where their gains are our losses and where their losses are our gains. In this context, every issue is seen as a dispute.

The very language in the system clearly underscores this. Terms like "the other side," or where the Summons or Petition uses the word "versus" to identify the litigants, reinforce this perspective. The two attorneys, who might even be good friends, are called "opposing counsel."

2. **This first basic systemic problem is compounded by the attorney's oath to represent one's client's interests to the best of one's ability.** The client does not fully understand this, but the attorney understands how the system works and usually begins a case with some assumptions about what is in the client's interests. For example, an attorney representing the higher income earner will usually start positioning from the beginning to keep spousal support to a minimum, or to maximize spousal support if representing the lower earner. This clearly represents what most people would conclude is in the client's best interests. However, what if it is not? What if the client would be better off paying higher spousal support? What if this better assuaged guilt, or fulfilled a personal goal to see the other spouse reach a certain financial goal, or simply was the kindest thing to do? If a client believes that it is "fair" to pay a higher level of spousal support than might be achieved through litigation, the attorney might say something like, "I know you feel that this is fair now, but I promise, five years from now you will regret this." What the family law attorney might fail to consider are the subjective payoffs in the situation, even with one's own client. A potentially high-payer client might feel that paying a higher level of spousal support than might have been accomplished in aggressive litigation was the fairer thing to do and actually accomplished much more for both parties in the long run (e.g., the receiver might have provided better opportunities for the children). The client will no doubt be balancing these more generous attitudes with the normal selfishness that would lead to aggressive litigation. Which way the client goes might depend mostly on guidance from the attorney.

3. **The dissatisfaction felt in both the attorney and the client is rooted in the second reason. A family law attorney can finish a case and feel it was a real win on the legal goals, but the client can finish the same case and feel nothing but loss and be**

further from his or her long-term goals. The family law attorney is operating in the legal arena and therefore naturally thinks of legal goals: property division, custody, residential schedules for the children, and the various support issues. The clients, however, are in the legal arena of their lives only temporarily and often against their wishes. For example, after a heated litigation battle over residential schedules for the children, the father might have "won" and gotten equal time with the children, but had he settled for less, he might have developed a much more cooperative relationship with the mother, much more flexibility in the schedule, better access to the children, and much happier children. Instead, he gets a rigid schedule, a bitter mother, and children who live in a family with parents who never talk and never change the schedule; plus, he is cut off from one-half of the children's lives. On court day, he might have been elated with the "win" but three years later be watching his children have difficulties and even litigating again. What the family law attorney sometimes fails to do is to look at the divorce case as a goal-based planning process.

The Family Law Attorney Challenge: Recapturing Market Share

Divorce is a time to plan for the future, where the legal outcomes of a divorce should be seen as means for achieving long-term goals in the parties' lives, not as goals in and of themselves.

A Kinder, Gentler Family Law System

What we explore in this book is whether or not a better system for divorce could be devised, relying heavily on game theory principles, in which clients have divorce lawyers assist them through the legal arena toward their long-term goals. We strongly believe that the best divorce is one in which family law attorneys serve as guides, providing "legal" advice, as defined and explained throughout this book. One can take a walk in a jungle without a guide, expose themselves to unknown dangers, and fail to see 90 percent of what the jungle has to offer. A guide with special knowledge and experience enhances almost every human activity. Our do-it-yourself culture with access to extensive online information can make the divorce process more efficient in many ways, but it is no substitute for a good guide. We believe that family law attorneys should recapture market share; their clients will be better off for it and in the long run can feel that the expense was worth it.

Game Theory: Background and Its potential Application to Divorce

Game theory has its roots in academia. The use of the word "game" is a little controversial, because the word connotes something light or fun. It can also connote deceit and manipulation, as in: "He is just playing games with me." The use of the word "game" arises, however, from the history of game theory. Game theory began as the mathematical study of decision making in parlor *games*. However, game theory has expanded to study human behavior in such diverse and complex arenas as macroeconomics, military strategy planning, and even marriage. Five Nobel Prizes have been awarded for the development and application of game theory to various aspects of economics: John Nash (1994) and Reinhardt Selten (1994); a shared prize by Robert Aumann and Thomas Schelling (2005); and Roger Myerson (2007).

Some authors have tried to rename game theory (e.g., decision theory), but unsuccessfully. One author went so far as to name game theory "strategic interactive decision making," but again, none of these alternatives have "stuck." Suffice it to say that "game," as we are using it, has a technical meaning, devoid of the light and humorous as well as the pejorative connotations.

We are introducing game theory in the divorce arena for its potential in explaining why divorcing spouses engage in disputes that appear to be self-defeating. Part of the reason is of course that people are at the peak of their marital problems when they are divorcing and control struggles are the norm. However, less obvious is that they are funneled into a legal system that might promote disputes rather than solutions to the restructuring of family relationships and developing constructive financial plans. Game theory helps explain why this is likely to be true in the legal system.

The Game Theory Challenges: Predicting Choices and Shaping Decision-Making

The ultimate test of game theory, and its usefulness, is whether it predicts the choices that people are likely to make under certain conditions and whether games can be played in such a way as to shape the manner in which people make decisions. Game theory is an analysis of human decision-making. It is important to keep in mind that most people are and will remain unaware of why they have made the choices they have made. Although a quarterback is unlikely to be consciously solving calculus equations when throwing the football, we can nevertheless use calculus equations to analyze the path that the football will take. This is where prediction comes in: to use the football metaphor, not only can we analyze why a football traveled the path that it did, but also we can predict that if the quarterback throws the ball with a certain amount of force in a certain direction and angle, the ball will travel a certain path to the receiver. Game theory is similar in that we can not only analyze past transactions (e.g., in a game theory experiment) and determine why people made the decisions that they made, but also look at the players, rules, and payoff structure of a future game and predict what the players are likely to choose as decisions and strategies.

Our Ambitious Purpose: Designing a Divorce Process with Rules and Payoffs that Increase the Likelihood of Making Good Decisions

The more ambitious purpose to which we can put game theory is designing a divorce process with rules and a payoff structure that increases the likelihood that people will make good choices for themselves and their children. It is our belief that this must be done within the existing structure of the legal system, because the legal system is founded on one of the most basic laws of organic life on the planet: tradition prevents chaos and change prevents extinction. Laws and the legal system (both statutory and case law), precedents, local rules, and local practice prevent the chaos of lawlessness. Change in the legal system is slow and arduous at times, but this prevents wild erratic experiments. But change is an inherent part of the legal system. Statutory laws are rewritten, as our Wisconsin example illustrates. The "system" converted what used to be marriage counseling centers (i.e., reconciliation programs) into mediation programs, with parent education classes added more recently. Social science has become an integral part of the divorce system, whether it be the psychological evaluations so common now or even at a broader level, the laws themselves. In current Wisconsin law, the court must consider several general factors in family law cases when there is a dispute over custody and residential schedules for children and a list of sixteen more individual factors. About one-half of those factors come from social science, from the developmental needs of children to the mental health of the parents.

Thus, we are not suggesting with this book that a whole new legal system be designed to guide people through divorce. Most of the suggestions we will be making have to do with minor changes in the process. Some of those are subtle, such as how family law attorneys think about the process of divorce, and some of them are dramatic, such as having a branch of family law in which the family law attorneys serve as transaction attorneys, each lawyer hired to represent clients in the transaction of their divorce. There are many examples in the current area: buying and selling a business or a home; setting up a business with two of more partners; etc. People do not approach these transactions with a mindset toward litigation if things do not work out. They plan to continue the negotiations until conflicts are resolved.

A Preview

In this book, we are going on a journey. We start at the trailhead by defining and describing game theory and the principles from game theory that we believe are necessary for the transformation of family law. Game theory is also like a stew, full of different ingredients— namely, branches of mathematics and decision theory findings. A game theorist has to apply algebra, calculus, set theory, geometry, and statistics. The mathematics is complex. However, we intend to extract the basic principles from game theory without requiring that the reader learn the undergirding mathematics.

We will present a few "games" with their math, at a simple level, for illustrative purposes, but our goal is to infuse the legal system with a simple way of thinking about how it does business. We gave two examples of this type of thinking when examining why the change of law in Washington State led to increased conflict and litigation at the temporary orders stage and when we analyzed why the law change in Wisconsin led to a decrease in settlement and an increase in litigation.

Following this intellectual exercise, we will use game theory to look more closely at traditional family law. We will not limit ourselves to examining the formal legal system, although that will be a focal point. We will also look at common practices of family law attorneys. Then we will use game theory to examine the trends in family law, such as the rise of collaborative divorce, and analyze their probable effect on divorce.

We will also explore how to design a divorce experience that reaches optimal outcomes for the parties and the parties' children using the game theory concepts introduced earlier. Finally, as a complement to that task, we will describe how game theory can be used in the settlement process between attorneys to reach optimal outcomes.

We understand that the optimism that this book suggests may have a flaw. Divorcing spouses have conflict or at least most do. This book or any changes that the family system might make will not eliminate conflict in divorces. We likely will never have a world without war, neighborhoods without crime, an economy without poverty, and divorce without conflict. Our premise, however, is that we have **unnecessary conflict** in the divorce system, which can be designed to make the payoffs for low conflict better than for high conflict. Rather than having 30 percent of divorces be amicable, perhaps we could reach 50 percent. Rather than 20 percent of cases with children being high conflict, perhaps we could get it down to 10 percent. With moderate conflict cases, perhaps parents could learn to protect their children from the destructive effects of divorce. The children deserve this, if the system can be redesigned.

We also believe that the use of game theory principles will add to the tools of family law attorneys in reaching optimal outcomes for their clients and the other spouse. This establishes not only a better working relationship between attorneys but also a better experience for the clients. The latter can produce lifelong positive effects on family life when children are involved.

We have been using these principles in mediation for many years with very positive results. We hope these principles will have widespread application. This is our goal and the purpose of this book.

Warning: For the reader not familiar with game theory, some of the material in this book might be challenging. Game theory is a different way of thinking about human relations; there are concepts that challenge the way we normally think about why people do what they do. We have tried to minimize the jargon, but some jargon is inevitable; jargon is a shortcut to a concept but can be like learning a different language. We have tried to minimize the use of mathematic principles, but some is necessary and efficient to explain concepts. We use other human situations such as poker games or a restaurant metaphor to illustrate concepts. We have assumed a knowledge of divorce dynamics and familiarity with the legal system as it addresses divorce. This is not a book for the lay public; it is a book for lawyers and mediators who work with separating spouses and, in some instances, paternity cases. So, put on your thinking cap and let's get started.

CHAPTER 1

A Primer on Game Theory Principles

Definition of a "Game"

At the simplest level a game is defined by its four elements: a *game* is when two or more *players* are strategically involved with one another where there are *rules* and the outcome of the game has *payoffs* that are based on the players' *decisions* and strategies.

Players

There must be two or more players who are strategically involved with one another. By strategic involvement, we mean that the relationship between the players includes the other conditions of a game described below and the outcome of the game affects both of them. Divorce has two players (the spouses).

Rules

A game has rules by which the players must play. In divorce, this means state and federal law, but also may include local court rules, the local legal environment, the historical relationships between the attorneys involved, and so on. For example, in one jurisdiction, it might be a law or "rule" that the parties attend mediation if they fail to settle some disputes prior to litigation in court. In another jurisdiction, it might be well known that a particular judge tends to order high levels of support. Some rules might be rigid and some might be flexible, but there are rules.

Payoffs

The outcome of a game, or a portion of a game, must have at least one payoff. We do not use the word "reward" here because a payoff might not be a reward. A payoff, for example, might simply be less of an aversive consequence. For example, a party might not gain a reward or advantage in the settlement, but may lessen the downside cost and/or risk. The term "payoff" can be a little misleading because it implies that one receives something. However, this is not always true. For example, a spousal support award of $1,000 per month is a positive payoff to the payer if the predicted amount was $2,000 per month.

A payoff can have a negative value. A spousal support award might be higher than anticipated, for example, and be a negative payoff. Also, a payoff can be a subjective experience. A mother who gets to continue to be the "primary parent" after the separation might have a very high subjective value payoff, even though it is intangible. We could assign artificial point values to subjective payoffs in order to do the math. The basic idea is that at the completion of a game or a portion of the game, one or both players receive a payoff.

In divorce, especially with children, the payoffs are complex and numerous. In games with multiple and complex payoffs, the payoff is called the "payoff structure," which will likely include payoffs for both parties. A marital settlement agreement, for example, delineates a payoff structure, providing numerous payoffs for both parties.

Decisions and Strategies

Each player must have a choice of actions available that involve at least one decision, but more commonly a series of decisions that combine to form a strategy. It is not a game if the outcome is primarily or solely determined by chance and/or there are no available choices to the players. The fact that players have choices, points at which they can choose different actions and strategies, makes it a game. Chance might play some role in the strategies (e.g., guessing what a judge might decide if litigated), but the game is primarily dominated by the choices and strategies of the parties.

Expanded Definition
of the Parts of a Game

Here we look at some of the more complex aspects to the definition of a game.

Players—How Many Players in Divorce

Although we are defining the game of divorce as having two players, the spouses, a more complex analysis with game theory would posit that it is more complicated and includes at least five and sometimes more players. In addition, each party preps for attorney meetings with family and friends, debriefing afterwards. Keeping family and friends out of the conference room does not keep them out of the negotiations. Especially with cell phones, parties often text and communicate with other interested (supportive) players in near-real time communication. Each attorney and client is also playing a game with one another; the attorneys, who most likely know one another, are playing a game; there are sometimes court-connected mediators and appointed guardians *ad litem*; and to some extent, everyone is playing a game with the judge, even long before the judge is directly involved. The attorneys, for example, might conduct the case differently depending on expectations based on experience with a particular judge. For our purposes, however, we are going to focus mostly on the game played between spouses and to view the spouse-attorney as one team player of the game.

Two Players in Our Schema

An advantage to seeing divorce as a two-person game, or perhaps as a two-team game, with attorneys, is in the analysis of choices. A common analysis in game theory is performed in a 2X2 grid, illustrated below:

Two-person, two-choice game

	Player 2 Choice A	Player 2 Choice B
Player 1 Choice A	Payoff for player 1 Payoff for player 2	Payoff for player 1 Payoff for player 2
Player 1 Choice B	Payoff for player 1 Payoff for player 2	Payoff for player 1 Payoff for player 2

Cooperation and Coordination Always Produce Better Outcomes

By defining the divorce game as a two-person game, we can make use of this form of analysis. As you might guess, few situations are this simple, and we will introduce other methods of analyzing some choices later in this book. This simple 2X2 grid method can be very illustrative of some basic principles. For example, this method is the one used in the famous prisoner's dilemma game to illustrate that while a certain choice is always the best for each individual player, a different choice would have been better for both players. The concept illustrated in the prisoner's dilemma game is that cooperation and coordination can achieve a better outcome for everyone when compared to self-serving individual choices. We will refer to the basic principle of the prisoner's dilemma several times in this book. As we shall see, using game theory can enhance the outcomes for both parties, whether in a game or in a real-life divorce. As in the prisoner's dilemma, we posit that the outcome for parties to a divorce is improved with the use of good information management, cooperation, and coordination. Later we will examine each of these ingredients.

The Prisoner's Dilemma

The prisoner's dilemma is presented in different ways, and the following is one of the iterations. In brief, two men are arrested who have robbed a store. The men have hidden the money taken from the store and wore masks, so that they cannot be identified. However, it was an armed robbery and both men retained their weapons, which were found on them when they were caught. The men are placed in separate interrogation rooms, and in each room, the interrogator presents the following, asking them to think about their choices, and that he will return in a few minutes: "We have you for carrying a concealed weapon for which you do not have a license. That will get you three years in prison, given your record. However, I will offer you a deal. If you confess and your partner does not, he will get seven years and you will get one year for cooperation in the investigation. If you both confess, each of you will save some court time and each will get five years. Let me know what you decide."

In our grid analysis previously discussed, this is the deal being offered.

Prisoner's Dilemma

	Prisoner 2 Maintain silence	Prisoner 2 Confess
Prisoner 1 Maintain silence	Prisoner 1 = 3 years Prisoner 2 = 3 years	Prisoner 1 = 7 years Prisoner 2 = 1 year
Prisoner 1 Confess	Prisoner 1 = 1 year Prisoner 2 = 7 years	Prisoner 1 = 5 years Prisoner 2 = 5 years

When each player examines the payoff structure—namely, the prison terms—if prisoner 1 takes the deal and confesses, he is better off no matter what prisoner 2 decides. If prisoner 2 remains silent, he gets one year, rather than three, and if prisoner 2 confesses, he gets five years rather than seven. Prisoner 2 has the same choices; he is better off choosing confess no matter what prisoner 1 does. Notice what happens if they both confess, which is the rational choice; they both do worse than if they both stayed silent. If they could communicate and had both of their interests at heart, they could agree to remain silent and take the three years each, which would be better than the five years. The principle is that when we add communication and cooperation to a negotiation, we can often enhance the outcome for both parties.

Rules

A game has rules by which the players must play. In divorce, the rules are an amalgam of legislative and case law, local rules, and the local custom of the jurisdiction. By this latter reference, we mean the informal rules understood, either consciously or unconsciously, by attorneys practicing in the area. For example, the attorneys might understand that their judge likes to settle cases at a status conference, by performing the role of mediator with some clout. The attorneys are likely going to organize their strategy in such a case to be ready to try to influence that judge at the status conference. This then becomes a rule by custom. In another jurisdiction, the judge might use status conferences solely for scheduling purposes. This is one of the key reasons that a divorce is more likely to have an optimal outcome if there are attorneys involved, or at least the parties are using a mediator.

Most divorcing spouses do not know many of the rules. Having attorneys enhances the knowledge base of the team. In family law, the "rules" are often known to the attorney and not to the client. Thus, the client is often playing a game of incomplete information, relying on the attorney to know and guide the client through the game without the client really knowing all of the rules. This is more complicated than it might seem, because in addition to the more obvious rules, such as statutes and case law, there might be local rules as to how the game is played (e.g., how much weight is given to temporary orders by a certain judge or which mental health professionals or appraisers lean in which directions) about which clients will never really know if representing themselves. As we intend to show, the more educated clients are, the better they will be able to work with their attorney as a part of a team. This is why "educated" is one of the five standards of an ideal settlement agreement, which we will introduce later; that is, the client, in addition to other information, is educated regarding the rules of the game.

Payoffs

The outcome of a game, or a portion of a game called a "node," must have at least one payoff for at least one player. In formal game theory, payoffs are called "utilities," but the more common and less technical term "payoff" is easier to understand. We do not use the word "reward" because a payoff might not be a reward. The reason "utility" is used in game theory is because it is a formal word to which value can be assigned. For example, in poker, the utility for a particular hand might be $6.00 for the winner, but -$1.50 for each of the other players. In a dispute over a property line, the utility of a particular outcome might have a combined utility: the utility of the actual value of the land and the subjective utility of personal pride at being right with a resented neighbor. For our purposes, we will call "utility" the "payoff," but keep in mind that this has a formal meaning to which positive and negative values can be assigned.

Again, we do not use "reward" because some payoffs are not pluses; they are simply limited negatives. For example, in the prisoner's dilemma game, all of the payoffs are prison time, but less prison time is a payoff with a higher value than more prison time.

Battle of the Sexes: Another Famous Game

In a famous illustrative game originally called "battle of the sexes," a husband wants to go to a sporting event while his wife wants to go to a concert; but both husband and wife would rather be together than go to their desired event alone. Thus, if the husband and wife both go to the concert, the husband is better off, has a higher payoff, than had he gone to the sporting event alone. This has value to him, because although he received a lower payoff value than had he and his wife gone to the sporting event together, he obtains a higher payoff value than had he been alone. There is no objective value that can be assigned to these payoffs (e.g., no financial value), and nothing concrete is received by either party. The payoffs of enjoying an event and of being together relative to being alone are all subjective experiences, but they drive the game. In game theory, "utiles" are assigned to these payoffs. The most common method is assigning points based on the subjective value. In this example, a game theorist would ask the husband, on a scale of one to ten, to rate being alone versus with his wife, independent of where they go, and to assign a value to going to the sporting event compared to the concert, independent of whether alone or with his wife. The wife would be given the same task. Then it is simple math to determine the relative payoff values for each of the players.

Objective and Subjective Payoffs

We will spend more time on this later, but this introduces the concept of objective and subjective payoffs. Objective payoffs are concrete positive (aversive or less aversive) outcomes. Subjective payoffs are subtler and reflect meaning to the individual that might not be easily observed. Yet a player might work much harder for payoffs that are subjective versus objective. Thus, to others, that player might appear irrational, yet actually be playing the game very rationally, given the subjective payoffs. There are ways to discover the relative subjective values of payoffs, such as an auction.

Dividing Cash and Auction Bidding—More Games

In a famous series of experiments, one player is asked to divide an amount of money (e.g., $100) and the other player must accept that portion to get any money, or reject that portion and then neither player gets anything. The most rational outcome would appear to be that player 1 splits the pot into $99 for herself and $1 for the other player and for player 2 to accept the $1. Player 1 has an obvious advantage to playing this way, but even player 2 does better to accept a $1 than reject it. However, in actual experiments, one of two things happened: player 1 split the pot close to evenly and player 2 accepted, or player 1 gave player 2 a much smaller portion and player 2 rejected it. Post-session interviews revealed that in the former case, player 1 felt that splitting close to even was "more fair," and in the latter case, player 2 rejected the money because of the perception that player 1 was simply too "unfair" and should not get anything. The subjective value of "fairness" drove the game more than the objective value of receiving money; that is, the subjective payoff was more important to the players than the objective payoff. This will be an important principle in our game theory approach to the divorce game.

One of the advantages of thinking in terms of game theory is that we can assign utiles (payoff values) to subjective payoffs. Some games do this automatically. For example, an auction for a famous painting assigns subjective value. A very nice painting to put up on a wall might cost $2,000. If at auction, someone agrees to pay $200,000 for a painting, we can say that $2,000 was for the painting and $198,000 was the subjective value that the buyer put on having a painting by a famous painter. An auction is a means of assigning value to subjective payoffs. If the person is buying the painting as an investment, he or she is hoping that later someone else will be willing to spend even more money for a subjective payoff.

Assigning Points to Goals

We can also assign payoff value by artificial means. For example, if a divorcing wife states that she wants to receive the homestead in the divorce, wants to receive the family cabin, and wants to continue to be a stay-at-home mother, her attorney can ask her to assign a number between 0 and 100 to each of these goals that reflects how important those goals are to her. Later we will discuss how to use this principle in actually settling disputes in cases. If we assume that both parents have an objective value of 50 points for each of those outcomes, if the wife assigns 60 points to retaining the homestead, 50 to retaining the family cabin, and 90 to maintaining her role as primary parent, we can say that the homestead has a 10 point subjective value, the cabin a 0 point subjective value, and the primary parenting role a 40 point subjective value. This provides the attorney with information to use in bargaining. For example, an offer could be made to pay a premium of 5 percent above market for the homestead; if accepted, she comes out 5 points to the good. Another offer could be that the husband retains the family cabin, but that the wife has the option of a two-week vacation with the children at the cabin each year. She gains the option of use but loses nothing in her subjective value of the cabin. Additionally, the lawyer knows that being primary placement parent has high value to the client and can bargain vigorously, even giving ground on other issues to satisfy the client's subjective values.

This point system, or the many like it used in game theory, is artificial but a good way to begin gathering information about the subjective value to a client of a certain outcome. When a doctor asks us on a scale of 1 to 10 how painful something is, perhaps with accompanying pictures or descriptions of what those numbers mean, he is essentially getting a numerical value of a subjective experience. Assigning numbers to subjective values is a means of communication so that the lawyer and client have a mutual understanding.

Strategies/Decisions

There are two basic types of games when it comes to choices. There are games in which the players essentially make simultaneous choices. This does not necessarily mean that the players make choices at exactly the same time. It simply means that both of the players must make a choice about something without knowing the choice of the other party. The child game "rock-paper-scissors" is an example of a simultaneous choice game. Second, there are games in which the choices are made sequentially; that is, before player B must make a choice, she will know the choice of player A. If the husband makes a settlement offer, for example, the wife will have that information in hand when she makes a choice to accept, reject, or make a counteroffer. The strategies that tend to be rational are very different in these two types of games. As we shall see later, sequential choice games generally reach optimal outcomes for both parties, because the exchange of information in the process creates a conversion of expectations to a solution. We will present more information about this later.

Summary
A game is defined by its ingredients:

- players
- rules
- payoffs
- choices/strategies

Game Forms

Games have different forms that affect the objective and subjective goals of the parties and the choices and strategies they will likely choose.

Normal Form Game

A normal form game is a game that is played one time with the payoff dependent on the combination of strategies used by each player. A hand of poker is a good example of a normal form game. Even though each of the players has several choices to make as a part of the hand strategy (e.g., how much to bet or whether to take more cards), each of these choices tends to be based on information known at the beginning of the hand or learned along the way, but with only one payoff. Keep in mind that the payoff might be folding early; that is, losing less money than might have been lost if the player stayed in the game. In a divorce, deciding who will retain the homestead is a normal form game. It is played one time and there is one payoff—for one party, the homestead, and usually for the other party, some share of the equity in the homestead.

Repeated Form Game

A repeated form game is a game in which time becomes an element. Each player has a time at which point he or she can take an action. Choices are available at different points in the game, and the information possessed by a player might change over time. This information might be "complete" in that the player knows all of the choices available at that time and all of the payoffs that might result, or "incomplete" if a player does not know all of the choices and potential payoffs. The information might also be "perfect" if both payers know all of the history of the game to that point, or "imperfect," if one of the players does not know all of the history. We will spend more time on the nature of information later. Think of a game in which there are n+1 players, like chess. ("N" stands for the number of players and the "+1" represents chance.) Let us say chance starts the game of chess with a 50/50 chance of each player being the white or black chess pieces. Player A wins the opportunity to go first and plays white pieces; player B plays black pieces. Chance is now no longer a player. Both players know all of the rules and both know the payoffs, so it is a game of complete information. Additionally, both players are present for the entire game and so it is a game of perfect information. In this game, time requires that the players take turns. On play one, white can make one of twenty moves. Player B does not decide which move to make until seeing player A's move. Each move, then, is a "decision node," defined as a point at which it is time for a player to make a decision, and the decision is based on the information available at the time it is made. This is a repeated form game.

Perhaps more easily seen is a poker example. One hand of poker is a normal form game. However, if the players play poker for a limited period of time (e.g., until midnight or until there is only one winner left), then we have a repeated form game. The end of each hand of poker is a node, with a payoff, and the payoff for the repeated form game is who has what winnings at the end of the night.

In divorce, child support is an example of a repeated form game. It is played at different nodes and has a time set for an end to the game—when the child reaches majority age (in most cases). The nodes might be whenever one of the parties applies for a change in child support or the nodes might be each year after the parties exchange tax returns.

Extensive Repeated Form Game

This is a special type of repeated form game in which the game is repeated, sometimes indefinitely. A poker hand played one time at a casino is a normal form game. An entire evening of poker with friends is a repeated form game (i.e., strategies for winning for the entire evening might include single hand strategies that one would not use for a one-time hand play at a casino). Playing poker with the same friends every Friday with no planned end is an extensive repeated form game. As different as a repeated form game is from a normal form game, an extensive repeated form game is different from a repeated form game. The rules might be the same for all forms, but the payoff structures are dramatically different. In our poker example, the objective payoff structure is the winning or loss of money. In our evening of poker, the payoff structure is the total of the winnings/ losses for the evening and the subjective payoffs of an evening having fun with friends. The payoffs for the Friday night game for many years are almost all subjective; the players might have little or no idea if they are ahead or behind in money. The emphasis in a normal form game is on the payoff; the emphasis in a repeated form game balances the payoff with the relationship; the emphasis in extensive repeated form games is on the relationship.

In divorce, many of the extensive repeated form games are what we would call co-parenting issues. For example, there will be a residential schedule for the children, the establishment of which is a normal form game, but also there is a repeated form game in that the schedule might require making revisions at various points until the children are majority age, and finally, there is at least one extensive repeated form game in that short-term flexibility in the schedule (e.g., switching weekends) that will go on throughout the life of the family. Even when the children are adults, the family will have to navigate schedules (e.g., when and where the children will celebrate holidays and the like with their parents) in this game. In other words, the residential placement schedule is a normal form game at the time of the divorce; it becomes an repeated form game after the divorce but while the children are still minors; and the co-parenting game is an extensive repeated form game that goes on as long as the parents and children are alive.

Single Games versus Multiple Games

A single game is one game, although there might be multiple payoffs for the single game. In family law, for example, determining how to handle the Thanksgiving holiday each year is a single game. A multiple game is when several games are being played at the same time, as though it were one game. Determining "legal custody" is a multiple game; determining a "residential placement schedule" is a multiple game. As we detail later, we will use this principle to examine actual residential placement schedules, but to illustrate here, the game is really a collection of games involving weekends, school days, weekdays in the summer, holidays, vacation periods, birthdays, and so on. As common sense would suggest, it is easier to play a single game than a multiple game, largely because the factors to be considered and the payoff structure (see below regarding simple versus mixed games) for each single game contained in the multiple game might be substantially different. Later in this book, examples of the practical application of separating multiple games into single games are given.

Objective and Subjective Payoffs

We have mentioned several times the concept that payoffs can have objective value, such as money, or subjective value, such as relief from guilt. We have also mentioned that game theory makes use of an area of mathematics called "utility theory." Every payoff has a "utile," i.e., value to the player, a value which has an *objective value* and a *subjective value*. Each type of value theoretically can be assigned an ordinal value, if somewhat arbitrary, and can be used to determine preferred outcomes to the game.

For example, player A might want to go to movie X and player B might want to go to movie Y. On the face of it, neither movie X nor movie Y have a quantifiable value, but we can assign an ordinal value to each by analyzing player A's and player B's relative interest in each of the movies. Thus, after careful inquiry, we might give movie X a value of 4 (on a scale of 1 to 5, from no preference to high preference) from player A's perspective and a value of 2 from player B's perspective, and we might also assign 2 and 4 values for each of the players for movie Y in the reverse. In this way, we can analyze and find the solution to the game. By understanding the preferred outcomes, theoretically, we can determine which strategies are likely to be chosen by the players, i.e., each player will choose strategies that have the highest likelihood of producing the preferred outcome. For example, if player A is indifferent to movie Y and movie X has a utile of 3 and player B ranks movie X as a 1 and movie Y as a 5, the strategies that the players are likely to employ will be different and the outcome predictable.

This might sound confusing because in day-to-day life we do not think like this. If a husband says he wants to go to the movies and would like to see movie X, and the wife says she would love to go but really wants to see movie Y, the husband, recognizing the wife's very strong preference and himself more indifferent to which movie they see, might just say, "Sure, let's go to movie Y." What has happened is that the husband very quickly did the calculations described in the prior paragraph, without knowing it. Our brains are capable of these complex calculations in an instant. All a game theorist is doing is detailing the calculations.

I return to an earlier metaphor, that of the football player throwing the ball to a receiver. An experienced quarterback will have thrown a ball to a receiver in practice and in games thousands of times. Each time, he analyzes the throw. Was it too high or low, was it thrown too hard or too soft, and was it thrown at the right angle given the movements of the receiver? What Sir Isaac Newton did when he invented calculus was simply develop a numerical way to analyze motion, depending on force, angle, and direction. The quarterback's brain is quickly making those calculations, without the awareness of the player, and adjusting the force, angle, and direction to get the payoff of a completed pass. All an observing mathematician is doing is assigning ordinal values to those calculations.

Behaviorists—that is, people who study behaviors—tell us that most of us do not really understand why we make many of the decisions we make, but that our brains make calculations as to which behaviors will produce a payoff, which might bring a positive outcome, but also which might help avoid an aversive outcome. Game theory experiments have consistently demonstrated that although people sometimes do not understand their decisions and strategies, there is a consistency behind those choices that is rational; that is, is aimed at producing the best payoffs.

Subjective values are critical considerations in game theory and this is especially true in family law, where subjective values are often a more important consideration for the parties than objective values. This is why attorneys will see clients make what appear to be irrational choices, such as spending $1,000 in attorney fees to obtain a property item worth $400. The player might on the surface appear irrational, but at the time of the game, the subjective value of the payoff to the player for winning the property is worth at least $600.

Psychological Importance of Prevailing

Subjective values can be difficult to detect, even those of one's own client, without careful inquiry. In the movie example above, the solution is simple, if we only weigh the objective value of the movie to each player: player A goes to movie X and player B to movie Y.

However, let us assume that player A is the husband and player B is the wife. Let us further assume that both prefer to go to the movies together rather than separately, but the husband's preference for being together is stronger than the wife's. We will quantify the husband's preference to be together on a five-point scale (low preference to high preference) as a 4 and the wife's as a 2. Let us further assume that the husband believes he has "given in" the last few times when they have decided to go out and that he believes that his wife should give in this time, whereas the wife believes that her husband spends a great deal of time engaging in his preferred activities with his friends and that he should defer to her choices when they are together. We will call this the psychological importance of prevailing, and after careful interviewing, we assign a 4 to the husband and a 3 to the wife. Now we see a situation dominated by subjective values. We could do the math and end up with total payoff values for the husband and wife and determine the strategies each is likely to use to "win" the dispute. However, this is a complicated process and unnecessary to make our point. The solution for the objective values was simple; the solution when adding in subjective values becomes complex, particularly when there are complex psychological subjective values operating. Contextual factors might be equally important. A person might be acting rationally when viewed contextually, but acting irrationally when viewed through the narrow and constricted lens of the legal system. This is particularly true in divorce! Most experienced family law attorneys have seen clients for whom the psychological importance of prevailing is the driving force, even if "prevailing" means "getting even" and is self-defeating.

Every Goal Has an Objective and Subjective Value

Just to spice this concept up a bit, we posit that nothing has an objective value alone. Everything has a subjective value. A house might be appraised at $200,000, but is that the objective value of the house? Take that exact same house and place it in a different neighborhood and it might be worth more or less, depending on the subjective values of the neighborhoods. One potential buyer might pay more because of the subjective value of being close to a school, and another might not be willing to buy at list because of the subjective value of being too close to a school. Even cash has subjective value. Ten dollars to Warren Buffet has a different subjective value than to a hungry poor person.

This book will emphasize the importance of the attorney thoroughly exploring and, in some instances, quantifying the subjective values his or her client assigns to payoffs in the divorce game. By doing so, the attorney might prevent later conflicts and disputes, even with his or her own client, and will be better able to seek settlement agreements in the bargaining process that maximize the value of the payoffs for his or her client. By thoroughly exploring our example client who is paying $1,000 for a property item worth $400, the attorney might find that the object is actually worth an additional $200 to the client purely for sentimental reasons (e.g., the client would pay $600, but no more, if the item was for sale by a third party) and that the client is willing to pay the additional $400 for the psychological payoff of knowing that the spouse does not have the property. Most attorneys have seen such disputes regarding wedding rings or Christmas ornaments, for example. Now the decision is understood by the attorney—the client is making a rational and informed choice, and neither will later resent the outcome if it had been explored before the offer. The client might later kick himself for making a stupid decision, but at least it was an informed one, not done with any unfair advantage. If when exploring the subjective value, the attorney and client discover that the total objective and subjective value is only $700, the client will likely be rational and not spend the $1,000 for it. Without having explored the objective and subjective value thoroughly, the client might get emotionally caught up in the bargaining process and pay more than something is both objectively and subjectively worth.

In Game Theory, the Pot Can Be 146 Percent Not 100 Percent

Understanding the objective and subjective values has another, perhaps even more important, function in bargaining. Game theory research finds that parties can achieve outcomes in games in which each party can receive up to 73 percent of the total value of payoffs. How can this be? How can two parties receive 146 percent of the pot? The answer lies in the subjective value of the payoffs.

A frequently given example in game theory of this principle is the "cut-the-cake" game. In the game, one player is told to cut a cake in two, and the other player gets to choose which piece she will receive. The rational solution is that player 1 cuts the cake in half and player 2 is indifferent to which half she receives. However, what if the cake is a marble cake and a third is mostly chocolate, which player 2 loves, and the other two thirds is vanilla, which player 1 prefers? Player 1 now cuts the cake in thirds, isolating the chocolate third from the vanilla two-thirds. Player 2 chooses the one-third chocolate cake and both are happy, both getting more value than if they received half the cake. Other more extensive and more easily quantifiable payoffs have found that a game can be played so that both players get up to 73 percent of the pot.

In reality, it might be impossible to determine an objective value devoid of subjective value. Let us examine the choice between two cars: an expensive luxury car (e.g., a high-model Mercedes) and a reliable mid-price car (e.g., a Toyota Camry). What is the objective value of the two cars? If we simply say the cost of buying the car, everyone would buy a Camry, which is of course not what happens. What if we calculate the cost per mile driven? We could add to the cost of the car the predicted total number of miles expected, the gas mileage each car gets, the total cost of expected service and repairs, and so on. If we divide the total number of expected miles by the total expected costs of driving, we could arrive at an expected cost per mile driven. People of course might only roughly figure this into their decision on which car to buy, but we could, presumably, arrive at a set of figures that we could call the objective value of the cars. Could this objective value be free of subjective value? Assume that the total cost per mile for the Camry is $1.78 and the total cost per mile for the Mercedes is $3.56. If this is the objective value, then again everyone would buy a Camry. Both cars are likely to have the same features (e.g., CD player or GPS), and the rides are likely fairly similar in comfort. Perhaps the aesthetics of the Mercedes are slightly better, perhaps the Mercedes in an accident is slightly safer, perhaps the sound system is slightly more pleasant, and so on, but is that worth paying twice the cost of the Camry per mile driven? Cars make statements about a person's values and priorities. The party who drives a mini-van lives in a very different world (and value paradigm) than the party who drives a sports car.

The subjective value is the answer. If the person choosing makes $500,000 per year, those subtle differences might well be worth a difference in cost that is hardly worth noting. If the person choosing makes $32,000 per year, the difference in cost per mile likely has a substantially higher subjective value. One might also factor in other subjective values. In one neighborhood, a Mercedes might suggest success and don prestige on the owner. In another neighborhood, a Mercedes might suggest drug dealing and instill fear in others. Both have a subjective value. People buy Mercedes for the subjective value of the car, not the objective value.

Auctions Reveal Subjective Payoffs to Parties

An auction is a game designed specifically to determine subjective values. An antique Globe oak filing cabinet might hold as many files as a cheap metal filing cabinet that costs $80. We might say, somewhat arbitrarily, that the objective value of the Globe is $80. If at auction, the final bid is $650, we can say that the subjective value of the Globe is $570. What is the bidder getting for $570? It could be the aesthetics of the filing cabinet, or it might match an oak lift-front bookshelf, or it might make the office appear more luxurious, and therefore the professional appears more successful to prospective clients and so on. Whatever the subjective values, the bidder is willing to pay for them, and if Globes typically go for $800, feel that he or she got a great deal.

One can translate the auction concept into divorce practice. If two parties want the same property, for example, there are several ways to establish an "auction" for the property. Let us assume that the property is household property, such as furniture, real silverware, a few special art objects, and so on. One could first distribute the household property for which there is no dispute, leaving only the disputed items. One could give each party 1,000 points to be divided and assigned to each item of property. A piece of art, for example might have 70 points from one party and 55 points from the other. After the parties have assigned all of their points to all of the disputed property, without the knowledge of the other party, the lists are compared and the highest bid gets the property item. If there are ties, a second auction could be held in which each party gets another 1,000 points to divide and assign to just those remaining items. In this way, the parties end up with payoffs, property items that were relatively more valuable to him and her. Monetary values might still need to be assigned to the property items and packaged into the property settlement, but in this way, the parties were able to express the subjective value of the items.

In brief, little attention is sometimes paid to the most important aspect of settlement issues, whether that is property, support, time with children, or even control of decisions affecting the children. Payoff outcomes have objective values, often established by statute or case law, but also have subjective value to the parties. By exploring the subjective value of payoffs, the parties can not only optimize their own payoff structure but also grow the pot to nearly 150 percent—to be divided between them.

Later in this book we will deal more with the mechanics of eliciting subjective values. Here, we want to emphasize their importance in reaching optimal outcomes for the parties.

Solution Concept

The solution concept is fundamental to game theory, because it predicts the likely strategies of the players. Once the preferred outcomes of the parties (i.e., the value of the combined objective and subjective payoffs) and the strategies available to each of the players are known, one can predict which strategies will be chosen and used. There are two sets of solution concepts: one for games of strategy, in which each player plays the game without bargaining (e.g., most card games), and one for games in which the parties have the opportunity to bargain. Because divorce is a game of bargaining, we will concern ourselves solely with solution concepts for bargaining games.

John Nash, Thomas Bayes, and Lloyd Shapley

There are a number of bargaining solution concepts, each with different levels of sophistication and points of emphasis. John Nash developed an equilibrium solution concept that is widely recognized, but others, such as Lloyd Shapley, have developed solution concepts that offer more flexibility in application. We will not explore these different models in detail. Suffice it to say that we will apply a Nash solution concept, slightly modified by the models developed by Shapley and by Bayes rule. Bayes rule is critical in our bargaining model.

Thomas Bayes is an interesting historical figure. I am not sure what post he held in the 1700s, but was an abbot or some such religious figure who was also a mathematician. He bucked the system at the time in working with probability mathematics and developed a theorem or rule which suggested that probability changes or at least the manner in which people perceive probability changes as they gain new information. For example, a person might begin with the perception that a coin flip will come up heads 50 percent of the time. However, if after the coin is tossed a number of times, heads comes up 70 percent of the time, the person might perceive that the coin might be biased and change the perception of future tosses to a 70 percent probability of heads. The basic notion is that a rational person changes beliefs when receiving new information.

This becomes a valuable tool in applying solution concepts to divorce bargaining because the basic principle is that with additional information, bargaining becomes increasingly fine-tuned to the facts. For example, if a wife makes an offer on property, the offer contains information with regard to the wife's subjective goals and priorities. The husband can use this information to adjust his perception of the desired outcome for the wife, reorganize his subjective goals and priorities, and make a counteroffer that also informs the wife. This process creates a convergence of expectations; that is, both parties can begin to see the ingredients of an optimal outcome for both.

Cooperative Bargaining and Compromise Bargaining Lead to Optimal Outcomes

The solution concept proffered in this book combines a cooperative bargaining process to a point (Nash and Shapley); followed by a dispute-based or, more properly, a non-cooperative or compromise bargaining process (Nash); and finally, where the strategies of the players can change with exposure to additional information (Bayes). This is particularly true in divorce bargaining, as each player learns more about the subjective payoff values of the other player. To reiterate, we posit that in order to reach optimal outcomes for both parties, the bargaining process goes through two phases: cooperative bargaining and then compromise bargaining, both of which are enhanced by Bayes rule—that is, the parties gain increasing amounts of information during the bargaining process about the subjective and objective payoff structure for both of them.

Cooperative bargaining by itself poses several important challenges for the attorney, CPA, mediator, or arbiter. For example, a game of perfect and compete information provides the best opportunity for cooperative bargaining success but might hinder a position-based dispute bargaining process, particularly if using hardball negotiating tactics. For example, if two players are deciding on a residential placement schedule for a child, in the cooperative stage, each will benefit from revealing all information, i.e., personal preferences and the reasons for them. However, if at the end of this stage, the parties have not agreed, the earlier revelations might harm the positional dispute that will likely follow. For example, if one parent reveals that his interest is not so much in having the child sleep at his house, and in fact because of his early work schedule would prefer not, but does want to be actively involved in the child's school life and extracurricular activities, the chances of improving payoff value for both parties is substantial in the cooperative bargaining phase. However, this information might later be used in hardball negotiating against his interests. This is one of the more brilliant aspects of Nash, who found a means by which the cooperative and non-cooperative[3] outcomes can be combined and are not in competition with one another.

Growing the Pot with Win-Win-Plus Bargaining

The defining characteristic of the cooperative bargaining phase is that the parties are growing the pot—the bargaining is improving the payoffs for both parties, or at least for one party while not diminishing the payoff for the other party. Non-cooperative bargaining, or what we have named compromise bargaining, does not imply animosity or conflict. It is simply a descriptive term that describes the phase of bargaining when in order to improve payoff value to one party, the payoff value for the other party necessarily is reduced. We will be going into this in more detail later in the book. We will also be describing a third bargaining phase, which we call "win-win-plus," which is a particular type of post-agreement value-added bargaining that aims to enhance the outcome for at least one if not both parties, without diminishing the outcome for either party.

The concept of "solution" is simply that there are optimal outcomes in games, including the divorce game, that are best achieved by applying the game theory principles to the bargaining process that we will be further exploring in later chapters.

Payoff Structure

Simple Game

A simple game is one in which the parties play one game for one payoff. A simple game lends itself to easy analysis and an easy resolution; i.e., the solution concepts for simple games usually determine a dominant

---

3. Cooperative and non-cooperative (compromise) bargaining are treated in more detail later in the book.

strategy and a more predictable outcome. A simple game might be a game played in an extensive form game at one node. For example, a hand of poker is a simple game, because there is one game with one payoff, but it might be occurring in an repeated form game, such as an evening of poker, which is a series of simple games that have payoff nodes and that combine into an repeated form game. In divorce, deciding what the schedule for Thanksgivings will be is a simple game. It is one game played for one payoff or a closely related set of payoffs that cannot be divided (e.g., food, family, post-dinner games).

Mixed Game

In contrast to a simple game, a mixed game is one in which the players play one game for more than one payoff. Not only might the payoffs be different for each of the players, but the relative utility (value) of each of the available payoffs might also be different for each player. This is especially true of the subjective values of the payoffs. Mixed games create numerous complications for both analysis and resolution. If a game has six or seven payoffs, each with different relative value to the players, and some of the payoffs are not even known to both players, the game is likely to be a complicated and messy one. In fact, mixed games promote competitive strategies as the best strategies. By confronting divorcing parties with mixed games in the legal system, therefore, the legal system promotes adversarial competitive strategies.

This is a major problem with the divorce game, as it applies to residential placement schedules for children; it is a mixed game for both players. Although each player is playing one game (i.e., trying to get the most time with the child), there are numerous payoffs, each with relatively different value to each of the players. Typical payoffs include the following:

- Time with the child. This by itself could be a mixed game. There might be certain types of time with the child that are more or less valuable for each of the players. The wife might highly value nighttime and dinners, but because she works, might value after-school time low, whereas the husband might put low values on nighttime, but very high values on after-school and dinner times. The payoff for getting a day, like Wednesday, might have different relative values to the players. The wife might traditionally bowl or attend a book club with good friends on Wednesdays and assign a low value to that day for placement of the children, whereas

Wednesday might be a half-day at work for the husband, giving him good after-school availability, and he might assign a high value to that day.

- Avoidance of loss of time with the child. Again, this might be mixed. The wife might not want a stepmom to have certain types of time with the child, for example, and thus the subjective value is not so much on getting that time as preventing certain types of relationships to develop between the child and the stepmom. Thus, getting time with the child has one payoff value, but avoiding the loss of time with the child might have a different payoff value. One parent might be indifferent to some loss of time whereas the other parent might find it very difficult not to see the child every day.

- Power to make certain decisions (e.g., choice of school).

- Possible retention of the homestead or other property settlement advantages.

- Levels of child support and possibly spousal support.

- Legal power or advantage (e.g., in a relocation dispute).

- Gender equity or status. The husband might be "fighting" the good battle for equal treatment under the law and fairness to both parents, whereas the wife might be fighting for the status of being the "mother" and all of the cultural meanings attached to this title.

- Retention of pre-divorce family roles. The wife might have put much more personal meaning into her role as parent than did the husband prior to the separation, organizing her life more around the role, and have a great deal of meaning in life to lose if substantial residential placement time is lost to the dad.

- Resolution of spousal conflicts. The husband might see getting substantial residential placement time as an opportunity to prove, finally, that his parenting ideas are superior to the wife's. The wife might resent that her husband did not help with the children during the marriage and now wants to exclude him as offering too little too late.

- A desire for involvement in certain aspects of the child's life. The husband might be fighting for placement because of an assumption, true or not, that if the child spends most of the time at the wife's home, the child will gravitate toward a social life near the wife's home and husband might not want to be left out of that part of the child's life, or might believe that the child will want to spend decreasing time with him as the child ages and peers become increasingly important.

As one might guess, the game of seeking a certain percentage of the residential placement time can be extremely contentious when one recognizes the complicated payoff structure. Each payoff might have more or less value to each player, and the parties might have only vague impressions, possibly based on inferential thinking rather than facts, of what the payoffs for the other player might be.

The resolution of financial issues can also be complicated by mixed games. Spousal support can often have many different payoffs for both parties. Like a residential placement schedule for children, while the outcome is a number, the payoffs associated with that number or some of the conditions associated with that number (e.g., remarriage) might be many. Retaining the homestead, for example, is at base a real estate deal, but it could have numerous subjective payoff values. Objectively, one of the parties is buying the house from the marriage. Subjectively, there might be neighbors who are close friends to both parties, and retaining the homestead might have the expected payoff of retaining/losing those friendships. Retaining the homestead might create an advantage in a dispute over residential placement of the children. The proximity to the children's school might be a logistic advantage or simply wanting to be the parent with the home with which the children are most familiar and comfortable might be a payoff.

As a rule, the more payoffs for each game played, the more complicated is the playing and the more intense and often contentious are the strategies chosen. We will be using this principle extensively in our bargaining model in order to achieve optimal outcomes for both parties.

Game Structures

Zero-Sum Games

In zero-sum games, there is a limit on the payoff that must be divided between players. For example, an often studied game is called "split the dollar," although it is played in various forms.

Split the Dollar: Another Game

Let us assume that I put $100 on a table and instruct the two players that they have five minutes to decide how to divide the money. If they have not agreed on a split in five minutes, the researcher will remove

$1 and they will have another five minutes to divide the remaining $99 and so on. One can imagine a number of scenarios to this game, but the defining characteristic is that any amount that one player gains is at the expense of the other player. There is a limit to the payoffs that each party receives. Interestingly, this game tends to prompt one of two solutions. Either parties divide the money in half in the first round or they tend to battle to the death, continuing until there is no money left.

Oddly, most parents in an intact marriage do not consider parenting a zero-sum game. Few parents count how much time they spend with their children and compare and compete over this. In fact, some of the "burdens" in a marriage, which the parents will often try to get the other parent to do (e.g., taking a child to the doctor), become a competitive "prize" after a divorce. Zero-sum games promote competitive strategies for the very reason that one person's gain is at least perceived as the other person's loss.

Non-Zero-Sum Games

There is no generally accepted term for the opposite of a zero-sum game. We describe these games simply as non-zero-sum games. In a non-zero-sum game, the payoffs can be quantified by assigning ordinal values. A non-zero-sum game occurs when the gain of one party does not necessarily lead to loss by the other party. As we stated above, happily married parents rarely count the percentage of time that each makes decisions and spends with the children. Most might have a general sense of who spends more time with the children and who is more responsible for child-related tasks, but beyond that, they do not compete or even pay much attention to the division of child-related "labor." In an ideal family system, if one includes providing for the financial needs of the children (and family as a whole), the division of time and decision-making authority is based on abilities, interests, the needs of the children, and practical considerations.

One could assign value to each of these factors. For example, out of a list of twenty parenting activities, each parent could assign an ordinal value to each activity. One could arbitrarily give each parent 1,000 points to spend on these activities and have them bid on each. In a sense, without the formality of bidding, many parents do this naturally. A dad who really enjoys and is good at helping with homework might end up doing the lion's share of that task, while the mom who enjoys the fun and intimacy of reading to the child might find herself doing much of that task. In a sense, they have unconsciously auctioned off the tasks to one another and ended up in a natural balance. One parent gains, but this is not at the expense of the other. The mother loses nothing when the dad is helping with homework any more than the dad loses when the mom is reading to the children.

Yet, at and after divorce, parenting often appears to become a zero-sum game, in large part because the court awards (perhaps inadvertently, "rewards") residential placement time and decision-making rights to each parent. Because the time available is limited, every hour gained by one player/parent is an hour lost by the other player/parent. This is an important concept because zero-sum games tend to be played with competitive rather than cooperative strategies. The court system transforms the non-zero-sum game of parenting during the marriage into a zero-sum game in the divorce, thus extending the "split" of the spousal relationship into a "split" of the parenting relationship. This interferes with the more natural split that might occur if the court did not treat child-rearing post-divorce in this manner.

In the same way that parents in a marriage might naturally gravitate to different parenting tasks in a cooperative manner, if parenting after divorce was not treated as a zero-sum game by the legal system, the parents might gravitate more naturally to an effective division of parenting labor under the new circumstance of having two residences instead of one. This might appear impossible, but really only involves some logistics obstacles. In a cooperative bargaining process, for example, parents could decide that maintaining their homework and reading tasks is a priority, make logistic decisions reflecting those priorities (e.g., end up in residences close to one another, shift work schedules slightly, etc.), and the father could end up with homework time every school day with the children, and the mother could end up with reading time (e.g., right before bedtime). By making residential placement schedules a zero-sum game, particularly focusing on overnights, the legal system becomes an obstacle to the more natural division of parenting labor and creates a game in which competitive, sometimes highly conflictual, strategies are the rational choice. On top of this, the legal system makes the zero-sum game a mixed one with numerous payoffs for "winning." Getting one more overnight might have substantial financial implications, for example.

How then do we account for those amicable divorces in which the parties divide up the child's time in a way that reflects a more natural division of parenting tasks? These players appear to be playing the game irrationally, but in fact are making rational decisions. The answer lies in the subjective payoff structure. The subjective value of an amicable, cooperative co-parenting relationship and of doing their best to arrange the child's life in a rational manner, playing to each of their strengths and availability, might outweigh the objective payoffs of child support amounts and so on. Because of the subjective goals of the parties, they appear to be irrational but are not. They simply have resisted the temptation by the legal system to view parenting as a zero-sum game.

Cooperative and Non-cooperative/ Compromise Bargaining

This is a counterintuitive concept, because the lay meaning of these terms is different from how they are used in game theory. Cooperative bargaining sets axioms that define what an agreement between rational players *should have* and then examines whether such solutions are possible (and technically, whether said agreements are unique). Compromise (non-cooperative) bargaining examines the rules in a bargaining environment and derives the likely solution by examining how rational parties would best advance their self-interest. In simpler terms, cooperative bargaining determines how many unique solutions exist that are *efficient*; that is, which provide the best outcome for each party without diminishing the value of the outcome for the other party—"win-win" solutions. The basic concept here is that the payoff structure can often be improved for one or both of the parties without diminishing the payoff structure for either party.

Compromise bargaining begins when in order for one party to gain ground (i.e., improve the payoff), the other party must lose ground (i.e., decrease the payoff). At this point in the bargaining, there is a "win-lose" solution.[4] This does not necessarily mean compromise in the form of traditional bargaining, however. For example, even though

---

4. Compromise bargaining does not imply conflict. Parties can bargain through this stage in an amicable and "cooperative" manner.

one party might lose ground in the payoff structure, there might be trade-offs that can be used to offset those losses.

Example:

Let's look at two examples to understand this principle. The first exemplifies cooperative bargaining. In the "split the dollar game: mentioned earlier, two players are told to split $100 within a time limit or face a reduction and possibly receive no money at all. The first step is cooperative bargaining. Before discussing how to divide the money, the players agree that the following axioms (standards) should apply to the solution: each player receives some money; player A should receive more money because player A found the game in the first place and without her efforts, player B would not have had the opportunity to receive money (i.e., there is a premium for having found the game); and neither player should receive more than 60 percent of the pot. This game can be solved in an axiomatic manner, although the solution is not unique (i.e., there are ten solutions that meet these criteria). This is cooperative bargaining; that is, that axioms considered fair, or "win-win," are applied so that both players know they will each receive money somewhere in the $40–$60 range. Now the players might bargain through the compromise stage (i.e., where in that $10 range they will make the split) and arrive at a solution.

An equilibrium solution (Nash) would suggest $55 for player A and $45 for player B, whereas a more complicated solution concept like Shapley would suggest has numbers closer to $53 and $47. What makes this game a cooperative bargaining game is that the players set axioms for the solution first and then bargain within the parameters of those axioms. When we address divorce bargaining, we will posit that starting with axioms enhances a cooperative bargaining process.

In a second example, let us assume that the parties take a hardball negotiation approach. In this pure non-cooperative bargaining approach to the split the dollar game, one looks at the solutions in which each player has the best chance of advancing his or her self-interest. For example, player B, a keen judge of character, decides that player A is non-competitive and wants to leave the table with money. Player B, then, might choose a *Boulwareism* approach; that is, make a "fair and reasonable, but final offer." Player B "bargains" by telling player A that he will take $70 and player A can have $30. Player B states that although it is not a fair division, player B would rather leave the table with no money than accept less than $70. Player A can then only accept $30 or walk away with nothing. If player B is correct—that player A is non-competitive and will rationalize the unequal division in order to get at least $30—player A will at the last minute take the deal. There are no mutually agreed-upon axioms by which to judge the solution to this game. Each player, given his and her character, chooses the strategy that best advances his and her personal interests. One can see a different emotional climate is likely to prevail in these two different examples.

The genius of the Nash equilibrium solutions is that they bridge the gap and account for both cooperative and compromise bargaining. His approach takes into account that each player plays the game most rationally if he and she endeavor first to maximize benefits to both players and then bargain within the narrow margins of the maximum solution. The authors will take this one step further by borrowing and modifying the concept of "value-created bargaining" (Mnookin, Peppet, and Tulumello). We will expand upon this concept later in a later chapter.

A Working Example to Illustrate Cooperative and Compromise Bargaining

A family law example might further illustrate this concept of how cooperative bargaining and compromise bargaining can interface. Let us assume that the wife wants to have the children ten of every fourteen days and wants the husband to have four of every fourteen days. Let us assume that she offers him every Wednesday and alternating weekends, from Friday to Sunday. Let us assume that the husband wants the children seven of every fourteen days and will accept several different equal time schedules. In traditional bargaining models, an assumption would be made that the solution lies somewhere between the husband having four and seven days, inclusive. Each party would determine a minimum (e.g., the wife might prefer to agree to five days rather than go to court), and the bargaining would begin. Both parties would begin to make the best case that they can for their individual positions, for themselves, and against the other. Strategies would include considerations of adding weight to one side or the other position. For example, the husband might realize that his travel for work is a hindrance and might change jobs to minimize travel, even though this substantially reduces family income. The wife might decide that a custody evaluation is likely to give her position more weight because she has had the traditional role of primary parent and she works as a teacher. This traditional bargaining model has predictable patterns. As in politics, the attacks on the other party are likely to escalate as decision time (a court date) approaches, creating an ugly family atmosphere, sometimes with levels of anger, hurt, and distrust that are difficult (sometimes impossible) to recover from. The case intensity will continue to build until either someone blinks on the courthouse steps or there is a trial. Keep in mind that the parties are treating this like a zero-sum game: there are fourteen nights, a limited pot, and any night that one parent gets, the other loses.

In the cooperative/compromise bargaining model, axioms (namely, standards or agreed-upon goals) would be set at the beginning.

Parties Agree to Axioms at the Beginning of Bargaining

Let us assume that the objective and subjective goals and interests of the parties are thoroughly examined by their attorneys and the following axioms are set:

- Both parents prefer a parent to care for the children rather than daycare or after- school care.
- Both parents want the children to have good relationships with both parents.
- Both parents want to maximize involvement with the children in ways that reflect each parent's skills and interests.
- Both parents want at least some involvement in all aspects of the child's life, including school, activities, and friendships.
- Both parents want to take vacations with the child and want the child to take vacations with the other parent.
- Both parents want to have each holiday be as good as it can be for all involved, including extended family.

Separating the Games: Multiple to Single; Mixed to Simple

At this point, the attorneys apply other game theory principles and separate multiple games into single games and mixed games into simple games.

1. The bargaining begins by focusing on each of the *holidays*, meeting the axiom of each holiday being planned—to maximize opportunities for the children and each parent to enjoy as good a holiday as possible, given limitations of reality. Let us assume that this ends up being an equal division of holiday time.

2. Once holidays schedules are completed, the attorneys begin to bargain regarding **vacations** and determine that each parent may take up to three weeks of vacation with the children each year and set the rules and procedures for this (e.g., periods of notification and how much school time can be missed for a vacation).

3. They then bargain relative to *weekends* and determine that an alternating weekend schedule best fits the lifestyles and goals of the parties and meets some of the axioms (e.g., both are able to participate in the extracurricular activities of the children).

4. Next, the attorneys bargain with a focus on *summers*. In discussing summer, additional axioms are discovered. First, both parties plan to take their vacation time in the summers. Because this is a repeated game (each summer is a node), they decide on procedures for identifying when their summer vacations will occur (more about the use of procedures later). After subtracting vacations and weekends from the total of summer days, and after investigating summer options while they work, they add an additional axiom. Because most summer camps and daytime programs operate on a weekly basis, they determine to equally divide the remaining weeks in a manner that allows each parent to enroll the children in desired activities and that accommodates the husband's travel schedule. This allows each of the parents to investigate programs and speak with the children about those programs without having to do a great deal of coordinating with one another. A final axiom that is added to summers is that neither parent wants to go a full week without seeing the children, so they add a midweek visit with the other parent. Similarly, breaks from school are planned, and it turns out, the additional school breaks will be shared equally. This has all been cooperative bargaining because the solutions are meeting the axioms and both parents are "winning" in that the payoff structure is meeting both their objective and subjective goals.

5. The parties are now focused on the single game of how to divide

school days. By taking this approach, the parties have eliminated about 200 days of each year and are left with about 165 school days (depending on school districts). The husband's original position is that he wants 82 of those days; the wife's position was that she wants 112 of those days and offered the husband 53 days. The "dispute" therefore has been reduced with cooperative bargaining to the difference between 53 and 82 days per year, a difference of 29 days per year.

We are still not done with cooperative bargaining. The attorneys ask the parties questions about what they are each trying to accomplish with their positions on these remaining 29 days. The husband asserts that he does not want to go a full week every two weeks without seeing his children; he wants to be more active in helping the children with their homework and being an important part of their school lives. The husband is concerned that the wife will, if she has a legal advantage, move out of the area to be near her family of origin. He wants to play a pivotal role in their extracurricular activities, which he considers critical to the development of the children and about which he thinks that the wife minimizes and will be too passive about. The wife asserts that she is available after school every day; historically has been the primary person helping with schoolwork, for which she feels particularly qualified as a teacher; has been almost solely responsible for getting the children to medical and dental appointments; and the children are used to seeing her every day and would suffer if they did not. The husband is indifferent to the wife continuing in some of these roles, and the wife is indifferent to the husband taking the lead on the extracurricular activities.

With this information, the attorneys bargain to the following solution: the wife will continue to take the children *every day after school*, independent of the residential placement schedule, meeting several of the axioms, including the wife's desire for almost daily contact with the children. The husband will take the lead in enrolling the children in *extracurricular activities*, after discussions with the wife, and will be able to take the children to those activities on school days, if he is available, independent of the residential placement schedule. This, too, meets several axioms and the interests of the husband. Thus, through cooperative bargaining, most of the waking hours of the children during school days have been decided. Next the parties come down to dividing those remaining 29 evenings and overnights. Now we are at the compromise bargaining phase. One or both of the parties must give in, so the gain of one must include a loss to the other. However, we have so reduced the payoff value of those days (now only 29 evenings) through the cooperative bargaining phase that the parties are practically indifferent to the outcome. The wife now asserts that she thinks it is disruptive if the schedule not only changes when the husband travels but also when they try to find makeup times. The husband asserts that it is still important to him that he be considered by the children as their equal parent. They agree that the husband will get all 29 evenings and overnights, thus having an equal residential placement schedule, but that the wife will get all days that he travels for work and he will forfeit all days lost for travel for work, without makeup days, a trade-off that trades higher value payoffs for lower value payoffs for each party. The wife gets the additional days per year when the husband travels for work, without the disruption of having makeup times; the husband gets an equal residential placement schedule. The wife also accepts limitations and presumptions regarding any future relocation.

Separating the Issues: Mixed to Simple Games

The parties separate the issue of child support from the outcome of the agreements on residential placement, further separating a mixed game into simple games. They agree that child support is determined on the equal residential placement schedule, but the husband pays a per diem amount for days that he travels for work and she takes the children. The wife agrees to certain presumptions regarding relocation, after asserting that she has no plans to move in any event. Again, we still see improvements in the payoff structure for each of the parties without diminishing the payoff structure of the other party; that is, we are still in the cooperative bargaining phase.

In this example, we have applied several of the principles of game theory to show how in a very practical manner they can facilitate settlement, while at the same time protecting the extensive repeated game of co-parenting. Not only has the "ugly" process of traditional bargaining and litigation been avoided, but also settlement approaches have been modeled and practiced that the parents can use in the future to resolve disagreements. Rather than competitive bargaining strategies, they have learned to separate multiple games and mixed games into single and simple games, to identify objective and subjective payoffs, and use cooperative bargaining strategies and effective compromise strategies in the process.

High-Conflict Families

Some parents will not benefit from this approach. In the group of parents that fall into the lowest category on communication and cooperation and highest category of open conflict, there is a deeply held different philosophy at work. In most cases, parents will, if only grudgingly, acknowledge that the children should have a substantial, meaningful relationship with both of them, that the children benefit from what each has to offer, and that they are both at least fit parents. This is often accompanied by concerns and some real problems, but the basic philosophy is supportive of both parents reaching objective and subjective goals for the children's lives. In high-conflict families, there is a substantially different, also deeply held philosophy at work, one that says the children would be better off with a minimum or no influence and involvement with the other parent. They rarely see that water seeks its own level and that they, too, are likely doing more harm to their children than good. Trying to force parents with this philosophy into a cooperative bargaining process is like sticking a square peg into a round hole. The goals in these families are very different from our middle group of parents who might benefit from the bargaining approach proffered here.

Bayes Rule

Bayes rule is sometimes referred to as Bayes theorem or Bayes law. Although we have mentioned Bayes and Bayesian bargaining elsewhere, for our purposes, it is important to understand Bayes rule. The technical definition is a complex mathematical probability model developed by mathematician Thomas Bayes in the early eighteenth century. The probability model essentially states numerically that people start with a belief that a certain event will happen with a certain probability, but that with new information, rational people change their belief as to that probability.

The Coin Flip Game

For example, there are three coins, two of which are fair (will come up heads 50 percent of the time if flipped) and an unfair one that is weighted to come up heads every time. If handed a coin, a rational person will calculate and believe that the odds that the single coin is unfair is one in three. If the person flips the coin three times and it comes up heads each time, the additional information changes the belief. It still could be a fair coin, but the probability of the coin being unfair has changed. We could show the calculation, but suffice it to say that the probability that the coin is unfair is now four in five.

Convergence of Expectations

In game theory, Bayes rule has come to mean that a person's beliefs about the other party/position change with new information. Bayesian bargaining posits that as the parties receive new information in the bargaining process, their beliefs about the objective and subjective goals of the other party change. Their beliefs about their own objective and subjective goals might also change, as they monitor their reactions to proposals. These changing beliefs result in a convergence of expectations with regard to the outcome of the bargaining.

For example, let player A, in a dispute over choice of school, have a belief that player B eventually wants to gain an advantage in a future residential schedule dispute. This is because player B first proposes a school near his house and distant from hers. Because player A does not want to be at such a disadvantage, player A proposes a different school, not for the purposes of gaining the proposed school for the child, but for the purposes of preventing a disadvantage in a future residential placement dispute. However, in response, player B provides additional information that the primary reason for his school choice was a problem of morning transportation; i.e., because of his work schedule, he would not be able to take the children to school in the morning to a different school, and the children would have no way to get there themselves. Player B was concerned that this logistic problem would lead to losing time with the children and reports no intention of attempting to gain time in the future. Player A now can change her belief system by recognizing that player B might accept a number of different proposals, assuming those proposals solve the transportation problem, and can make the proposals that best protect her position in a future residential placement dispute, should one arise. Thus, the new information from player B allows player A to update her beliefs and make win-win proposals.

Providing Information Changes Beliefs

Bayesian bargaining generally works more effectively in reaching axiomatic or cooperative bargaining solutions. What this means is that players who update their beliefs about one another with new information are more likely to reach mutually satisfying results. This is called a "convergence of expectations"; that is, more information allows a modification of beliefs and, thereby, a change in expectations. Without a convergence of expectations, players might choose the worst payoff structure for both of them. A player, who rigidly maintains beliefs about the other player, independent of new information, is more likely to press for payoff outcomes that serve neither party's interests. Attorneys and CPAs can play a critical role in helping clients recognize and follow Bayes rule by providing additional information that changes beliefs. For example, an attorney could tell a client who asserted that winning on a particular issue is "a matter of principle" that his retainer for cases with a "principle" involved is double because, he explains, "In my experience, principles are expensive." This information gives a clear message—that by being rigid in the bargaining process, the transaction costs will be much higher. In another example, an accountant might provide information about a present value calculation of a future spousal support proposal that changes the party's belief.

Many beliefs are maintained not with information but with inferential thinking. Thus, a spouse might assert that she has a vested interest in maintaining all of her retirement income in the settlement and wants that considered in the bargaining. Rather than changing the husband's belief that she is trying to get him to concede a larger share of the estate than to which he is entitled, he might infer that the wife is trying to trick him into giving her an early advantage, because her retirement is substantial. He is inclined to ignore her interest and demand an equal division of her retirement. This is of course an inference on his part, ignoring the new information. His attorney, recognizing that his client is not allowing Bayes rule to facilitate an optimal solution, tells his client that he could be right but that there is no harm in doing a little more exploring. So, the attorney sends a letter to the other attorney indicating that his client, the husband, is willing to explore the wife's interest but first, what is the wife trying to accomplish in her future life by retaining the retirement account (her subjective goals) and will the Wife accede at the beginning of the bargaining process that the division of the total estate will be equitable? A response will provide more information that will help to update the husband's beliefs.

Definitions and Concepts—Summary

Game theory is rich with terms and concepts that can be employed by attorneys and mediators to understand how and why parties behave the way they do in the divorce game. We have also offered hints on how these principles can be used to facilitate settlement, although we will expand on this further in later chapters. In this chapter, we have introduced terms and concepts, setting the stage of analyzing traditional divorce and introducing a game theory model of negotiating. In summary, here are those terms and concepts:

a. **Definition of a game**
   1) Players
   2) Rules
   3) Payoffs
   4) Decisions and strategies

b. **Game forms**
   1) Normal form game
   2) Extensive form game
   3) Repeated extensive form game
   4) Single games versus multiple games

c. **Objective and subjective payoffs**

d. **Solution concept**

e. **Payoff structure**
   1) Simple games versus mixed game

f. **Game structures**
   1) Zero-sum games
   2) Non-zero-sum games

g. **Cooperative and non-cooperative/compromise bargaining**

h. **Bayes rule and a convergence of expectations**

In Chapter 2, we will apply these terms to analyzing the divorce game in more depth.

CHAPTER 2

Game Theory Principles and the Divorce Game—General

The Divorce Game: Multiple Games at Play

When a marriage ends, the parties play one major game, the "divorce game." When the parties have minor children, within the divorce game are two major subgames: one, a game in which the post-divorce care of the children is established (**child game**); and the other, a game in which the financial issues of property and support are resolved (**financial game**). Within each of these subgames, the parties play two additional subgames. In the child game, the parties play the legal game, which addresses issues of legal custody, residential placement schedules, and other legal requirements relative to these two issues (e.g., relocation), and they play the child planning game, which addresses communication and cooperation between the parties and other aspects of their continuing relationship with one another as separated parents (often called the "co-parenting relationship").

Co-parenting surprisingly receives little attention in the legal system. However, this may change, as many divorcing parents are required to attend parenting classes and co-parenting training programs for high-conflict parents. Perhaps this is recognition of the importance of this game. Interestingly, while the legal game focuses on the decision-making, residential placement schedule, child support, and relocation, social science tells us that these are much less important as predictors of outcomes for children than is the co-parenting relationship. Of a list of the seven most important predictors, the co-parenting relationship is number one, and the residential placement schedule is number seven. Yet the legal system focuses largely on the legal game rather than the child planning game.

Parties who successfully raise well-adjusted children are those who play *both* the legal game and the child planning games well. There is some overlap between the two games, although most elements of each game are distinct. Some of the overlap conflicts and some does not. For example, determining a residential placement schedule for children is part of the legal game and the child planning game. In the legal game, the task is to come up with a residential placement schedule, designating when the children will be with one parent and when they will be with the other parent (at least in terms of responsibility for the children). In the child planning game, the task is to decide on a blueprint schedule that maximizes benefit to the child (e.g., takes advantage of parental availability) and provides sufficient flexibility. Both require a schedule describing when the child is expected to be in each home.

In the financial game, the parties play two subgames: the legal game, in which property division and support issues are addressed at the time of the divorce, and the financial planning game, in which the process of how the parties will interact over financial issues in the future is addressed. The financial planning game sometimes receives little attention, although experienced attorneys recognize the importance of this game in the bargaining process. For example, while the law might presume an equal division of property, the two parties, with the assistance of their attorneys, might negotiate an unequal division in exchange for a non-traditional support package. This might be a better "plan" for both parties when compared to what the law presumes.

Repeated Form Games Promote Cooperative Strategies

Because the rules and payoffs are different in the legal game and in the child planning game, conflict can arise. The legal game determines a residential placement schedule, which is a "normal form game" and a "mixed game," both often treated as zero-sum game. Also in the legal game, legal custody (i.e., decision making) is treated as a normal form game but recognizes that most of the decisions to be made are in the future and therefore has an element of a repeated form game. The child planning game is an "extensive repeated form game" and a collection of "simple games." Normal form games promote competitive strategies, whereas extensive form games promote cooperative strategies. The reason for this is that in normal form games, the focus is on winning the payoff. In repeated form games, the emphasis is on having a relationship that leads to positive long-term payoff structures.

This is a crucial concept in applying game theory to divorce; that is, that repeated form games promote cooperative behavior as the most rational strategy. To illustrate this, assume that a salesperson is attempting to make a onetime sale, a normal form game. The rational strategy is to be deceitful and competitive. A used car salesperson, for example, will do better to keep quiet on unfavorable information about the car, such as the cost to the dealer, a prior history of accidents, and possible malfunctioning in the engine. The desired outcome is to make the sale at the highest price. Tactics such as acting like the advocate for the potential buyer and pretending to go into the back office to talk to the manager about an offer are manipulative and deceitful, but good strategies. In a normal form game, the salesperson is indifferent to the customer's outcome. However, assume that a different salesperson is attempting to establish a long-term relationship with the potential buyer; that is, having repeated sales over a long period of time. The best strategies are more likely to be cooperative, providing good information about the product, backing it up with guarantees and good service, and so on. In this latter scenario, the salesperson is very concerned about the customer's perception of the relationship and satisfaction with the product. In a sense, the salesperson is most concerned about reputation.

In normal form games, the focus is on the content of the situation. In divorce, the content is the fact-situation at the time of the divorce. In repeated form games, the focus is on the procedures to be used at future nodes in the game. Thus, the normal form game of a residential placement schedule, played at the time of the divorce, will focus on the fact-situation (e.g., parental availability). The repeated form game of the legal custody recognizes that most of the decisions are in the future and needs procedures in place for making those decisions.

The residential placement game, played at the time of the divorce as a normal form game, has elements of an repeated form game. A rigid residential placement schedule is difficult to follow without some flexibility. Opportunities might arise that can only be taken advantage of by going "off schedule." A parent might have to travel for work on occasion and that might clash with the schedule. In order to have flexibility at future nodes in the schedule game, therefore, procedures for going off schedule need to be in place.

Focusing on the repeated form games at the time of the divorce and developing procedures for the future nodes, therefore, increases the chances that the parents will engage in cooperative strategies in order to optimize outcomes for both of them and, when children are involved, for their children.

Who Is Being Served in the Divorce Game and Are They Being Properly Served?

The obvious answer is that the divorcing spouses are being served, but *who* are these divorcing spouses? Social science tells us that they are usually people who had positive impressions of and feelings for one another at one time and high hopes for their relationship. Over time, they were unable to resolve the persisting problems in the marriage, whether that was on how to deal with money, how to achieve satisfactory affection, how to manage extended family involvement, and so on. They ended up in power struggles and might even have ended up using very damaging strategies as they escalated (e.g., avoidance, bullying, affairs,). At some point, they likely lost their empathic connection to one another or, as John Gottman and his colleagues indicate in their research, reached a point of contempt for one another. Social science tells us that the point of no return in a marriage gone sour usually occurs about two years before one of the parties initiates a divorce. Because they are so vulnerable in those last two years, and because they have lost their empathic connection to one another, they might well have engaged in out-of-character behavior, such as affairs, secrets, excessive drinking, and even incidents of domestic violence. Non-pathological people can appear pathological in those last two years and during the process of the divorce.

Pathological people also get divorces. Most divorcing people appear narcissistic at the time, but people with narcissistic personality disorders divorce at a much higher rate than people without that disorder. This book is not about managing pathological people; it is about guiding non-pathological people, who might appear to be pathological at the time, through the divorce game.

An inherent problem facing the attorney or mediator who is trying to guide a party through the divorce process is that usually one or both of the parties are coming in the door with a recent history of power struggles with a person for whom they likely have little empathic concern and possibly for whom they have contempt. The parties, therefore, might be prone to be competitive with one another in the divorce game rather than cooperative—even though their long-term interests are better served in a cooperative process. Adding to this paradox is that most training of attorneys is how to win in competition. In his wonderful book *The Joy of Settlement,* editor and attorney Gregg Herman points out that while about 90 percent of divorce cases settle without a trial, most of the training for lawyers is on how to litigate.

We have already commented on a fundamental assumption in family law: that the interests of the parties are at odds with one another. From the beginning, therefore, a spouse who has been at odds with the other spouse and who has little or no empathic concern for the other person meets with an attorney who has been trained to win power struggles in a system that assumes that the parties are in a dispute with "the other side," the other spouse, and who is represented by "opposing" counsel. Thus, the parties are vulnerable to getting locked into intractable conflict with one another.

A common misconception is that the family law litigation system is a mismatch with families, but a more objective analysis of this starting point is that the litigation system is a perfect fit for divorcing spouses, at least at the time of divorce. Thus, although we intuitively understand that the litigation system often makes matters worse, on an emotional level the system often fits the spousal dynamic at the time. Now the spouses have champions (attorneys) to help them win power struggles with one another and a third party (the judge) to prove them "right." This is at least the fantasy of many parties entering the system.

Some divorcing spouses have maintained an empathic connection to one another, negotiate in good faith, accept the losses inevitable in a divorce, and part relatively amicably. This book only partially addresses this type of divorce. The bargaining principles in this book might enhance the payoff packages each party receives, focusing them on objective and subjective goals. Some amicable spouses might focus on what is "fair" but would do better to focus on achieving their long-term goals.

This book is largely intended for the middle 60 percent of divorcing spouses who are neither in the 20 percent high-conflict group nor in the 20 percent highly amicable group. It is people in this middle group who are vulnerable to making important mistakes in the divorce process and who might have a difficult time negotiating as rational players without guidance.

Applying Game Theory to Divorce
Theoretical Considerations

Game theory predicts the strategies that people are likely to use and decisions people are likely to make. If a person familiar with game theory understands the rules and payoffs of a game, then that person could predict the strategies that *rational* players are likely to use.

Rational?

That players are "rational" is an assumption of game theory, an assumption that has been controversial in game theory literature. Opponents to the application of game theory to real-life situations argue that players are often not rational and often do not choose strategies that lead to optimal outcomes. They also argue that often real-life situations are much too complex and ambiguous to expect players to understand which strategies will lead to the best payoff structures. Proponents of the application of game theory to real-life situations assert that a rational player is one who will choose the decision or strategy most likely to maximize the payoff. Not all game players are rational, at least not all of the time. Therefore, another meaning of "rational" players is probabilistic. This means that, on average, players will play the game a certain way because a rational player would play the game that way; that is, playing the game a certain way increases the probability of a positive payoff structure. So is a divorcing spouse a rational player or an irrational player?

Game theory research suggests that proponents appear to have the upper hand; that is, in actual experiments in which the players can become emotional and appear "irrational," in fact they play games generally in a rational manner. Real-life applications of game theory have found the same outcome, such as the application of game theory to economic situations. The government auction of air space in recent years to broadcasters and cell phone companies, for example, was structured with input from game theorists and was quite successful, with only a few anomalies.

Rational does not necessarily mean knowledgeable, calculating, or shrewd. As we pointed out earlier in the book, people often do not know why they make some decisions and yet their decisions optimize outcomes more often than not. Divorcing parties might not understand all of the rules and payoffs of the divorce game and might also be in emotional and mental states that make it difficult for them to play the game as "rational" players. However, in addition to providing legal advice, their attorneys are in a position to understand the rules and payoffs and to remain "rational" players through the game. CPAs can greatly assist in this process when examining the financial aspects of the divorce by remaining rational when looking at the payoff structure. A social scientist can also aid by being a rational player in the tasks involved in restructuring the family.

Thus, we see each party and his or her attorney, and perhaps a CPA and social scientist, working as a team, as the "rational" players in the game. In fact, this is one of the major benefits to playing the divorce game with each party having an attorney. The attorneys know the rules, understand important aspects of the payoff structure, and are able to remain "rational" when the parties, for emotional reasons, might be inclined to make choices that are not rational approaches to the game.[5]

The answer to the question as to whether the players in the divorce game are rational is this: when working with an attorney and perhaps with the assistance of other professionals, "yes, on average," the players are rational.

Game Changer

Changing the "game" alters the strategies and decisions likely to be chosen by rational players. There are two ways to change a game: (1) change the rules; or (2) change the payoff structure. It is more accurate to describe "payoffs" as a "payoff structure" because in most games, there are multiple payoffs, often one dependent on the other. This is

---

5. Two strategies that are in essence negative tit-for-tat strategies are called the "grim strategy" and the "battle-to-the-death strategy." As the names suggest, these are strategies in which the negative interactions lead to self-defeating outcomes. Left to their own resources or in the company of problem attorneys, many divorcing spouses might be inclined to play the divorce game this way; that is, incurring so many transaction costs in the process of the divorce as to lead them into a lose-lose outcome.

particularly true in the divorce game. A marital settlement agreement (MSA) outlines a complete package of payoffs for each of the parties. A payoff structure allows for flexibility; that is, one party might lose one game in order to win in another in which the payoff is objectively or subjectively more valuable.

In our earlier poker analogy, a payoff for a single hand might be less important to a player than the payoff for an entire evening. A player might therefore be willing to lose the payoff for a given hand, by bluffing, if it promotes the overall payoff structure of winning other payoffs and the big payoff of the entire game (total winnings).

Similarly, in the divorce game, a party might choose to give in on a particular issue, sacrificing the payoff on that issue, in order to gain another payoff of equal or better value, thus improving the overall payoff structure of the Marital Settlement Agreement, potentially for both parties. For example, assume that a mother asserts that she would like to have the children every Christmas Eve and Day to spend with her extended family, who live some miles away. If this were litigated, it is very unlikely that a court would award her every Christmas Eve and Day. However, the father might be willing to accept her proposal if he has another proposal that is of more importance to him as a trade-off for his Christmas concession. Assume he proposes that she have every Christmas Eve and Day but that he has from December 26 to January 1 to take the children on a ski trip. This might enhance the payoff value for both parties.

The rules and payoffs of a game can be designed to promote conflict and dishonesty. In our poker analogy, the ideal hand occurs if a player has completely concealed the value of his or her hand but knows the value of the other hands. The rules and winner-take-all payoff promote competition (conflict).

A game can be designed to promote problem solving and honesty. At least for partners, the card game "bridge" is an example of promoting an honest exchange of information (e.g., bidding conventions) and cooperation (arriving at a makeable bid), even though this honesty gives opponents important information. Thus, poker and bridge have different rules and payoff structures that promote very different decisions and strategies.

Disputes between parties in traditional divorce are predictable, given the rules and payoffs of the game. Game theory explains what it is about litigation that promotes conflict as the most rational strategy.

When one looks at the laws and payoff structure in current family law, one can see, paradoxically, that high-conflict disputes are the most rational strategy, i.e., the strategy most likely to produce the biggest payoffs. As we pointed out earlier, amicable spouses going through a divorce are resisting the temptation to engage in conflict because their subjective payoff goals outweigh the objective goals of the legal system.

By understanding the game, and how to modify it, attorneys and mediators can increase the chances of resolving disputes and preventing escalation of the divorce conflict. In other words, by redefining the rules and payoff structure, the professional can create a game in which the most rational strategy is cooperative behavior. These changes in the game can be accomplished in the context of existing laws and local rules in most jurisdictions. For example, collaborative divorce and cooperative divorce do this with private contracting between parties and their attorneys, without addressing statutes or case law.

Taking a more traditional approach to the divorce game will sometimes generate a game analogous to "chicken." In a conventional approach to family law, the two attorneys will sometimes play the game, with court dates serving as the "crash!" Some of the "tough guy" posturing that occurs can set the game in motion, which might end on the "courthouse steps"; that is, at the very last moment before a trial (swerve). Once started, the payoff structure of chicken is uncertain, because there are multiple Nash equilibrium solutions. The problem for the parties is that in the game of chicken, all four of the outcomes have high transaction costs and no assurance of producing the best payoff structure for either of them. The same is true of a traditional approach to divorce, such as bargaining in the shadow of the law, playing chicken to the courthouse steps and then crashing (a trial with high transaction costs and disruption of important relationships), or swerving with a last-minute deal that might not serve anyone's long-term interests well.

We suggest the consistent application of five basic game theory principles throughout the divorce bargaining process to improve the likelihood of success in realizing a fair, reasonable, and optimal settlement.

BASIC GAME THEORY PRINCIPLES:

1. Differentiate between and address normal form games and repeated form games. With normal form games, focus on the content, and with repeated form games, focus on procedures.
2. Separate multiple games into single games.
3. Separate mixed games into simple games.
4. Manage information so that it is public, verifiable, complete and perfect, thus allowing Bayes Rule to apply.
5. Set axiomatic standards for each appropriate agreement, but more important, set axiomatic standards for the payoff structure of the Marital Settlement Agreement—for a total divorce package.

The Case Planning Goal: Create Non-Zero-Sum Games Promoting Cooperative Strategies

Emphasizing repeated form games in addition to the normal form games, separating multiple games into single games, and separating mixed games into simple games tends to generate non-zero-sum games, promoting cooperative rather than competitive strategies. Even when resolving disputes, therefore, the transaction costs are likely to be less. Bayes rule allows a convergence of expectations to optimal solutions. We intend to show how this assertion works.

1. Differentiating Between and Addressing Normal Form Games and Repeated Form Games

There are two forms of analysis of games: a game table and game trees. The type of analysis chosen depends on the nature of the game. There are two dimensions to games which determine their type. One is whether the game is a simultaneous move game or a sequential move game. In a simultaneous move game, both players must make a move without knowing the choice of the other party. In a silent bid auction, for example, players make bids without knowing the moves (bids) of the other players. In a sequential move game, players take turns making moves. An open auction is an example of a sequential move game. Before making a move, the player will know the move made by the other player(s) and have this information to determine strategy and make the choice.

The second dimension defining the type of analysis appropriate to the game is whether the game is a onetime game, a "normal form" game (see definitions), or a game that will be repeated to an end point, a "repeated form" game. (A repeated form game can be repeated without any clear end in sight, called a "extensive repeated form" game.) An example of a normal form game in a divorce is the disposition of the cars. If the parties are satisfied to each take a different car, there is no dispute. What happens if both parties want the same car? This becomes a normal form game, winner takes all, and there is a tendency for the game to become competitive rather than cooperative. It has the appearance of a dispute because the formal definition of conflict/dispute is when there is no compromise solution available. One spouse gets the car and the other does not.

In our bargaining model, using game theory principles, there are two optimal solutions: in the first solution, a party gives in, losing the payoff value of the car, but gets a trade-off in return of equal or greater payoff value to the party. Remember, here we mean not only the "objective" value but also the subjective value of the trade-off. In the second solution, the parties explore the subjective goals involved: why each of them wants the car. A careful exploration of the subjective goals can suggest alternative solutions. For example, if the subjective goal of both parties is to have a high-status car (e.g., the old Mercedes convertible), then an alternative solution is to work with the property division so that both parties end up with a high-status car (e.g., one party gets the Mercedes convertible but the marital property is used to buy the other party a high-status car).

An example of a repeated form game in divorce might be child support or spousal support. An example of an infinite extensive repeated form game in divorce is the co-parenting relationship, which extends well into the adult lives of the children. In a repeated form game, the end of each subgame is called a "node." In the co-parenting game, every time the parties share important information with one another or make temporary schedule changes, they are at a node. In a battle-to-the-death game, a parent refuses to change the schedule, regardless of the reason, because the other parent refused to be flexible the time before. This is a negative tit-for-tat game. In a positive tit-for-tat game, the parent agrees to the change, presuming there are no competing plans, anticipating reciprocity the next time he or she wants a change. In the information sharing game, when a parent leaves a conversation with the other parent better informed, the payoff value rewards the activity. If the node had a negative payoff, such as an argument, criticism, or name-calling, the parties are likely to change strategies to avoidance of one another.

Simultaneous choice games are best analyzed with a game table, like we illustrated earlier with the prisoner's dilemma game. In that game, there was a Nash equilibrium with both prisoners confessing. We could complicate matters a bit with the following table, with the higher number representing better payoffs.

In this variation on the famous prisoner's dilemma game, player

The Game

	Player 2 Choice A	Player 2 Choice B
Player 1 Choice X	Player 1: 6 Player 2: 6	Player 1: 15 Player 2: 2
Player 1 Choice Y	Player 1: 2 Player 2: 15	Player 1: 10 Player 2: 10

1 does best, no matter what player B chooses, by choosing X (6 is better than 2, and 15 is better than 10). Likewise, player 2 does best with A, no matter what player 1 chooses. However, as one can see the solution, then, is box 1 (6, 6) even though both players could have done better by cooperating and choosing Y and B (10, 10). This shows somewhat graphically that a cooperative strategy can often promote the best outcomes for both parties. However, the only way that they can discover the best outcome is by communicating and cooperating.

However, look at the following table:

The Game

	Player 2 Choice A	Player 2 Choice B
Player 1 Choice X	Player 1: 6 Player 2: 6	Player 1: 4 Player 2: 8
Player 1 Choice Y	Player 1: 2 Player 2: 15	Player 1: 10 Player 2: 4

This situation has two Nash equilibria: if player 1 chooses X, player 2 does better to choose B, but if player 1 chooses Y, player 2 does better to choose A. The reverse is true for player 1. There is no way to pre-determine the choices that the parties will make, unless they communicate and cooperate with one another to maximize the outcome for both of them. This is a fundamental flaw with simultaneous choice games. Simultaneous choice games often create multiple Nash equilibria and a lack of predictability with regard to best choices.

Since this is often the game played in divorce traditional bargaining models, conditions are ripe for lose/lose outcomes. In traditional bargaining, both attorneys ask their clients to identify a position on the legal issues and then begin the bargaining process. In essence, both clients have made a simultaneous choice, each identifying positions without knowing, other than by guessing, the choice of the other party. In our game table above, if player 1 chooses Y and player 2 chooses A, they are now locked into a competitive game where they attempt to gain the desired outcome and avoid the undesired outcome. By starting with client positions, the attorney is creating a simultaneous choice game, promoting disputes and conflict and reducing the chances of an optimal outcome for the parties.

A game tree is a means of analyzing sequential moves in either a normal form or a repeated form game. Below is an example of a normal form game tree and an example of an repeated form game tree.

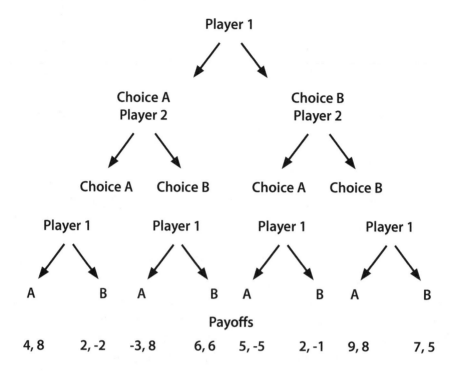

Payoffs							
4, 8	2, -2	-3, 8	6, 6	5, -5	2, -1	9, 8	7, 5

By examining the payoffs, one can backtrack, or more technically roll back, and see the best strategies for each player. When one examines the payoffs above, for example, player 1 has the best payoff of 9 and chooses B. Given that choice, player 2 has the best payoff of 8 by choosing B and then player 1 chooses A. Player 1 receives 9 and player 2 receives 8.

One can combine these approaches to analyzing games by sequencing game tables into a tree of tables or, in the reverse, by combining branches of a tree into tables. We do not want to make this too technical but do want to make a point:

Sequential move games have a much higher chance of reaching optimal outcomes than do simultaneous choice games.

Thus, when starting to bargain, rather than the attorneys talking to their clients about their preferred legal outcomes or positions on legal issues, by focusing on their goals and then entering the bargaining process with sequential moves they are more likely to optimize outcomes, for both clients. On a more practical level, attorney A makes a proposal on some facet of the divorce (first move) and then attorney B makes a counterproposal (second move) and so on. In our car example, attorney A proposes that his client receives the Mercedes because she wants the status of the old sports car. Attorney B responds that his client would also like the car for much the same reason. Attorney A then proposes that in the settlement of the estate, funds are used to purchase a similar car so that both receive a comparable asset.

Divorces include both normal form games and repeated form games. They might also combine moments when simultaneous choice moves are made and others when sequential moves are made. Analyzing payoffs using tables and trees can be helpful in the bargaining process. In game tables, for example, there is usually a Nash equilibrium solution, or a mini-max solution.[6] In game trees, there is usually a roll-back equilibrium solution; that is, by looking at all of the possible outcomes at the end of the decision tree, one can see the one that most favors one or both players and roll back the decisions to the first move to maximize the chances of reaching that desired outcome.

Some Games Are Normal Form Games and Some Are Repeated Form Games

It is important to understand that some games are normal form games and some are repeated form games. If the legal system tries to turn an repeated form game (e.g., parenting after a divorce) into a normal form game (a onetime determined residential placement schedule), there is likely to be conflict. The authors encourage attorneys and mediators to recognize which type of game model is most appropriate to use, given the issues in the divorce.

CPAs can be enormously helpful to the attorneys and parties by performing some of these analyses. For example, let us assume that an accountant was given the following axioms:

- Set an outcome date five years from the date of the divorce.

- Look at all of the assets and expected incomes of the parties.

- Analyze the reasonable choices available to each party during the five years (e.g., get a job now or seek a higher education degree first; buy a residence versus rent and keep money in a retirement account; etc.).

- Include in the analysis tax ramifications, opportunity costs, and transaction costs.

---

6. In highly complex games with many choices, a form of finding the point of equilibrium is called "mini-max." This is more complex than we need to display here.

- Prepare a decision tree analyzing the potential financial positions of each of the parties at the five-year date.

- Identify the roll-back equilibrium solution that maximizes the benefits to both parties.

The results of such an analysis could help shape the final settlement in a real win-win solution to the game. By pointing out to the parties the likely five-year outcome, emotionally driven objections might be more easily overcome. For example, simply telling a spouse that the other party has proposed a maintenance support of $2,000 per month for ten years might raise substantial objections and a good deal of litigation. However, if an accountant were able to show that same spouse that by paying $3,000 per month for five years, the financial position for both parties will be better, the proposed payer might be willing to accept this proposal if the analysis is convincing.

Taking Turns Leads to Optimal Outcomes

We can also use this type of information to influence the bargaining process. For example, game theory research informs us that sequential move games have the best chance of maximizing the payoff structure for both parties. Thus, the process of the two divorcing parties taking turns making offers and counteroffers, without fixed ideas prior to receiving an offer, will likely produce optimal outcomes. This will certainly work better when compared to each player taking a position and sticking with it through a trial. The primary reason taking turns tends to lead to optimal outcomes is because Bayes rule is involved. Every offer and counteroffer provides information, including information about the subjective values and goals of the parties. This information can be incorporated into future offers and counteroffers to enhance the outcome—the final deal. Also, sequential choice games use decision trees, which are easier to analyze than tables. In tables, the parties can make the rational choice, but it may be the least optimal payoff, such as occurs in the prisoner's dilemma game.

Focusing on Content and Process Is Critical

The approach to normal form games is different from the approach to repeated repeated games. In a normal form game, the focus is on the *content*; that is, the facts and getting to the payoffs. In a residential placement schedule game, for example, the focus is on the current factors and establishing the schedule. In repeated form games, the focus is on the *process*; that is, on rules and procedures. Child support can be both a content and a process decision. Maintenance might only be content decision. It is important to plan for each, because the only certainty is that the family will evolve and the needs/resources will change. Thus, the focus in the extensive repeated form game of co-parenting is on how parents can make decisions together regarding the residential placement schedule, with the presumption that they will have to change the schedule as the family circumstances change. Another example is developing procedures for making decisions about going off schedule at times for special opportunities, such as how to have the children on the other person's residential placement time. Thus, rules of conduct, information exchange, criteria and procedures for making decisions are the focus, not the schedule itself (which in a healthy family will change over time). What this illustrates is that some games in divorce are both normal form games and repeated form games. Establishing a schedule at the time of the divorce is played one time, with a focus on content (i.e., the facts at the time of the divorce), but changing the schedule in the future is a repeated form game, for which including procedures and axioms at the time of the divorce can prevent future conflict.

Another example in the residential schedule game is vacation time. A decision at the time of the divorce might be that the parties can each take vacations, perhaps with some parameters (e.g., no longer than ten days). However, the vacation schedule year after year is a repeated form game, so procedures not content are the issue. The procedures might include axioms (e.g., only a certain number of missed school days per year for vacations) and involve notification rules and procedures for resolving a conflict in the vacation times chosen by the parties. Rather than going with easy cookie-cutter procedures, such as in odd years, mother has impasse-breaking authority, it might improve the payoff value by exploring the objective and subjective goals of the parties.

In the normal form game on the disposition of cars, the focus is on content, such as who gets which car and the values of the cars. In the repeated game of support, the focus is on procedures (e.g., exchanging tax returns by a date certain or conditions under which support ends).

Conclusion

To facilitate an effective bargaining process and to prevent conflicts from arising, an attorney, often in consultation with an accountant, should differentiate between normal form games and repeated form games and analyze each differently. The authors encourage attorneys and CPAs to ask this question at each stage of the bargaining process: "Is this issue a normal form game or a repeated form game?" The worst mistake is to treat a repeated form game as though it were a normal form game. Spousal support, for example, is a repeated form game, and to bargain as if it were a onetime decision fails to design creatively optimal payoff structures for the parties. When a game is both a normal form game at the time of the divorce, but also has future nodes making it also a repeated form game, the focus should not only be on content for the normal form game (addressing decisions at the time of the divorce) but also on process (preventing future conflict and litigation by including procedures in the MSA) for the repeated form game.

As an example, in a real mediation case, assume that the wife has not worked for a number of years and the husband earns a good deal of money. Assume that the objective and subjective goals of the parties are identified and that they include the wife becoming financially independent of support. Assume that the parties share this goal and are even able to develop the wife's budget to see what income she will need to reach this goal and also maintain a reasonable lifestyle for the children when they are with her, again a shared goal. In other words, the parties start the bargaining process by identifying long-term objective and subjective goals. The, the parties, each knowing what the goals are, take turns making proposals, some of which are creative. The outcome is an agreement that the husband will pay a certain support level while the wife goes to school to obtain a certain degree and then pays a reduced amount dependent on the wife's income level, with a date certain by which she should be able to reach the income level determined at the beginning. The parties also discuss what to do if she does not reach that income level by that date and agree to a procedure involving further mediation. In this real case, the wife did complete the schooling and began to build her income per the agreement, but she did not reach the goal in the time estimated in the original plan and returned to mediation. Many of the facts had changed (e.g., the husband had remarried and had a dual-income home) and it became evident that the wife was approaching the income goal and had made a sincere effort to get there in the amount of time initially estimated. They agreed on continuing support at a certain level for additional time, which now was a bit more certain than the initial estimate. Thus, they reached a solution to the normal form game but built in procedures for future nodes.

By viewing the game as a repeated form game based on planning to meet goals, rather than as a zero-sum normal form game played at the time of the divorce, both parties were satisfied with optimizing the outcomes for both of them and were able to avoid competition and conflict. We also note that the interests of the parties, the long-term goals, were not at odds with one another. In a traditional bargaining model, the husband would be attempting to keep his total support as limited as possible, demanding that the wife meet with a career appraiser, and the wife would be fighting to get the highest amount of support possible. The payoff structure of the outcome might have been less than optimal for one or both of the parties, and also the payoff structure of their emotions and relationship as parents would likely be negative. In our example, the parties had maintained an amicable co-parenting relationship, working as a parenting team, but also as a team to meet their long-term income and career goals. By treating the "problem" of support as a goal-based planning "problem" with a plan at the time of the divorce (the normal form game) and a procedure for the future repeated form game, both parties reached higher payoff values.

2. Separating Multiple Games into Single Games

As a reminder, multiple games are a package of single games played as though collectively they were one single game. The best example in divorce is the residential placement schedule for children, but there are many other examples, such as custodial decision making, which is usually a collection of six to twelve custodial decisions, or six to twelve single games. There are also financial multiple games. Although settlement offers often list specific assets and debts, the game is often played as a single game (e.g., a total distribution of the estate). Support is often played as a single game, when in fact it might involve a number of single games collected into the multiple game of support.

Multiple games are divided into single games because single games are easier to solve than multiple games. Single games generally promote better payoff values to both parties as compared to playing the multiple game as if it were a single game. We gave an example earlier with the residential placement schedule for children. By playing each single game, starting with the easiest to solve (e.g., the holiday schedule) and working up to the most difficult to solve (typically, the schedule for school days), not only is the scope of the problem greatly reduced, but also the information exchanged during the process informs the parties of possible settlements when the game reaches the compromise phase of bargaining. For example, if one of the subjective payoffs for a parent pressing for school day placement of the child is participation in the child's athletic activities, a single game can be played on the participation of that parent, independent of the placement schedule. In this case, the solution to the participation game might be that the parent can take the child to half of the practices and games, independent of the residential placement of the child. Many jurisdictions play the residential placement game by counting overnights, largely because they are easy to count. However, an ideal schedule that enhances everyone's lives might be to play a separate game for overnights.

Focus on Solutions to Disputes

As an example, we mediated a case in which the husband was pressing for equal residential placement time with the two children. His goals involved a genuine interest in the lives of the children. The wife, however, lived closer to the school, but even more important, she asserted that the husband's job was not conducive to a shared residential placement schedule. He was a construction job boss, who often had to travel up to an hour to a job site and worked from about 6:00 a.m. to 2:30 p.m. She could not comprehend school mornings at his home. He proposed waking the children and dropping them off at her home before he went to work. He refused to play a marginal role in the children's lives, and she refused to put the children through the proposed school mornings one-half of the time. Her opposition was not to his involvement with the children; it was to the "cost" to the children on school mornings. Heading to custody study and trial, the attorneys recommended mediation. It became clear that they were playing a multiple game: the waking hours game, which broke down into the two subgames of after-school time and dinner and evening time, and the overnight game. We separated the multiple game into single games. By playing the waking hours game first, coming to an agreement was easy. Playing the overnight game second also led to an easy solution; the result was that they had a substantially equal residential placement schedule: The husband's afternoon availability had him with the children every school day after school. On Monday and Tuesday, he kept them until near bedtime and then took them to the wife's home. On Wednesday and Thursday, she picked them up on the way home from her job at 5:00 p.m. They alternated weekends, but his weekends ended near bedtime on Sunday. The wife had the children twelve of the fourteen overnights (all but Friday and Saturday on his weekends). He had ten of ten after-school periods. Because they shared the waking hours equally, child support was calculated as though they had an equal schedule with equal expenses, although the wife had the lion's share of overnights. The impossible-to-solve multiple game became an easy-to-solve set of single games, which maximized the payoff value to both parties. The father achieved his goal of being an active part of the children's lives; the mother achieved her goal of sensible school mornings; both achieved their goal of parent-care rather than after-school care; and they developed a way to focus on disputes with solutions.

When facing a dispute, inquiring as to the subjective goals and values of the parties leads to a separation of a multiple game into single games. A dispute over spousal support, for example, might become a set of single games when the parties are each asked questions about their subjective goals and values for the money. For example, if the wife reports after inquiry that she needs a certain guaranteed income to purchase the homestead from the marriage and to qualify for a certain mortgage, the support game could be played separate from the real estate game. At the same time, the husband reports not only that his plans for the future include changing jobs to a more desirable career but also that he will earn less than he is at present. The support game needs to be played separate from the career change game. In this real example, the husband was a successful financial advisor, but previously had been a teacher and wanted to return to teaching. When played as single games, creative solutions to each game might resolve the dispute on the multiple game with optimal solutions for both parties. In this example, investigating the retirement benefits for teachers and combining that with the husband's goal of teaching for some time gave the importance of his existing retirement account less weight to him. The parties agreed that he would provide a sufficient amount of money from his retirement account to the wife to reduce her mortgage to an amount that required a substantially lower income.

The wife won the real estate game; the husband won the support game that allowed him to win the career game.

Conclusion

Some multiple games are easily identified, such as the residential schedule game. Others are subtler and might require a probing exploration of objective and subjective values and goals. However, when an apparent dispute or impasse is reached, identifying the single games involved in a multiple game can lead to solutions with high-value payoffs for both parties. When reaching the appearance of an impasse in bargaining, analyzing whether there is a multiple game being played can lead to solutions.

3. Separating Mixed Games into Simple Games

It is helpful to understand the effects of separating mixed games into simple games. Some games have payoff structures that are simple and some that are complex. A simple payoff structure is one in which there is either a single payoff (e.g., the pot at the end of a hand of poker) or in which the payoffs are multiple but so directly related that they are similar to a single payoff (e.g., getting a job with a certain pay package that includes pay, retirement, sick and vacation pay, and health insurance). A complex payoff structure is one in which there are multiple payoffs, each of which has independent value. Simple payoff structures form simple games whereas complex payoff structures form mixed games. The strategies used to play simple games tend to be different from those that are chosen to play mixed games. As one might guess, simple games are easier to solve than mixed games, where the optimal strategies tend to be more cooperative than competitive and where the payoff value for the game tends to be higher for both parties.

For example if politics were a simple game, the only payoff for running for an office might be a job that pays $60,000 per year and lasts two years. A person would be a fool to spend $200,000 campaigning for such a job. However, let us see what happens if we add other payoffs to the game of running for office and make it a mixed game. Let us assume that although the job is only for two years, once one has the job, the odds of getting the job renewed for two more years increase substantially, and, for two more years after that, the odds increase yet again. Thus, in addition to obtaining the job, one attains a high probability of retaining that job for a long period of time. Now we have a job that might only pay $60,000 per year, but there is a high likelihood that it will pay that rate for many years. The campaign costs begin to look a little more sensible. Let us further assume that once one has the job, one gains power to make decisions that affect one's friends and other people in one's community, increases one's status in the community, and increases opportunities for benefiting friends and others. Let us further assume that the job has numerous benefits, including free travel and a generous retirement package. Finally, let us add that after one has held the job for the first two years, the money for future campaigning increasingly comes from others and the personal expenditures decrease, perhaps to nothing. Now, the $60,000 job looks like it might be worth the initial $200,000 investment.

The principle here is that by adding payoffs to the game, we increase the chances that people will play the game more intensely. Winning a gold medal at the Olympics is enough to strive for, but what happens when we add the public exposure and the high likelihood of product endorsements that will make one wealthy? Top sports stars will often make more money through endorsements than for their athletic achievements. Suddenly, the years of hard work for the few minutes of glory and a gold medal look like a good investment in the future. Even if one does not get the gold medal, simply being on the Olympic Team might assure easy entry into a rewarding career.

In divorce, for example, we add numerous payoffs to the game of getting the most residential placement time with the children. We call this a "mixed game" because we are mixing payoffs for the one game (see earlier for a list of payoffs associated with the residential placement schedule). The game for gaining residential time with the children is fairly straightforward; parents gain or lose time with their children. The utility of spending more time with the children and the utility of avoiding lost time with the children is enough to make playing what appears to be a zero-sum game intense. However, if the only payoff was time with or away from the children, it might be easier to focus on what residential placement schedule would make the most sense, given practical factors, for both the parents and for the child. When we design this as a mixed game, by adding financial implications, power and control over certain decisions, relocation advantages, gender equity, status, and so on, we can turn the mixed game into a nightmare.

By separating the mixed game into simple games, optimal solutions become easier to find. A simple game could be played addressing relocation power by building into the agreement legal presumptions. A simple game could be played for school choice. A simple game could even be played for child support. In an actual mediation, the wife kept accusing the husband of wanting more time with the children to reduce child support, an inference not unusual in addressing schedule disputes. However, when she brought it up for the third or fourth time, even though the husband kept protesting that the money was not that important to him (he was part owner and manager of a successful business), it occurred to us that perhaps she was playing a mixed game. We realized that perhaps child support was important to her, not him. We separated the two games, playing the child support game first. The wife acknowledged that her budget was dependent on the current child support level and the implications of a loss of child support were substantial to her. The husband, who had been sincere in his denials that the money was important, offered to keep child support at its current level, even if higher than local child support guidelines. Once the wife won the child support game, she was willing to "lose" the residential placement game to the husband.

The same analysis can be done for many of the financial games played in divorce. Spousal support, for example, might appear to be a simple game of one party paying support to the other, but there can be many payoffs, both positive and negative to both parties. For example, one could look at a monthly support order for $3,000 as a payoff. However, if we were to ask the recipient probing questions, we might find that what that $3,000 accomplishes a whole set of payoffs. An anxious recipient might find that $3,000 prevents having to face changing careers or challenging oneself with financial necessity. Or, in the reverse, a recipient might find that the $3,000 allows for further education and a longed-for career change. The payer might have any one of several aversive payoffs: having to live with a new wife who resents seeing the money go to the prior wife; having to experience the payment as an easing of personal guilt; finding the payment a salve for bitterness; facing long-term support extremely restrictive on his or her choices to pursue a different career in which income might be lower; and so on. What the support should be for both parties is a simple dollar amount that propels each party into the future as well as it can be done. It should be an investment in the future of both parties. By separating the payoffs and addressing each one as a simple game (e.g., having a plan for a party to obtain the education to begin a longed-for career), the parties can often prevent the inevitable disputes that come with mixed games.

These examples also underscore another advantage of this bargaining tool. By reaching solutions to simple games that are creative and address the objective and subjective goals of the parties, the parties have available to them agreements not available through litigation. However, creative agreements are available in mediation, collaborative divorce, etc. Game Theory is a technique that can be used in multiple separation facilitation models. In the earlier example of the father wanting more time with the children and the mother resisting for financial reasons, by playing the simple games separately, the parties avoided a long, drawn-out residential schedule dispute, with transaction costs that might have been higher than the support amount involved, which would have ended in a schedule that may or may not have worked and a child support order by formula based on that schedule that might not have achieved their goals.[7]

A final effect of playing mixed games, rather than simple games, is that the payoff structure is almost always worse than had the game been divided into simple games. Engaging in a major dispute over a residential placement schedule, for example, is a poor approach to financial planning for both parties. First, the transaction costs make the game itself very expensive, eating up at least some if not all of the gain associated with a win or partial win of the dispute. Second, the financial outcome of a residential placement dispute—that is, perceiving child support as a source of income for one party and an expense to the other party—might not be the most effective and efficient use of family resources for either party or for the child. Finally, the players might be playing different games. One might be playing the game for status and to avoid loss of time with the child, while the other party might be playing the game for child support and to avoid the risk of a later relocation. When people are essentially playing for different payoff priorities, there is no win-win bargaining if the game is played as a mixed game. Both parties might do more poorly in terms

---

7. Wisconsin, where this mediation occurred, has child support guidelines that are almost always followed by courts.

of the final payoff structure compared to breaking down the mixed games into simple games.

The True Costs of Playing Mixed Games

We have identified three major negative effects of playing mixed games versus simple games. First, the game is played most rationally by playing it dishonestly. The second effect flows directly from the first; that is, dishonesty creates a game of incomplete and imperfect information, which promotes negative strategies and conflict. Finally, the payoff structures achieved by both parties when playing mixed games are almost always inferior, sometimes substantially so, when compared to playing the simple games involved, to which better solutions are usually achieved.

The solution to these drawbacks is to separate mixed games into their component simple games. Using our residential placement game as an example, we could separate the support payoff from the residential placement schedule. The child support payoff might better be addressed in a financial planning game in which the parties make goal-based decisions about how to divide property and develop the best use of family income. The care and welfare of the children will fit into this discussion (e.g., it might work out well for both parents if one of them continues to work part-time and be primarily responsible for the care of the child after school, not only in terms of quality of care but also in child care expense savings).

The same could be said of the spousal support game mentioned earlier. If one of the payoffs is for a party to obtain an additional degree and start a new career, developing a plan specific to this payoff could be more effective and efficient than making this one of the payoffs of a support dispute. If a payoff is the aversive one of restricting a party to an unwanted job, reducing this aversive outcome with a different plan could benefit both parties.

Conclusion

By playing each of these simple games, the payoff structure of all the games collectively is likely to be superior, when compared to playing the mixed game. The information can be honest, complete, and perfect, including the disclosure of subjective values and goals, and disputes can be kept to a minimum. Effective and efficient win-win-plus bargaining strategies can be applied to achieve superior outcomes.

4. Managing Information So That It is Public, Verifiable, Complete, and Perfect

We have made references to different types of information, or qualities that information might have. We have mentioned information that is "perfect" and "complete." Consistently, we have asserted that information management is essential to successful game theory bargaining.

Information management is a key concept in game theory. The amount of information each player has about all aspects of the game and how players gain information affects the strategies each player will choose. As we have illustrated with poker, player A's perfect playing position is one in which no other player knows what cards she holds and she knows exactly what cards the other players hold. These strategies used by a poker player are solely focused on information management. Likewise, a health insurance company understands that there are financial incentives for high-cost users to sign up for insurance and for low-cost users not to sign up. Thus, the insurance company must have rules governing the management of information in order to "win" the insurance game, such as obtaining medical records, requiring full disclosure from applicants, and limiting payments for pre-existing conditions whether or not disclosed.

In the divorce game, successful bargaining requires information to be effectively managed. There are four basic principles to information management in the game theory approach:

- private versus public information
- verifiable versus non-verifiable information
- complete versus incomplete
- perfect versus imperfect

Private versus Public Information

In the divorce game, each player has information. There are disclosure rules and procedures for obtaining information from the other player and from other sources. The goal of each player is to receive, and thereby make "public," the relevant information known by the other party. However, each player will usually keep some information private. Private information is that which is possessed by fewer than all of the players in a game. Public information is information that is possessed by all of the players. Private information is tricky in divorce negotiations because there are really more than two players, when one includes the attorneys and, in some cases, a mediator, and of course the judge. Using the simplest model in divorce, let us assume that private information is information that one party and his or her attorney possesses but is unknown to the other party and his or her attorney. For example, private information might include a long-term plan to relocate after the divorce is final, or a party might know that he or she will be receiving a large raise in several months. Private information might include that one party has been having an affair and plans to live with the new partner once the divorce is final. Private information might be that the one party has secretly planned to quit work and move to Guatemala and work in a micro-financing program. Subjective goals can be private.

Private information is an obstacle to a cooperative bargaining approach, but might be an asset in hardball negotiating. For example, revealing a probable but not yet executed promotion at work, with a substantial increase in income, provides an opportunity for value-added bargaining but serves to disadvantage the party revealing this information in hardball negotiations.

A common form of private information is the subjective value players place on certain payoffs. A player might place more subjective value on support or property outcomes than is disclosed to the other player. Private information that reflects subjective values can greatly affect outcomes. For example, a homestead might have a public market value, but one party might give the homestead additional subjective value (e.g., keeping a familiar residence for the children, a house into which one of the parties put a great deal of creative effort, or proximity to friends). Revealing this private subjective value works well in a cooperative bargaining protocol, but might put the party at a disadvantage in hardball negotiations. In a cooperative bargaining process, solutions take into account the subjective values and include them in solutions to maximize the payoff values to the parties. In a competitive bargaining process, or hardball negotiations, one party might take advantage of that information in order to maximize his or her payoff, diminishing the payoff to the other party.

Rules that increase the value of making private information public increase the probability of achieving optimal bargaining outcomes.

That is, if the divorce game has rules that increase the value of revealing private information, both parties can achieve a better outcome than would occur if the information were kept private. We remind the reader of the prisoner's dilemma presented earlier, in which both parties end up with a better solution when they communicate and cooperate, making private information public between them. As another example, in the card game of bridge, a better outcome for team A is likely if, during the bidding phase, each member of team A has a good idea of what cards the other player on team A holds. This is true, even if revealing information to one another also discloses information to team B. Thus, bidding conventions have been developed that reveal information about cards. The incentive to reveal cards to a teammate outweighs the drawbacks to revealing cards to opponents. We can see that the rules of bridge, which promote public information, contrasts with the rules of poker, which promote private information.

Collaborative divorce developed the affirmative duty to disclose in an attempt to make a rule change in the game to promote public information in the bargaining process. From a game theory perspective, this is a good rule change. However, one party might have information that he or she is very reluctant to share. In an actual example, a husband, who was a successful businessman, had never told his wife that during their marriage, he had an affair and, as a result of the affair, had another child. He and the mother of that child struck a private arrangement that she would raise the child without his involvement but also that he would pay a certain amount of child support. He was able to pay this out of his business without his wife's knowledge. He entered into collaborative divorce and told his attorney this story but did not want it revealed to his wife, in part for protective reasons—his agreement with the mother of the child stipulated that he not tell anyone about the child, to keep the child out of other unwanted situations. The attorney now had the dilemma of how to handle this information in light of a contract that included an affirmative duty to disclose.

Mediation offers a solution to the private information disclosure issue. However, we still have this conundrum that making information public facilitates more positive payoff structures for both parties in cooperative bargaining, yet puts a party at a disadvantage in hardball bargaining. There is a solution. If parties agree to first attempt cooperative bargaining, and only failing, move on to hardball bargaining or even litigation, the disadvantage of making information public can be managed by hiring a neutral third party (e.g., a mediator) and conducting the mediation with each party and his and her attorney separately. The agreement to do so could include the rule that the parties make public all of the information to the mediator, but that the mediator will not make any information tagged as private public to the other party. For example, if a mediator knew that the wife has a great deal of subjective payoff value for obtaining the homestead, the mediator could use this information in the negotiations without revealing it to the husband. This has the potential of enhancing the payoff structure for the wife without putting her at a disadvantage should cooperative bargaining fail.

Research on collaborative divorce suggests that settlement is reached about 85 percent of the time and, in most cases, making private information public is not a problem. However, for the 15 percent that proceed to litigation, the revelation of some private information might turn into a disadvantage. In the game theory bargaining model, making the private information public increases the chances of optimal outcomes for both parties and in cases in which revealing some private information could disadvantage a party, introducing a mediator with rules about information management can be a solution.

Verifiable versus Non-verifiable Information

This concept is as simple as the name suggests. Information is verifiable when the party possessing the information is able to convey it in a credible manner to the other party or to a third party (e.g., by providing supporting documents). Non-verifiable information, which may or may not be public, can only be verified (except by inference) by the party who possesses the information. For example, a party might say that it is a crucial goal that his or her retirement account remains undivided. This is public information, but no one other than the party making the assertion can verify that the information is accurate (e.g., it might be a bargaining ploy).

Non-verifiable information becomes an obstacle if and when the parties distrust one another. If the parties trust one another, assertions by one party will be considered verified because the assertion is considered credible. If trust is absent, however, non-verifiable information becomes at best neutral or possibly an obstacle to optimal cooperative solutions.

Inference is a legitimate form of verifying information. If a party behaves as if a position is important, the inference that the position is important is considered in game theory as verification. For example, party A states that child support is not an important consideration and yet consistently behaves as if child support is an important factor. Party B can consider this verified information in making the inference. However, this relies on Bayes rule (see definitions) regarding the beliefs of the parties and inferences as to the other party's beliefs/motives (i.e., concerned with child support, in this example) and must be subject to modification if additional behavior reveals that an earlier inference is likely incorrect. Bayes rule essentially state that through the bargaining process, each of the parties modifies his and her beliefs as to the other party's type (i.e., style of bargaining) and as to the objective and subjective value of the payoffs to the other party.

Information is also considered verified if the party revealing the information is considered a reliable reporter. If the husband considers his wife rigorously honest and frank, then when she reveals that she would like to remain in the homestead and gives credible reasons for wanting to do so, the information that the homestead has additional subjective value to her is considered verified.

Information is most useful in achieving optimal outcomes if it is verifiable, if only through trust. Thus, rules and procedures that increase the credibility of the information shared will facilitate an optimal bargaining process. If information is revealed in the cooperative bargaining process that is not verified, by documents, reasonable inference, or trust, the players will do best to focus on verifying the information before going forward. An attorney can meet privately with his or her client and discuss the importance to the cooperative bargaining process of having information verifiable, and even at that point to suggest the type of mediation mentioned in the earlier section on public information. Additionally, the attorney, or perhaps a counselor, might probe more deeply with the client for objective and subjective values and goals and then be able to verify the information.

Complete versus Incomplete Information

Information is complete when the rules and payoffs of the game are known to all the players. It is not necessary to know the choices of each player to have a game of complete information. In divorce, this is complicated because the rules and payoffs might be known to each party, but in mixed form. For example, the attorney might know all of the rules in the legal game and might even know some of the payoffs, as presumed by law. The client might know much about the payoffs (e.g., property values) but little about the rules. Between attorney A and the husband, there might be complete information and the same might be true of attorney B and the wife. As a team, therefore, each party has complete information. How true this is depends on how each team conducts itself and the thoroughness of the discovery process. An attorney might not know all of the rules, for example, in an unfamiliar jurisdiction (e.g., a judge expects certain actions to be taken by the attorneys prior to a hearing). Likewise, the husband might not have complete information about the payoffs because the wife is a partner in a firm about which the husband knows little.

Games with complete information provide conditions that facilitate optimal outcomes. Additionally, complete information facilitates value-added bargaining in the win-win-plus phase of the bargaining model proposed by the authors. For example, attorney A and the husband, by knowing the rules and payoff structure, can develop a value-added proposal that improves the payoff structure for both the husband and the wife. If attorney B and the wife also know the rules and payoffs, they can respond to such an offer in a reasonable fashion and may include additional value-added options, which improve the payoff structure for the husband.

Perfect versus Imperfect Information

This is one of the more complex concepts in game theory and information management. Perfect information occurs when both players know the complete history of the game. Conversely, imperfect information occurs when at least one party does not know the full history of the game prior to making a choice. For example, when a car dealer asks a potential party to make an offer, the person making the offer does not know the history of the game (e.g., what the dealer really paid for the car or what the dealer has already decided to accept for the car). This is a game of complete but imperfect information, i.e., where both parties know all of the strategies and payoffs, but do not know the history of the game.

In family law, if each party is required to make a move without knowing what the other party has chosen, the game is one of imperfect information. To achieve optimal outcomes, the rules of the game should make perfect information the dominant strategy. What this means is that the rules must be such that the incentives for revealing the history of the game and the punishments for not doing so make doing so the rational choice.

If one party has been planning a divorce for some time and has deliberately taken action to thwart the interests of the other party (e.g., the husband has his family of origin put the family farm into a family trust) and does not reveal these actions, this is a game of imperfect information. A more obvious example of dealing with imperfect information is what insurance companies do. When someone signs up for health insurance, they are asked to reveal pre-existing conditions. If a party fails to reveal such a condition, the insurance company has a rule that it will not pay for future medical services for that condition. Thus, the insurance company establishes a rule that provides an incentive for revealing the complete medical history of an applicant, creating a game of perfect information.[8]

Family law attempts to accomplish the same through disclosure rules and consequences for failure to disclose. Collaborative divorce has taken this a step further by creating a contractual affirmative duty to disclose relevant information. This reflects the recognition of the value of perfect information to collaborative bargaining. In the game theory bargaining model, there is an additional step taken to make the game one of perfect information. The parties reveal their subjective goals when making a proposal. The subjective goals undergirding a proposal helps make the bargaining process one of perfect information.

Perfect information enhances the bargaining process by making the application of Bayes rule possible, which in turn allows for a convergence of expectations on the optimal outcome. If in the example above the husband reveals a subjective payoff value of maintaining the value and control of the family farm in his family of origin, the bargaining process can include that payoff in the settlement. The end cost to the husband might be the same, but the subjective payoff in the payoff structure might be better, if only because it increases the level of trust in the settlement process. Greater trust also will help with the issue of verifiable versus non-verifiable information. In our bargaining model, the attorneys and parties will do best if they believe in the basic premise that the overall payoff structure for both of them has a better chance of being optimal if they play the game with perfect information.

---

8. We are aware that this has changed, but find the "old" rule illustrative.

Conclusion

Bargaining is more likely to achieve optimal outcomes for both parties to a divorce if information is managed effectively. This includes creating rules and procedures for making relevant information public, verifiable, complete, and perfect. We have described a specific role that a mediator can play to facilitate the development of perfect, complete, and verifiable information while protecting privacy. This becomes necessary in order to protect the rights of the clients to some privacy in the bargaining process and to keep options open for hardball negotiating should cooperative bargaining fail. It also protects one party from being taken advantage of by an unscrupulous party who might use the bargaining model presented here for the sole purpose of gathering information for later use in hardball negotiations or litigation.

---

5. Setting Axiomatic Standards for Each Agreement and for the Payoff Structure of the Marital Settlement Agreement

---

Having axiomatic standards at the beginning of bargaining on an individual issue (a single simple game) helps guide the bargaining to the optimal solution. For example, if a party raises questions about the other party introducing children to new romantic partners, making it a topic of bargaining, it would be helpful to obtain the objective and subjective goals of the parties and to use those goals to establish axioms for any agreements reached. One of the lawyers does some quick social science research and brings up several issues to determine if those issues might be subjective goals of the parties, and the parties bring up their own goals.

The following axiomatic standards may be applicable:

- The children should not develop bonds with new romantic partners that they then lose, increasing the effects of the parental separation and causing relationship instability for the children.
- The children should be given new sources of stress slowly so that they do not get overwhelmed.
- The children should not be exposed to situations that might sexualize them, by seeing their parents in sexual or quasi-sexual behavior.

- New romantic partners should not usurp parental roles, such as disciplining them, making medical decisions, giving haircuts, and enrolling the children in activities.
- The children should not be exposed to substantial blended family problems.
- Parents should know from one another when a new romantic partner is going to become involved with the children and should plan together how and when that will happen, so that there are no surprises.

The parties bargain with these axioms as standards and arrive at the following possible agreement:

- Neither parent will introduce the children to new romantic partners for at least eight months following the final divorce.
- Neither parent will introduce the children to new romantic partners until they have been seeing the person for at least six months and are fairly certain that there is a good possibility that the relationship will be long term.
- Both parents will include the other parent in planning how the new romantic partner will be introduced to the children (not when).
- If the new romantic partner has children, before living together, the parent and new romantic partner will attend at least two sessions with an expert on blended families to get some guidance.
- New romantic partners will not take on parental roles, except to discipline the children with the parents' rules and methods of discipline if alone with the children and responsible for their care at that time.

After arriving at these agreements, the parties measure them against the axioms to see if they have arrived at an optimal agreement. When doing so, they might add one more agreement:

- Each parent shall have an opportunity to meet the new romantic partner before the other parent begins living with him or her.

When the entire package of divorce agreements are reached, by applying what we call the Five E's as axiomatic standards, we can determine if the Marital Settlement Agreement (MSA) is optimal for both parties.

THE FIVE E's:

1. Educated
2. Equitable
3. Effective
4. Equilibrant
5. Envy Free

The Five E's

1. Educated

The parties are "educated" if they have had public, verifiable, perfect, and complete information through the divorce process, including fundamental rules in the legal system and the long-term implications of their agreements.

2. Equitable

Although an individual agreement might favor one party over the other, it is "equitable" if both parties agree that the overall payoff structure, the MSA, is reasonably fair. Here, fairness does not focus solely on the objective value of payoffs. In fact, the objective value of the payoffs might not be equitable in that one of the parties might have a much larger share of the objective payoffs. Fairness here refers to the objective *and* subjective payoffs. Thus, while one party might have more of the objective payoffs, this might seem fair to both parties if the other party achieved substantial subjective payoffs. For example, one party might have received 75 percent of the estate, but the other party might have received sufficient value to live comfortably and also be freed from obligations that allow the party to pursue some important goals, like being a yoga instructor or living in Chile for a while. The parties might consider this payoff package as equitable.

3. Effective

The agreements reached are effective if they achieve the goals of the parties with a minimum of ambiguity. For example, assume that an agreement includes a holiday schedule where the children are with their father every Labor Day to the following morning and also assume that the schedule allows the mother to take the children to school the first day of school each year. What if school starts the day after Labor Day? Without addressing this possibility, the agreement is not effective.

Another meaning of effective relative to divorce is with regard to the repeated form games involved. A MSA that does not include procedures and axioms for repeated form games is not effective. For example, if the MSA does not explicitly state what constitutes a "change of circumstance" for the adjustment of child support, the parties are left to guess. Some jurisdictions have such standards, but often the parents are not made aware of these. For example, one jurisdiction has the standard that if a parent's income goes up or down by more than 10 percent relative to the prior twenty-three months, there has been a change of circumstance. By using a running average like this, the jurisdiction avoids the problem of seasonal incomes. Parents are often not aware of this rule and, therefore, if they suspect the other parent's income has increased, or if his or her income has gone down, they have no standard to determine whether or not an adjustment in child support is warranted. This agreement is not effective.

As an interesting aside, one of the authors was aware of this rule in the child support office of the jurisdiction in question; this was the standard applied by the attorneys in the child support office. He mentioned this in a presentation to attorneys in that jurisdiction, and they did not know of the standard. Thus, the family law attorneys in the jurisdiction did not have complete information.

A child-related example might be what to do if the parties have a dispute about enrollment in an extracurricular activity that runs across residential time in both homes or requires financial contributions from both parents. If during the bargaining process, probing questions are asked about this issue and the parents assert that they might well have some of these disagreements, the bargaining process should include a solution procedure for handling such an issue. Then the agreement is effective. Carefully examining a MSA for repeated form games and developing procedures for them is critical to this axiom.

4. Equilibrant

Technically, in game theory language, the standard is called "efficient," but the term efficient has too many non–game theory connotations to use here without confusion. We name it "equilibrant". The concept is that the payoff package cannot be improved for either or both parties without diminishing the value to one of the parties. If a party can increase the payoff value without the other person losing any payoff values, the agreement is not equilibrant. For example, assume that the parties have agreed to a term of eight years for spousal support at a certain amount. Then assume that one of the parties would like that to be assured, that there will not be a modification later if circumstances change. Assume that the party believes this is needed in order to qualify for a mortgage amount. Proposing that the spousal support be converted to a fixed, non-modifiable Section 71 Payment agreement would accomplish this goal without diminishing the value of the agreement for the other party and perhaps even improving the subjective value of the agreement for the other party. Although the agreement ensures that the amount will not go down for the party making the proposal, it also ensures that the amount will not go up for the other party.

In an example that is child related, assume that the parties live about five miles from one another, with the mother living closer to the children's school but having a relatively shared residential placement schedule with the two young children. The father worries that over time, the children's interests will increasing drift toward the mother's home, because much of the social activity occurs near her. He worries that this might mean that the children will express increasing preferences to live full time with her and that she might even pursue this goal in a future schedule dispute. He proposes that he be able to enroll the children in most of the extracurricular activities in order to ensure that the children maintain interests and social connections with peers near his residence. The mother agrees, because she has less interest in extracurricular activities than does the father. Her payoff package does not diminish, but his improves.

5. Envy Free

Most spouses going through a divorce are realistic enough to know that they will lose value. They will lose some time with the children, and they will lose some property. There are also other losses involved. They will lose some control over the lives of the children and will probably lose some friendships, such as couple's friends. They will lose some connections to the extended family of the other spouse, and perhaps most emotionally difficult, they will lose the dreams they had for the marriage. In addition, when there are children, they will lose the dreams of the kind of family they would like their children to have when they grow up. Many of the emotions in a divorce emerge from these losses. Much of the anger and blame that often accompanies a divorce are covers for this deep sense of loss. The legal process of the divorce reifies these losses. A legal divorce directly confronts any reconciliation hopes, for example, and drives home the permanence of the divorce. The MSA identifies the loss of time with the children and the loss of property. If a party finishes the divorce process believing that he or she lost more than the other party, optimal solutions were not achieved.

The axiom that directly measures this is one where the payoff package for each party is envy free, meaning that while there is loss, neither party would trade his or her payoff package for that received by the other party. If one of the parties would trade his or her package for the other party's, this axiom has not been met, and it is time to go back to the bargaining table. A quick solution is of course for the other party to simply offer to trade packages, but this is often very unrealistic.

Probing questions will likely yield new subjective goals and values that were not included in the bargaining process. For example, assume that the mother says that the package is not envy free because the father has a block of time of seven days each month with the children, and although the time with the children is generally shared, she does not have such a block and does not want to go seven days without seeing the children. This subjective value is now introduced into the bargaining on the residential placement schedule, which is adjusted to meet these goals without diminishing the value to the father. Perhaps a plan is included that the mother will attend activities during that seven days and be allowed to take the children for dinner on one of those days, or perhaps they both end up with a block of seven days with a day in the middle when the children are with the other parent. If the parties are asked again if the entire agreement is envy free, and they agree, then the MSA is envy free.

It is important for parties to know about the Five E's at the beginning of the bargaining process. This provides them with a form of assurance that they will not be taken advantage of in the process, while also assuring them that the goal of the bargaining process is to achieve these axioms for both parties—that is, to reach optimal solutions. Doing this sets the tone of the bargaining and reinforces a balance of narcissistic and altruistic interests (more about this in later chapters). The parties should understand that the bargaining process is designed not only to address their self-interests but also to address the interests of the other party. Thus, if one party must give in some on one issue in the compromise bargaining stage, he or she has some assurance that in order to achieve the Five E's axioms, the other party will be giving in on another issue.

Proposals during the bargaining process have the best chance of being acceptable if they address the interests of both parties in order to meet the Five E's axiom.

Summary—Bargaining Standards

1. Recognize that the divorce game is made up of subgames, some of which are normal form games and some of which are repeated form games. As we shall expand on later in the book, normal form games require a focus on the *content* of the game, the facts of the situation. Repeated form games require a focus on *procedures* for how future decisions will be made.

2. Identify *multiple games and separate them into single games.*

3. Identify *mixed games and separate them into simple games.*

4. Employ *Bayes rule* in the bargaining process. Ideally, this means taking turns making proposals and counterproposals. By taking turns, each move reveals additional information about objective and subjective values and goals, with the opportunity for each party to change beliefs, creating a convergence of expectations and optimal solutions for both players.

5. Employ *good information management* by making information public, verifiable, complete, and perfect. By doing so, Bayes rule is enhanced, leading to optimal solutions for both players.

6. Establish *axioms for each appropriate individual issue* addressed in the bargaining process, based on the *objective and subjective* values and goals of the parties, and maintain the overall axiom of the *Five E's for the entire payoff package*—namely, the marital settlement agreement.

By applying game theory principles to the divorce process, with or without the use of mathematics in the calculation, parties to the divorce, with guidance and assistance by their attorneys, become rational players who can achieve optimal payoff structures for both of them.

Why Use Game Theory Principles?

We have provided information about principles derived from game theory and have steered away from the use of mathematics and jargon as much as possible, to keep these principles simple and easily applied. Skilled mediators and experienced family law attorneys will recognize some of these principles in their existent approaches to their cases. They might reasonably ask, Why complicate matters with game theory? Earlier drafts of this book included more mathematic proofs and more jargon, but those made it virtually unreadable except by a game theory expert. A "saddle solution," for example, is a complex solution that requires substantial mathematical calculations but also can serve as a guide to solving a complex game like divorce. However, few, if any, attorneys or mediators are going to develop a MSA by going through these complicated mathematics.

So, what is the point? Why introduce game theory and not just a few bargaining tools? The answer is that while a few new tools might be helpful, they would not transform the experience of divorce by the spouses and, when children are involved.

Game theory is a way of thinking about the process that differs from traditional divorce.

- The assumptions are different.
- The process is different.
- The outcomes are different.

When a proposal is made, the goal is not only to maximize the objective and subjective payoff for the party making the proposal but also to maximize the objective and subjective payoff for the other party. When an MSA is evaluated by the parties and the attorneys, the Five E's ensure that the best plan for going forward has been achieved for both parties. A divorce is an unfortunate, sometimes tragic event in people's lives. When they interface with the professionals involved, if the event can move the parties and, if a family, the children, in a positive direction, society improves.

There is a more pragmatic purpose to introducing game theory into the family law system. Divorce *with* attorneys should become the norm, especially when children are involved. For attorneys to recapture market share, divorcing spouses should assume and expect that they are hiring guides through a difficult process and that, by doing so, the outcomes for them and their children will be better and well worth the price. Traditional law promotes selfishness and conflict; family law should promote cooperation and positive outcomes for all involved.

CHAPTER 3

Traditional Divorce Analyzed

Examining a Business Case Study Using Game Theory Principles

Before analyzing a traditional divorce using game theory, it might be illustrative to analyze a business—the Tupulo Restaurant—using game theory principles. Henry, the owner of Tupulo Restaurant, is a rational player in the restaurant business. He is experienced in the business, seeks good advice, and plays the game well. He understands that having dinner at a restaurant is a complex experience that begins with the call to the restaurant and ends when the parties drive away after their meal. It is not just good food that matters. Before opening the restaurant, he first develops a value proposition. In game theory, this is called the "axiom" or "group of axioms" that are the standards by which decisions are made. Henry's value proposition is that from the first call to the restaurant through the entire dining experience, customers will be treated with warmth, good listening, guidance, and accommodation and provided with good food that is presented well and in a timely manner. Timeliness in the restaurant business is provided without uncomfortable waiting periods, but never rushed. Henry also realizes that the type of food provided and the cost of the meals must fit the context of the restaurant location.

In our first analysis, Henry is setting axiomatic standards for his decisions. In game theory, this establishes the foundation of success. Success is dependent on three basic ingredients (double entendre intended):

- Is there a market for this type of restaurant?
- Can they attract a sufficient number of first-time customers to reach a tipping point (that is, can they get enough initial attention to create good word-of-mouth advertising)?

- Does the objective/subjective payoff surpass the objective/subjective cost? This balance is crucial to any business. To be successful in business, the value offered must exceed the cost involved. Some costs are obvious, such as the price of a meal, and others are subtle, such as the hassle involved in parking at the restaurant.

Note: In our experience, the last of these axioms is all too often neglected by attorneys practicing in family law. In a sense, having a satisfied customer involves an analysis of the objective and subjective payoffs relative to the costs. This is one of the key reasons for the growth in pro se cases and the loss of market share by attorneys.

Let us follow Joan through the "dining experience" offered at Henry's restaurant and analyze her experience by using game theory. Joan and her husband, James, are celebrating their fifth wedding anniversary, and she decides to treat them to a nice dinner. She saw an article in a local paper touting a new restaurant, Tupulo. She decides to give it a try and calls for a reservation. She is greeted by a pleasant voice, which is her first payoff, because she does not have to leave a message and wait for a callback. The time that she requests for their dinner reservation is unavailable, but the voice on the telephone assures her that she will find an opening close to that desired time and does. This is her second payoff, being treated as an important person. Next, the voice asks her if Joan has been there before. When she reports that she has not, the voice provides her with information on where the restaurant is located and, because it is downtown, where to park. The voice also informs her that there is free valet parking available. She has now received two more payoffs. The voice asks if this is a special occasion, and when the voice discovers that it is an anniversary, she asks how long they have been married and finishes by telling Joan that they look forward to seeing her. Joan receives another payoff by feeling that the reservation process was made personal. In game theory, Henry realizes that he is playing an extensive repeated form game, which requires a focus on procedures rather than content. The meal is the content, but the initial phone call is a procedure. He has trained his staff that when receiving a call, first try to accommodate the desired reservation time or come close to it. The staff is then to ask a series of questions, gathering information, some of which will be used later to enhance the experience, and to get personal in order to build a relationship with the customer. Henry does not just want the customer to enjoy the meal; he wants one meal to be the beginning of many—with Joan and with others to whom she recommends his restaurant. He wants Joan to spread the word. In game theory, one meal is a node in an extensive repeated form game with Joan and others, whom she tells about the restaurant. So far, the payoffs Joan received, all subjective, in making the reservation exceed the cost (e.g., the time and hassle of a phone call).

Joan and James easily find parking and locate the restaurant, because they were directed in the initial call. They arrive a little early, but the hostess takes them to a small table in the bar to sit while they wait for their table—and even takes their drink order. Here again, we see another payoff in that they are welcomed, even though early, and treated as special. We see the axiomatic standards at work in the training of the hostess. Rather than have to wait for a server, the hostess takes their order. When their table is ready, they are led there, they are given menus, and the process continues. The waiter, rather than reeling off the specials like a recording, greets them and asks them if they have any questions and whether or not they would like to hear the specials. By individualizing the experience, the waiter is providing more payoffs. The meal progresses, not only without a rush, but also without any great wait. At the end of the meal, the waiter brings a couple of small dessert plates "on the house" and wishes them a happy anniversary. The waiter knows what they are celebrating because there is a note by the reservation book. Joan and James have just received another payoff, both objective (the dessert) and subjective (someone listened when Joan told them about their anniversary).

The Tupulo Experience: Henry Setting up Procedures, Establishing Axiomatic Standards, and Playing an Extensive Repeated Form Game

The restaurant's menu included prices, and that is what the bill reflected, so there were no surprises. This is another payoff, because the couple got what they thought they were going to get for the price they expected to pay. The restaurant is able to price the meals (and wine, etc.) because there is a formula for doing so. Depending on the location and the menu, a restaurant owner understands the fixed costs (e.g., lease), the costs of the initial investment spaced over the time that the restaurant is expected to be open, and the expected profit. These costs usually run about one-third of the cost of a meal. The food costs usually run about one-third and the personnel another one-third. The restaurant then determines how many meals on average it needs to serve to break even. When the restaurant serves more meals, only the food cost increases, so the restaurant makes more money. When the establishment serves less, the reverse happens, and the restaurant loses money.

By playing the game as an extensive repeated form game, Henry hopes for repeat business, and with word-of-mouth advertising, increasing the chance of success. Had he played the game as a normal form game, he might have made a profit on Joan and James, but fail in business because they do not return and do not recommend the restaurant to others.

In game theory, we would assign points to the utility or, more formally, to each utile. The utility includes both the costs and the payoffs. The costs are the difficulties getting to the restaurant and the parking. Henry has reduced those costs by negotiating with a local parking garage and by providing directions and guidance regarding the parking. Once in the restaurant, the costs are chiefly the dollar cost of the meal, but might include potential subjective costs. If Joan and James had had to stand near a door while they waited for their table, for example, there would have been costs compared to being taken to a waiting area where they could have a pre-dinner drink. If the meal had been rushed or too slow, there would have been costs. Again, we see that Henry has designed the experience to minimize those subjective costs. He has also minimized the subjective costs of the dollar amount by having a menu with a range of pricing. A wealthy person might have no difficulty paying for a $35 entrée, but someone for whom money is a bit tighter might be more comfortable with an entrée costing $18. Henry has taken into consideration this subjective value of the dollar cost. If we assign points to these costs, we might find that Joan and James have spent sixteen points for their dinner. Although Henry minimized the parking problem, his downtown location did make getting there more difficult. If we assign points to the payoffs, we might find that Joan and James received twenty-eight points in value, with the payoffs pointed out above, including the additional payoff of a good meal. Subjectively, Joan and James will leave the restaurant pleased with their experience because the payoff value greatly exceeds the payoff costs. This is the end of the node. If Joan and James return or tell others about their positive experience, the extensive repeated game begins to favor Henry.

Will a rational player, Joan, go back to Tupulo and recommend it to others? The answer depends on the one additional question asked earlier: is there a market for the restaurant style (a sushi restaurant in a mining town might have difficulty getting established). Presuming that there is a market, Henry can count on two characteristics of humans: (1) they like the familiar if they know they are getting quality; and (2) they like to share positive experiences, especially when there is status involved, such as being "in the know" about a new restaurant.

It is no accident that some restaurants flourish while others fail. It is the balance of payoffs to costs that predicts success. Nowhere is this more naked than in the restaurant business because few businesses are as exposed to these game theory principles.

A more formal game theory analysis would look at the entire experience, determining where each node is—that is, those points in the experience where Joan and James have a choice and the same for the restaurant, the two players in the game. Points would be assigned to each choice. The number of points is arbitrary but relative to other choices. For example, when Joan calls the restaurant, the restaurant has a choice in how to take the call. They could have a recording saying that someone will call her back; they could have a recording giving information about the restaurant (e.g., location and hours of operation); or they could direct the person calling to the restaurant's website for more information and to make reservations. One could construct a chart assigning relative points to each of these choices as payoffs to Joan; that is, each choice would be given a number of points relative to each of the other choices. We could conduct a mini-pilot study and poll thirty people and ask them to assign points to each choice, take an average, and use that result. The next node might be in what the person answering the telephone call says. We could list a number of choices, assign points to each choice, and so on.

It is very unlikely that Henry had done this type of analysis, but his experience in the business led to intuitive choices that, if we were to do a retrospective analysis, suggest this type of thinking. First, his focus is on the experience of the person calling for a reservation through each step, beginning with the meal and ending at the point of them walking out of door. He intuitively made good decisions regarding the customer's personal experiences and choices throughout the process. Perhaps most important, Henry recognized that he was entering into an extensive repeated form game, with a focus on procedures and axiomatic standards, with Joan and James, which will either lead to success or failure. Serving a single dinner to Joan and James means nothing to his success; their repeat business and the people they tell about the restaurant are what will lead to his success.

Examining a Divorce Case Study Using Game Theory Principles

John and Mary are married and live in the State of Ambiguity and the County of Confusion. Mary wants to initiate a divorce. She asks some of her friends if anyone knows a lawyer she can go to and manages to get a couple of names. She calls Attorney Dispute. What is the value proposition of Attorney Dispute? Is it, "If you have the money, I will take your case?" Attorney Dispute's secretary makes an appointment for an initial consultation and tells Mary to bring $5,000 for a fee in advance of service, "just in case you hire Attorney Dispute." From a game theory perspective, what payoff points does this beginning have for Mary? What if Attorney Dispute had set an axiom that clients will at each stage of the process be educated? The secretary's response to the initial phone call might be very different.

- *"Attorney Dispute likes his clients to have a good overview of the legal process, the tasks involved in a divorce, and to see if you and he are a good fit, based on your goals and his procedures."*
- *"He offers a free one-hour meeting."*
- *"After that, you can decide if you would like to hire him, or if you would rather not, he can give you the names of other attorneys who might be a better fit."*
- *"Would you like to schedule a free initial consultation?"*

Compare these two choices and in your own mind, assign relative points to each choice. How much weight would you give to being greeted with the statement of an axiom of education? How much weight would you give the emphasis on "free" rather than "bring $5,000"? How much weight would you give a statement of interest in the client's goals and the importance of a good fit in the attorney-client relationship? Remember that in game theory analysis, we are always comparing choices and the relative payoff value of those choices.

In the first meeting between Mary and Attorney Dispute, each player will be making numerous strategy choices. Attorney Dispute will need to decide the following:

- whether to focus immediately on background for the legal process (e.g., finding out what property is involved and how many children and their ages) or whether to focus on Mary's emotional state

- whether to have Mary explore her decision with an experienced counselor/coach (for example, the probable impact of a divorce on her children) that he works with before engaging Attorney Dispute or to go forward with filing a divorce petition

- whether he advises Mary to tell John about the divorce right away or to wait and tell him when they are prepared to take the first steps of the case

- whether to advise Mary to tell the children, wait to them tell, tell them with John, or other options

Mary will have many of her own choices and decisions to make. Mary and Attorney Dispute are playing the "will you hire me?" game.

However, they are playing the game in the context of a legal system that has no clear-cut value propositions. Most family law statutes include legal procedures and factors to be considered in decisions, but no clear-cut value proposition on what the divorcing spouse's experience should be like and no clear axiomatic standards by which agreements/rulings should be judged. From a game theory perspective, there are several inherent problems for divorcing spouses in this approach.

The Fight Begins (Perhaps without Knowing It)

As we focused on earlier in this book, the fundamental presumption of the current legal system is that the interests of the parties are adverse to one another and that the legal system is a vehicle for resolving these presumed disputes, through settlement negotiations, mediation, or litigation. The theme permeating the legal process is that new disputes are to be created at each step along the way. Getting a certain outcome becomes paramount. For example, the attorney representing a business owner may seek the services of an appraiser who is known to lean in one direction, while the other attorney may seek the services of an appraiser who typically leans in a different direction. Thus, what starts as an ambiguity—that is, how much is a business worth?—becomes a battle of the experts and a dispute. A common practice in law is the "letter for home consumption." Simply, this is when one attorney sends a provocative letter to the other attorney, copying the client, not so much for the other attorney but to demonstrate how the attorney is championing the client's cause against "the other side." The other side, of course, responds with an equally provocative letter, copying his or her client. The lawyers understand the strategy but the parties do not. In the context of the assumptions undergirding the system, this is a reasonable strategy, even though doing so tends to escalate the conflict between the spouses. Spouses often personalize such letters as if they were coming directly from the other spouse, increasing the conflict between them.

Parties Need to Accomplish Goals; Lawyers Work to Achieve Legal Outcomes (Perhaps without Knowing It)

Attorneys and the legal system identify property division, income sharing, custody, and residential placement schedules as goals, because they are the end product of the attorney's work, possible court orders, and the final marital settlement agreement. However, the lives of the spouses and their children go on after the final judgment of divorce as ordered by the court. To divorcing spouses, an MSA is not a goal; it is a tool for trying to accomplish goals. With the focus on the legal outcomes as goals, the parties walk out of a final hearing just beginning to live the rest of their lives and to raise their children. We know of one case in which at the end of the hearing the attorney congratulated his client for what on the whole was a "win." The client left the court not feeling like he won; he felt like he had just experienced a death. For the attorney, the goals had been reached, but these were not the client's goals.

The Payoff Structure for Attorneys/Mediators and Spouses Are Different

Transaction costs typically benefit the attorney but are negative payoffs for the divorcing spouses. Winning a legal argument might have a positive payoff for the attorney but create increased conflict, bitterness, and aversion for the spouses, while reducing the assets available to the spouses and their children. One of the authors once asked an experienced attorney why attorneys want to settle when going to trial is so much more lucrative. The attorney replied that on average trials are not more lucrative, because clients often refuse to pay their bill for litigation. Here we see the balance of costs and payoffs tip into the negative direction. Only if a customer in a restaurant had an awful meal would he or she refuse to pay the bill.

This is compounded by the law, which typically focuses on solely the legal outcomes at the time of the divorce and provides prescriptive guidance for reaching those outcomes. For example, when law prescribes an equitable division of marital property, the law is focusing on the short-term objective goal, rather than the long-term objective and subjective goals of the parties. To the degree attorneys and mediators focus on these prescriptive outcomes, they direct parties to do so also, which can lead to playing the divorce game in a rational but self-defeating manner.

Rules That May Be Unknown to the Spouses Create Payoffs for the Attorney but Have Adverse Effects on the Spouses

In one county, attorneys are considered as having failed if they do not settle and end up litigating. Attorneys in this jurisdiction have an incentive to pressure their clients into a settlement, when doing so might not be in the interests of the clients or even the whole family. In another jurisdiction, the most successful attorneys are the ones best known for intense levels of litigation. The incentives in that county are to disrupt settlement and get the case to litigation and trial. In both counties, the divorcing spouses are likely unaware of these "rules" and the payoff structure for the attorneys.

Without a Clear Value Proposition, Neither the Parties nor Their Attorneys Know What a Divorce Is Supposed to Accomplish

In theory, divorce should be a solution: the reorganization of a family that dissolves the problematic marriage, divides the assets and debts of the marriage, places parents in two residences, and allows for the successful raising of children. How often do we see parties giving up any positive parts of the marriage, keeping the problems, sometimes escalating them through the divorce process, *and* getting no permanent solution? In our restaurant example (Tupulo), by having a clear value proposition, Henry was able to design each step of the process of a dining experience with standards. Without such a value proposition, the design of the experience of divorcing parties is a mishmash of steps, some attempting to promote communication and cooperation (such as required parent education), some attempting to help encourage settlement (such as required mediation), but some promoting conflict and disputes (such as an attorney advising the client not to budge from a position in mediation).

Without Clear Axiomatic Standards Against Which to Measure an Outcome (the MSA), Parties Have No Way to Judge the Payoff Structure

One standard that exists in some jurisdictions is that the property division must be equitable, which helps, but is vague and incomplete. Child support guidelines and even presumptions with regard to custody and residential schedules for children might also help. However, there are no clear axiomatic standards for outcomes that predict positive long-term outcomes for the parties and the children in the family, including financial outcomes.

Traditional Divorce Treats Most Games as Normal Form Games and Zero-Sum Games, Which Promotes Competition and Conflict

Property division, income sharing, custody, and residential placement schedules are viewed as goals by the legal system rather than tools to help the parties reach goals. When asked what a good residential placement schedule is for children, an attorney should respond in this way:

- "It depends on how you want it to turn out for your children."
- "This is what you need to decide."

For example, the attorney might ask the client if he or she wants:

1. Strong relationships with both parents
2. Both parents actively involved in the child's life
3. A stable childhood with the consistency of conducting a life outside of the family from one home
4. A situation that minimizes the hassles of children going back and forth between two homes
5. A more marginal relationship with one of their parents
6. The children living mostly in one home but have ways of actively including the other parent in all aspects of their lives
7. Parents actively dealing with one another or avoiding each other

The Court System May Not Be Friendly (Perhaps Without Knowing It)

The court system inadvertently turns the non-zero-sum game of parenting into a zero-sum game by making the prize the number of overnights with the child and creating numerous payoffs for getting as many of those nights as possible. Because there are only 365 nights in a year, it is a zero-sum game. Every night one parent gets is a night lost to the other parent. We earlier discussed the extensive list of payoffs that come with winning this mixed game.

Non-Zero-Sum Games and Repeated Form Games Can Be Played in Divorce (Perhaps Without Knowing It)

Property division and income sharing are not inherently zero-sum games, although they might appear to be so. On the face of property division, it looks like the marriage has a total net worth in assets that have to be split. Thus, there is an illusion that views each dollar one party wins as one dollar that the other party loses. The same could be said of income sharing. The parties have a total income that is to be allocated, either as child support or as spousal support. However, are these games really zero-sum games? Another way to view property division and income sharing is to look at them as means of reaching long-term goals for both parties. Perhaps both parties might want to be financially independent of one another as soon as possible, say within five years. From this perspective, the net worth and income are viewed as tools to reach these financial goals. How to best use those tools is not a zero-sum game; it is a financial planning game. Every dollar one gets is not seen as a dollar lost to the other party, but rather as a step closer to meeting the goals of both parties

As a result of treating these non-zero-sum games as zero-sum games, and these repeated form games as normal form games, traditional divorce promotes strategies aimed at *winning rather than planning*. The strategies best suited to winning normal form zero-sum games are aggressive, competitive, mud-slinging, and dishonest. Where do these ex-spouses go when the game is over for the attorneys? It is no accident that re-litigation rates are highest for parties who litigated the first time when compared to using alternatives such as mediation, collaborative divorce, cooperative divorce, or simply pro se settlement.

Conclusion

When we analyze traditional divorce using game theory principles, we see that the most rational strategy is provoking conflictual disputes. When parties behave rationally, however, they are met with ever-increasing transaction costs, psychological costs to the parties and their children, damage to the co-parenting relationship, disrupted relationships between spouses and extended family members, and an increasing number of cooks in the kitchen (e.g., custody evaluators), none of whom love the children and none of whom will be there when the children are twenty-five years old to see how it all turned out. Ironically, although traditional divorce promotes self-defeating strategies, such as battle-to-the-death disputes over support, the professionals in the legal system often look at the parties with distaste, even though in the context of the divorce they are behaving rationally.

It is with a keen awareness of the problems associated with traditional divorce that we see the development of alternatives. Mediation is as old as the court system, although its use in family law is a little more recent. Mediation has its own body of research and theory that we will not discuss in great detail here. However, it is noteworthy that some game theory principles have been incorporated into many forms of mediation. Interest-based mediation as opposed to position-based mediation, for example, incorporates the notion of subjective goals as well as objective goals. A mediator does not represent one party, and most mediators do not see the decisions in divorce as zero-sum games or necessarily that the interests of the parties are opposed to each other.

Collaborative divorce has also attempted to incorporate some game theory principles into the settlement process. By taking away the ability to litigate from the attorneys, should the collaborative process fail, for example, collaborative divorce removes the chicken game dynamic. By collaborating on the use of experts, and utilizing coaches and child specialists, collaborative divorce reduces dependence on traditional competitive bargaining. By having an affirmative duty to disclose, better information management is encouraged. However, while not bargaining in the shadow of the law, the parties in collaborative divorce are now bargaining in the shadow of losing their attorney. This puts pressure on the parties to settle to avoid the loss of the attorney, onto whom the party might have placed a good deal of transference dependence. It also puts additional pressure on that same party, who must consider the loss of the transaction costs incurred to that point and the specter of starting the divorce process all over. Cooperative divorce attempts to remove this obstacle while avoiding the pressure of the game of chicken, but it is too early to know how successful that attempt has been.

Although not specifically analyzing each of these alternatives to the traditional divorce model with game theory, each of these attempts to offer alternatives to traditional divorce reflect at least an intuitive understanding that traditional divorce can all too easily lead parties into a process for which the costs are too high for the positive payoffs achieved.

ALTERNATIVES TO THE TRADITIONAL DIVORCE MODEL:

1. Create a value proposition-- a clear understanding of what the divorce is supposed to accomplish.
2. Assume that the interests of the parties are more in concert than adverse.
3. Have a focus on the long-term objective and subjective goals of the parties, not the legal outcomes.
4. Have a focus on the node in every repeated form game, be cause action is required at each node. The case does not end with the Court order.
5. Avoid turning non-zero-sum games into zero-sum games.
6. Define differences as disagreements about how to achieve goals— not disputes on legal outcomes.
7. Establish clear axiomatic standards that guide the bargaining process by which the MSA can be judged.

CHAPTER 4

Game Theory: Applied to Custody, Residential Placement Schedules and Co-Parenting

---

Introduction

Knowing what is most important when playing the children's game is a good starting point. Whether or not they are aware of it, separating and divorcing parents play two parallel games simultaneously relative to their children. One is obvious and often receives the most attention: the "legal game." Parents know that they play the legal game. This game includes the tasks of establishing legal custody (decision-making authority for the children), residential placement schedules (where the children spend time with each parent), rules about relocation, grandparent involvement, and so on. As necessary as the legal game is, it is not what is most important to long-term outcomes for children and, indirectly, for parents.

The Legal Game Is Well Known
The legal game is a normal form game played once (i.e., at the time of the divorce), but does *not* include decisions that correlate highly with long-term outcomes for children. More often than not, the parents do not know this (nor do many attorneys or judges). Residential schedules, for example, are important, but not as important as other factors, like the support systems in place for parents and children (e.g., grandparents, supportive teachers, good daycare), the quality of parenting in each of the homes, or the most important factor—how well parents communicate and cooperate with each other.

The Child Planning Game Is Less Well Known

After many years of study and research, social scientists discovered that all parents also play what we call the "child planning game," although parents might be unaware that they are doing so. Interestingly, this is as true for parents who live together (e.g., are married) as it is for parents who are separated.

All separated parents play the game; the only difference between families is how well they play it. Some parents play it well and have children who turn out well; these parents also enjoy the process of parenting together. They develop a flexible family system that includes at least a moderate level of communication and cooperation. Some parents play it from moderately well to poorly. These parents have children who have higher risks of many different types of problems. They find the process of parenting together frustrating, even hateful, and often miss out on major portions of their children's lives because of their failure to communicate and cooperate. They feel helpless and powerless to address concerns about the other home, live with inflexible schedules, miss out on wonderful opportunities, and find their lives dominated by bitter disputes and resentments. Even parents who do everything in their power to avoid each other are playing the game, because they still send messages to one another, sometimes through the children or sometimes through simply ignoring important issues, and place heavy burdens on others, including their children, as the cost of this avoidance. For example, costs of education often include sending double mailers for the same child to separated parents who have not designed a system for sharing school information, and teachers are forced to hold double meetings with parents who cannot sit through a parent-teacher conference together.

Parents Cannot Avoid Playing the Child Planning Game—They Can Only Control How Well They Play It

Some parents live in a fantasy world, believing they can just create two families, never deal with one another, and have that work out. When it does not work out, they blame the other parent for the problems and get frustrated when they see their children suffer for it. Parents always communicate with each other. Parents who play the game well communicate directly and constructively. Parents who play it poorly communicate through the children, or nasty notes, or by failing to take the children to their scheduled activities (message: "You cannot control me by signing the children up without my permission"), and so on. Because there is always parental communication, all that parents can control is how successful and constructive it is.

It is not *pie-in-the-sky* idealism to assert that bitterly divorcing parents can play the child planning game well. Some parents, and even some professionals, support this myth with statements like, "If we could communicate (or get along), they wouldn't be getting a divorce." Perhaps the most impressive proof that this reasoning is false logic is the fact that about one-third of separating parents, after a sometimes bitter and conflict-filled divorce period, play the child planning game very well; and another one-third, again after a bad period around the time of the divorce, play it moderately well. If it were inherently true that people who could not get along as spouses cannot get along as parents, more than one-half of separating parents could not accomplish this, yet they do.

Communication and Cooperation after Divorce Is an Achievable Goal

The explanation for this paradox—that is, how people who failed to be effective in their marriage can be effective as parents after their separation—is that working together as separated parents is not as complicated or as emotionally challenging as having a successful marriage. There are psychological needs and emotions that come up in a marriage that simply do not exist in a successful parenting relationship. Thus, parents who failed to make the spousal relationship work well can, and many do, make the child planning relationship work very well. The myth that a failure in the marital relationship necessarily means that parents cannot communicate well is not only false on the face of it, but also false because many parents who were unable to maintain a good marriage prove it wrong by actively and constructively communicating and cooperating as parents after their separation.

As an analogy, many people perform well in workplaces or on athletic teams with other people with whom they might neither want nor be able to maintain good friendships. A good friendship requires a unique set of interpersonal skills and a wide variety of emotional ties that are simply not required to do good teamwork. Good teamwork requires simply having a shared set of goals (accomplishing certain work tasks or winning a game), a plan, and follow through. The child planning game is much more like teamwork than a friendship or a marriage. It requires having shared goals (e.g., having the children do well), a plan, and follow through.

It might be frightening for parents to try playing the child planning game at the time of a separation and divorce. The thought of communicating with the other parent, with all that might have gone on—including affairs, near-violent episodes, bitter frustration, terrible criticisms of one another, guilt, shame, and intense fear—might seem overwhelming and perhaps abhorrent. It is understandable that parents would like to avoid one another when emotions are intensely negative.

Divorcing Parents Should Start Communicating as Soon as Possible, or at Least Learn How to Do It

Nevertheless, to start playing the child planning game at the time of the separation and divorce has the best payoff down the road, in spite of how emotionally difficult it might seem at the outset. Research has shown that the sooner parents begin communicating as separated parents, the better their co-parenting relationship will be in the long term.

It is very important for parents to understand this game and how to play it well. If they try to coparent without understanding how to do it well, they might only compound the pain and frustration of their divorce and intensify the fear that they have for their children. Even if parents are unable to start effectively co-parenting right away, knowing how to do it will help down the road when emotions are not running so high. It will be harder to start later and some unnecessary damage might have been done. Nevertheless, even if they start playing well six months or a year after the separation, their children's lives will be substantially better for it, as will theirs. To delay playing it well (or at all) means playing it poorly for a while and perhaps developing more bitterness and bad habits over time. Again, while it is difficult to play the Child Planning Game well right away after a separation, parents will be grateful down the road if they do so.

Separating parents often hear general advice, such as, "You have to communicate," but they receive little guidance about what that should include or not include. Traditional divorce historically has not addressed this important parallel child planning game to the legal game. More recently, the court system has initiated programs to address this, mostly parent education programs that identify parental conflict as harmful to children, but also some programs that focus on the importance of communicating constructively.

The child planning relationship between two parents will last the lives of the parents and will have more impact on the lives of their children than almost any other aspect of their divorce. The parents will be grandparents to the same children someday too. The marital relationship ends, but this relationship continues. Successful separated parents—that is, parents who successfully raise well-adjusted children in spite of the separation—on average, play this game well enough (it does not have to be perfect). Researchers have studied these successful parents and found that they did a few things modestly well, and this made the difference. We call this the "child planning game."

Parents and professionals focus a good deal on the *legal* tasks of a divorce as it relates to children. We call this the "legal game." It largely consists of determining how major decisions will be made about the children (legal custody) and what residential schedule the children will follow (i.e., when they will be staying at their mother's residence and when they will be staying at their father's residence). There might be other legal tasks, depending on the facts of the case and the jurisdiction. Relocation issues might arise, for example, or the involvement of grandparents.

Goal-Based Planning

A good child-focused plan cannot be developed unless parents know what their basic goals are for their children. For example, if the parents want a child to have a strong bond to both parents, where the child grows up having both parents involved in all aspects of the child's life, then a schedule that has the child living with one parent and having occasional (e.g., every other weekend) visits with the other parent will not work. If the goals of the parents are to create as little stress, to provide as much stability of location in residence as possible, and to minimize the logistics problems for the child, then every other weekend can work well. If the goal is to have the child spend as much time as possible with parents rather than with daycare and other providers, then the work schedules of parents become a major planning factor.

A good exercise for separated parents is to ask themselves what they would like their child to say about growing up with separated parents when they are older (e.g., twenty-five years old). This can help parents begin to identify their goals for their child. From the beginning of the bargaining process, it is important to identify not only the "content" of the decisions, such as work schedules of the parents, but also the subjective values and goals of the parents. Parents will have some goals that contradict one another. This is true of many child-based decisions; that is, that some factors lean in one direction and some in another. Balancing all of the goals of the parents is the task at hand. We hope that by introducing game theory principles, parents will be focusing on ways to achieve as many of both parents' goals as possible, rather than the either/or disputes that we sometimes see in traditional divorce.

Thus, when parents begin to talk about their goals, asking questions about what their career goals are, what they would like their children to say about growing up in their family and how the children will describe the relationship between their parents when they are older, and do they want their child to do well in school, be social, be a good friend and problem solver, and so on begins the process of identifying how custody and residential schedules can be used as tools to accomplish those goals. Starting by asking what type of custody the parent wants implies that custody and a residential schedule is a goal. It also establishes a position that undermines the negotiating process and the important effect of Bayes rule on the process.

For example, if the mother says she would like the children to think of their lives as stable, even after the separation of the parents, but also to have strong relationships with both parents and to have both parents be actively involved in their lives, the attorney can say that there are several ways to set up custody and residential schedules to accomplish that goal. There is no position, just a narrowing of possible outcomes to those that accomplish the long-term goals. Further questioning regarding "stable" might reveal that the mother is mostly concerned with disruptions during school weeks. Again, there are a number of schedules that accomplish this goal. Because there is no position, there is no dispute yet. In fact, the father's goals might be very similar and the parties might start exploring schedules that meet these standards.

The point is that what type of custody and residential schedule the family should have is not the starting point; it is the end point and is based on the goals of the parents for the family experience for themselves and for their children.

Legal Game:
Custody/Decision Making and
Residential Placement Schedule

The Legal Game

Laws vary from state to state and country to country with regard to the child game, but most have two basic legal tasks: decision-making authority and a residential placement schedule. In some jurisdictions, these two will be closely tied to one another. One parent will receive custody, which is the decision-making authority but also specifies that the children will live primarily with that parent and have visitation[9] with the other parent on some schedule. In other jurisdictions, the two are completely separate. One parent may have the children living mostly with them, while the other parent may have decision-making authority. With regard to decision-making authority, most jurisdictions at this point have some form of joint custody in which both parents have decision-making authority, although the implications of those laws vary in form to some extent. In some jurisdictions, joint custody suggests that a decision has to be mutual, whereas in others, joint custody simply means that the parents are on equal legal footing. In the latter case, parents have the legal authority to make unilateral decisions, but the other parent has equal legal authority to make a different decision or to veto the decision made by the other parent. This can prompt a custody dispute that is resolved by a court or some alternative dispute resolution system. Most jurisdictions also identify what decisions fall under custodial authority. That list might be as long as eleven or twelve decisions or as short as six decisions. In Wisconsin, for example, there are six custodial decisions:

1. Choice of religion
2. Choice of school
3. Elective medical care
4. Obtaining a driver's license
5. Joining the military as a minor

---

9. Visitation is referred to by different names in different jurisdictions (e.g., parenting time).

6. Marrying as a minor

Other states include additional custodial decisions, such as enrollment in extracurricular activities that include the parenting time of both parents or daycare or after-school care required for work.

Focusing solely on the legal game is misdirected.

The "legal game" is a parallel "game" with the Child Planning Game. Sometimes, the court system's sole focus on the legal game is what frustrates all concerned and steers parents down destructive paths. The legal game is essential and important but is only one-half of the task facing separating parents. The professional who assists parents in playing both games well, including coordinating the legal game with the child planning game as much as possible, will have more satisfied clients and a more satisfying experience in representing them.

One of the more frustrating experiences for those who play the legal game is the degree to which laws have connected the support of the child to the residential schedule, usually through child support formulas linked to overnights. In addition, and worse yet, sometimes these connections include other financial planning decisions (e.g., who will retain the homestead). Experienced family law professionals are well aware that tying these financial payoffs directly to the residential schedule often (more accurately, almost always) interferes with parents designing a child-focused residential schedule. However, the real costs of raising children are tied to the schedule. Although efforts have been made to develop approaches for financially supporting children in ways that do not create incentives for disputes over the schedule, none have taken hold, at least not universally.

Legal Custody/Major Decisions

Legal Custody

"Legal custody" might be described with different terminology in different states. The basic concept, however, is similar in all states. Legal custody is the legal authority to make *major decisions* regarding a child after a divorce. Major decisions include such decisions as which school the child will attend or in what religion the child will be raised.

Although joint custody has become more common and even a presumption in many states, there are statutory exceptions to the presumption of joint legal custody. For example, in many states, if there has been a finding of domestic violence, there is a presumption that joint legal custody is *not* in the child's best interests. Joint legal custody makes sense in many situations, but is usually wise to have some sort of decision-making procedure in place *should there be a dispute.* The goal of such a provision is to avoid parents having to file petitions and pursue court action if and when there is a disagreement. Potential solutions are becoming more common: e.g., give one parent impasse-breaking authority or agree to have an arbiter or a parenting coordinator settle disputes. However, we have little research on these alternatives to trial.

Establishing legal custody is a normal form game and a repeated form game. In the normal form game, the focus is on the *list of decisions* that are either joint or not joint. The parties should carefully examine which decisions are statutorily included on the list of major decisions and consider adding decisions to that list as part of their MSA. The *procedure for making a custodial decision* is the procedure for the repeated form game. Simply having a dispute resolution procedure is insufficient guidance. For example, assume that the mother wants to initiate a medical procedure for a child, such as medication for perceived attention deficit problems. The father disagrees and the parents do not have an agreed-upon procedure for making the decision. Thus, they now are in a dispute. A disagreement only becomes a dispute when the parties are unable to resolve the disagreement. Now, the father has to choose between initiating a dispute resolution process that is going to cost time and money and in which he might not prevail or simply giving in to the mother—two aversive choices. If they have a decision-making procedure for their private use and it is undergirded with game theory principles, they have a means of maximizing the payoff to both of them.

The marital settlement agreement should specify not only the decisions that will be major decisions, but also the decision-making procedures that the parties will follow. Making a list of the custodial decisions is the normal form game, and identifying decision-making procedures is the repeated form game. There are many research-based decision-making models. We have included one in chapter 7 that is formulated using game theory principles.

Major Decisions

Though by no means complete or exclusive, the following is a list of major decisions used in many states.

A. Choice of School

Local law is sometimes vague about exactly what this choice includes. It is relatively clear that the school the child attends is a major decision, but it is not clear whether or not this includes any other educationally related choices. For example, if a teacher recommends summer school because a child is behind in math skills, is the choice to enroll the child in summer school a major decision as defined by law? If a child is selected to participate in a "gifted and talented" program, must the parents confer and make the decision, presuming joint custody, or may one parent simply enroll the child? Tutoring and homeschooling are other possibilities. Parents might want to consider further defining this decision in order to prevent misunderstandings and conflict. Attorneys can be very helpful in working with the parents to define this aspect of their custodial relationship. Statutory law and local rules might also define which parent has access to educational records or if both parents have such access. Discussing this issue at the time of the divorce can establish expectations and procedures that might prevent misunderstandings and conflict.

B. Choice of Religion

Courts find themselves in an unusual and difficult position relative to the question of religion. The separation of church and state would seem to suggest that the court might not have jurisdiction over religious choices. At the same time, the law in many states suggests that the court has this authority in divorce cases when there is a dispute between parents. On a practical level, this issue rarely comes up with separated parents; most either practice the same religion, neither actively practices a religion, or both respect the religious differences between them and allow the other parent to expose the child to his or her religion. Many separated parents will have already addressed this difference while married; that is, they have made a decision on religious training for the child. The court often finds a way to slip off the hook of this issue, if it is challenged by one of the parties, by simply recognizing the decision made during the marriage. If the parents agreed to raise the children in the Lutheran religion, for example, during the marriage, the Court often will simply enforce this decision post-divorce, even when one of the parents challenges the marital choice.

Despite this, religion does occasionally come up as an important point of disagreement in divorce and can even be the source of family turmoil. In a case in which the author did an evaluation, the parties belonged to an exclusive religion. When the mother left that religion following the divorce, the father and his church "condemned" the mother and informed the children that she was going to go to hell. Parents should discuss their plans and religious values at the time of the divorce and try to avoid turning an important part of parenting into a nightmarish dispute. Above all, they should not look to the courts for a solution. This factor might even be included in the design of a residential schedule. One parent might request every Sunday so that the children attend church or every Tuesday for confirmation classes.

C. Elective Medical Care

This is one of the simpler issues in legal custody. Yet, it can also be one of the more contentious ones. For example, one parent might believe that the child has attention deficit disorder and wants to try a regimen of medication, on advice from a doctor. The other parent sees the child as energetic, believes that the other parent simply has poor parenting practices, and does not want the child on medication. Another example that comes up frequently is whether or not a child needs counseling. Some medical decisions are affected by the cost involved. For example, one parent might want the child to have braces but the other might object, not so much to the idea of braces, but because of the cost. Many medical decisions have the potential to improve the life of the child but are not necessary; each parent must weigh the benefit relative to the cost. Unfortunately, there are no clear answers to questions such as these. A judge might have no clearer idea about what to do in these situations than the parents. Reasonable people might disagree about what is best for children.

Parents in intact marriages face these same decisions, often with the same disagreements but have no judge to whom to turn. How do they successfully make these decisions? Researchers have found people successfully resolve disagreements by following certain steps. In other words, they have a procedure. If separated parents can jointly use these procedures to reach decisions, they might be able to avoid bringing in third parties and escalating the level of conflict. Chapter 7 includes science-based procedures.

D. Military

Whether or not parents want their child to join the military, as a minor, is what is addressed in this decision-making area. This situation is rare, but in many ways parallels all of the other decisions parents face. It involves gathering information, including information about the child's temperament, behavior, coping mechanisms, and so on; looking at options; and choosing the one most likely to produce the best outcome for the child.

E. Marriage

Whether or not parents want their child to marry, as a minor, is rare.

F. Driver's License

Although the law focuses on whether or not a parent will give the child permission to obtain a driver's license, the issue is more complicated. Parents would do well to discuss with each other, well in advance, the conditions under which they will allow their child to obtain and use a driver's license. In essence, parents are pre-deciding the axioms for the decision. Those axioms might include academic standards, conditions of use of a vehicle, whether the parents intend to buy the child a car or expect the child to pay for some or all of a car, expenses associated with driving, and other conditions of driving. Experience teaches us that problems sometimes arise solely because of a failure to discuss these axioms in advance.

For example, one parent might ground the child from driving because the child abused the privilege (e.g., broke curfew). The other parent might continue to let the child drive, thinking that the first parent has been too harsh. Suddenly, we have a child who is developing a strong preference for one home and who feels bolstered by the one parent against the other parent, and the situation might even escalate to a dispute over where the child lives. Worse yet, the child did not learn the lesson of responsibility on which the parents based these decisions. The child has learned to escape personal responsibility and to use one parent as a tool against the other. Having an agreed-upon axiom for vehicle use in such situations prevents this escalation.

G. Daycare and After-School Care

Part of providing continuity of care for a child is having both parents use the same institutions. While we can readily see how foolish it would be for parents to have the same child attend two different schools according to the residential placement schedule, we sometimes see parents using two different preschool programs or different after-school care programs. We see one parent using a relative and the other an organized daycare program. We even see one parent using after-school care or babysitters when the other parent is available to care for the child.

These different combinations of child care might make sense in some family situations, but in others, they are likely to cause the child confusion, disrupt the child's social development, and interfere with the child's ability to participate in extracurricular activities. Having a procedure for making these decisions will likely help.

H. Enrollment in Extracurricular Activities

This can become one of the more complicated decisions that parents must deal with, in part because the decisions come up many times and often reflect deeply held feelings, beliefs, and personal meaning for the parents. Social science research does not help much here. While social science tells us that the children most likely to do well socially and academically are those involved in extracurricular activities, it does not tell us which activities might be better than others, and it does not tell us how much of the child's time should be spent in extracurricular activities.

Most parents should consider a number of dimensions when making these decisions.

1. How much input should the child have in the choice of extracurricular activities?

2. Should the parents jointly decide on activities if they include residential time from both homes? In some family situations, the primary residential parent makes these decisions, and the other parent is happy to go along. In others, the non-primary residence parent resents the intrusions on his or her "time" and will passively or openly defy such decisions.

3. Some activities occur solely on one parent's residential time, but could eventually lead to a mutual commitment (e.g., a Tuesday dance class might eventually lead to three or four classes and recitals). Should these be joint decisions at the onset or solely when they reach the point of including both parties' parenting time.

4. Should parents have input over activities that occur solely during the other parent's residential time but to which the parent disagrees? For example, what if one parent opposes martial arts training for an aggressive child?

5. How much of the child's time should be devoted to extracurricular activities? Time is a limited commodity, and a certain amount must be spent on sleep and school. After that, children and parents have a good deal of latitude.

6. How should the child's extracurricular activity schedule be balanced with the interests and activities of other children in the family, including stepchildren, and of the parents?

Major decisions cover an important aspect of the child's life. Children do best when their parents are thoughtful in their planning, discuss their goals for the child, and both participate in making the choices involved. Pre-deciding on axioms and procedures might prevent future conflict between parents and confusion and frustration for the child.

Additional Major Decisions

The decisions that are by law considered "major" vary from state to state. Often, on a practical level, parents might face a number of additional decisions that if made together will simply work better for everyone in the family. When deciding what type of custody makes sense, it is important to discuss other decisions that might be added to the list provided in the law. We have provided above a list of some of the more common major decisions. Below, we have listed additional decisions parents might at least want to discuss:

- Discipline. Some discipline approaches works best if consistent between households. Children also do better and learn faster when both households use similar discipline methods with similar rules. Decisions regarding corporal punishment and decisions about third parties providing discipline (e.g., stepparents) are sometimes added by parents.

- Moral/values formation.

- Recreational Activities. This may involve planning summer enrollments, rules about which movies a child may see, etc.

- Romantic Partners. This includes how and when to introduce children to new romantic partners of the parents.

- Appearance. One of the oddly frequent issues that parents raise in mediation is the child's modification in appearance. Some parents want control over haircuts. Some disapprove of pierced ears (or other piercing) until a certain age. Similarly, some object to tattoos.

- Stays Away from Home. Some parents like to include stays away from home to the list of major decisions. In most instances, they approve of the other parent's decisions (e.g., sending the child to a grandparent), but in some instances they might disagree and want some input. For example, spending the night at a home of a friend without adult supervision might be a point of contention. Having the child spend time at the home of a relative who is an alcoholic or has a criminal record is another example.

- Babysitters. This is sometimes an issue for parents. In most instances, parents find their own babysitters, but in some instances, both want some input or an agreement to select from a list of mutually agreed-upon babysitters.

The MSA should include provisions to facilitate future communication and cooperation and provide guidelines (axioms) and procedures to cover future decision-making. Although there is a temptation to decide quickly on joint legal custody and move on, giving this part of parenting serious consideration in advance, and inclusion in the MSA, will likely lead to greater parental cooperation and a more coherent experience for the child. The child will likely benefit from the values and goals both parents have and turn out better. Separated parents with good communication discuss these issues on an ongoing basis: talking each week about what kind of curfew makes sense, how long groundings should last, and how to teach the child to be responsible. Many separated parents do not achieve this level of communication and cooperation. However, they can accomplish a similar experience for the child by having these discussions at the time of the divorce and establishing some basic ground rules and guidelines (axioms) and procedures for making these decisions when the issues do arise.

Residential Placement Schedules: Traditional Approach

Understanding history should prove helpful: Children are not property! First, in the typical legal game, the traditional approach for residential schedules is thought of as a single decision; that is, some division of the child's time between two homes. Thus, parents often find themselves discussing or disputing such oddities as a "9/5 schedule" or "primary versus 50/50 schedules." Holidays, summers, and vacations are thought of as modifications to this main schedule. This "divide the pie" approach to residential placement lies in the legal roots of "custody" itself. The original legal meaning of custody is to have, control, and hold property. Custody decisions historically involved awarding the child to a parent as property, because children were historically considered family property. Children could be sold, for example. Only in the late nineteenth and early twentieth centuries did children become a legal class of citizens receiving special protections in law. However, the principle of awarding custody of the children has continued to haunt family law. At first, custody was awarded to fathers, because mothers could not own property. Then the "tender-years" doctrine evolved out of new psychological theories and new economic trends, which left children in the care of mothers. Young children were awarded to mothers and older children to fathers. Again, largely because of cultural and economic trends, this evolved into a system in which 90 percent of custodial awards of children of all ages were to mothers by the 1950s. Since the 1970s, we have seen a shift to awards of joint custody. However, the principle of awarding property persists. A 50/50 schedule is awarding "property" equally to both parents. It is not a residential placement schedule carefully designed to meet the needs and interests of the child, taking into consideration the facts of the family.

There is a second major problem with this conventional approach to the legal task of awarding custody as it applies to the residential schedule. Combining different child-focused considerations into a single game of deciding on a residential schedule treats a group of single games as a multiple game and simple games as mixed games. The single, simple game of designing a good Thanksgiving becomes part of a mixed game, the common approach to which is the simplistic solution of alternating holidays. Turning the single, simple games into a multiple and mixed game likely substantially reduces the quality of everyone's life in the family.

A third problem is that the traditional approach turns an extensive repeated form game into a normal form game. A normal form game is a game played and solved one time, based on the facts at the time the game is played. Those strategies and decisions tend to be competitive and conflictual because they are designed for a onetime interaction between the players. The players are not focused on reputation and relationship; they are focused on winning. This approach is at odds with the realities of post-divorce families. The facts of a family are constantly changing, requiring new decisions about residential schedule issues on an ongoing basis. When faced with the need for another change, the approach is likely to be the strategy learned and practiced at the first node, which was treated as a normal form game. Some of the early research on mediation versus litigation found, not surprisingly, that mediation had significantly lower re-litigation rates than did litigation. In a sense, the legal system teaches parents how to make these decisions. Teaching them the competitive strategy leads to further competition when facing a future decision node relative to the schedule.

Designing a child-focused, family-specific residential schedule recognizes that this is repeated form game requiring procedures for future decision making.

A by-product of playing the residential schedule game as a normal form game is that the strategies for winning a normal form game cause increased conflict. Normal form games promote competitive winner-take-all strategies, lessening the likelihood that the parents will develop a good co-parenting relationship. A repeated form game is based on procedures that can be reapplied to any change in circumstances and the strategies that work best in a repeated form game promote cooperation, not conflict. Thus, a repeated form game is a substantially better match for the decision-making that goes into designing a residential schedule. In addition to making the decisions for the current residential schedule, the parties will do better to also design procedures for changing that schedule as circumstances change.

Residential Placement Schedules: Game Theory Approach

By separating the many multiple and mixed games of residential placement into simple and single games, the parties can design a family-friendlier schedule. Rather than begin with the general schedule, therefore, it will work best for the family to begin with as simple and as single a game as possible: planning good holidays. Actually, it is important to begin with one holiday, and often it is best to pick a holiday that the parties are unlikely to disagree about, such as Father's Day or Mother's Day.

Holiday Schedule Game

Parents should avoid the temptation simply to alternate holidays and make sure they both get their "fair share" of holiday time with the children. A formulaic approach can be simple, but also can lead to substantially inferior holiday experiences for all concerned. As tedious and fraught with feelings of loss and tension as it might be to do so, parents will do best if they think through *each* holiday with the objective of producing the best experience for everyone. This might include the children having every Thanksgiving with the same parent every year, for example, because of a family tradition in that parent's extended family, and having a different day on the weekend with the other parent.

A procedure should be established for dealing with holiday residential schedules. The planning process can include honoring existing family traditions. It can also be a time to begin new family traditions that will become a rich part of the child's life and memories. Again, while this approach is tedious, engaging in these discussions sets the stage for a style of interacting with one another that will serve the parties well down the road. The very process of looking at a particular holiday, examining all of the factors that might go into making it as good a holiday for the children and the parents as possible, and making some of the necessary compromises, is a procedure. In a sense, the separating parents are learning and practicing a procedure that can be used again at future decision nodes.

The procedure should identify the content of the game (e.g., how many days are involved in the holiday, whether the parents have time off from work, and family traditions) and the objective and subjective values and goals of the parents for that holiday.

One of the most potent reminders of how important planning is, compared to simply dividing holidays or any other type of residential time, is to count. If parents try to divide holidays by some type of formula (e.g., every other Thanksgiving), it is easy to focus on devising the formula so it is fair to the parents. If parents focus on the fact that they might have control over only six or eight more Thanksgivings for their children (i.e., with a twelve- and ten-year-old child), planning those six or eight Thanksgivings is more likely to be focused on the children's experience. Also, two is often better than one that is split in two. Having two birthday parties on different days might be better than a hectic split of the actual birthday. Teaching children to honor their parents on their parents' birthdays might better achieve the parents' goals (e.g., having an agreement that each parent will help the children buy/make cards for the other parent) than arguing about whether the parent with the birthday will get a two or three hour visit.

A good starting point for many parents is Mother's Day[10]. Few parents dispute that the children should have at least some time with their mother on Mother's Day. However, even though the parties seem to agree, it is important to avoid proceeding too quickly through this. It is important to follow a procedure that will be effective later when discussing more difficult holidays and other residential schedule issues. For example, the discussion might include the following:

1. Should Mother's Day just be the day or the whole weekend?
2. Can the mother travel to be with her own mother and family on that day? If she wants this option, should there be a procedure in place for her to exercise the option?
3. What are good start and stop times?
4. Does the father want some time with the children to celebrate with his mother (e.g., breakfast)?
5. If the whole weekend is involved, and the parents end up with a weekend rotation, should there be a procedure for switching weekends so that the father does not lose a weekend?
6. Can the father be involved in the planning (e.g., helping the children to prepare cards or gifts)?

As this one example demonstrates, planning good Mother's Days can be an involved process. This issue (and many others like it) deserves a process that focuses everyone on planning good Mother's Days and on teaching children the importance of honoring their mother.

The next holiday might be Father's Day, following similar procedures. The parents then continue through the list of holidays, adding to the list days that are special to the family (e.g., annual family reunion days). As holidays are discussed, parents can decide whether they need to design a plan. For example, in one family, July 4th might be important, with an extended family get-together at a lake, fireworks, and other festivities. However, in another family, the parents might be fine just following the regular schedule for July 4th, figuring that over time they will each likely spend this holiday with

---

10. This Mother's Day is a good illustration of why planning content and procedures for residential schedules is really important for children and the family.

their children about half of the time. In one family, the parties might want plan for Halloween plan, and in another, not.

Christmas and the winter break from school can often be the most complicated and difficult holiday, and therefore might be best left to consider last. As each holiday is discussed, however, it should become clear that each can also be revisited. Thus, if getting one parent to compromise on a Christmas plan requires changing a prior agreement on a different holiday, then so be it. The goal is to create a whole package of holiday plans that fit the current fact situation, which is the best that can be done to provide as good a holiday as possible for all involved.

Game theory may be at work without the parties even knowing it. Without clearly identifying doing so, the professionals involved are engaging in game theory bargaining. They are separating multiple and mixed games into single and simple games, and playing each game for the expected payoff. They are engaging first in cooperative bargaining by focusing on the objective and subjective goals of the parties, which serve as axioms for the decision. They only resort to compromise bargaining if the cooperative process does not succeed and a disagreement remains. Perhaps most important, they are teaching and practicing a procedure for making decisions that can be used by the parties in future decisions, without explicitly stating that this is being done.

If the bargaining is done in four-way meetings, the attorneys can guide the process. If it does not involve such meetings, one attorney can guide the process. For example, one attorney could write the other attorney a letter something like the following:

> *My client would like to start putting together a residential schedule plan that works well for the children and takes into consideration the goals of the parents. We are starting with holidays. Our proposals for holidays are based on the following goals . . . Our proposal for Mother's Day and Father's Day takes into consideration that your client's mother . . . Please let us know your client's reactions to the proposals on holidays, including your client's goals for holidays and counterproposals that might enhance everyone's experience in this important part of the family's life. Ultimately, we will incorporate these agreements in the marital settlement agreement.*

This frames the bargaining process using game theory principles.

Vacation Game

Another aspect of the residential schedule that often involves planning but rarely includes substantial disagreement is the vacation schedule. As with holidays, more time should be taken with this issue to establish procedures and a process of communication between the parents. Thus, the parties should have an active discussion that includes what types of vacations they realistically can take in the future. All discussions should begin with exploring both parents' objective and subjective goals for vacations with the children. Axiom discussions might include the following:

1. How long should each vacation be?
2. Should there be any limits on vacations that interfere with the other parent's residential time (e.g., must include the weekend of the parent taking the vacation)?
3. Should there be a limit on how many school days each year the children can miss for vacations?
4. Do vacations take precedence over holidays, or the reverse?
5. Can a vacation that interferes with the residential placement schedule simply be spending time at home, or should it require going somewhere?
6. Should there be limitations on where the children can go or with whom they may go (e.g., a grandparent rather than a parent)?
7. Are itineraries to be shared?
8. Will the parent who is not going on the vacation have access to the children by phone, text messaging, email, and the like?
9. What will be the procedure for scheduling vacation time (e.g., how much notice should be given; how can the parties prevent vacations from interfering with other plans [such as Bible school and day camps])?
10. If both parents would like to have the children do special things (e.g., take a trip to Disneyland), which parent will do which trip (rather than both doing the same trip)?

Having these discussions not only trains the parents in a style of planning that might prevent future disputes (e.g., one parent thinks the other parent is taking the children out of school too much for vacations) but also allows them to practice an approach to joint decision making that they can use in the future with one another as they hit the inevitable nodes in the repeated extensive game of parenting.

Summer Schedule Game

The summer game is actually two games: the summer weekend game and the summer weekday game. However, it is difficult to separate the two in most families. If they can be separated, they should be, and they should be played separately, usually beginning with the weekend game.

When playing the summer weekend game, a good place to start is to count how many weekends there actually are, subtract the weekends taken by vacations, and then plan for the rest. Often, there are just eight or ten weekends left to consider. Again, because this game leans more heavily in the direction of a repeated form game, the focus should be on procedures, not content. Remember that a game theory procedure includes axioms, content, and procedure. The axioms might include that each parent will get one-half of the available weekends. Another might be the mother always gets the first weekend in August because that is when she has a family reunion. Another might be that if a parent can get off work on Friday, or at least early on Friday, that parent gets the children to have a longer weekend. The content issues are the total number of weekends available, the part of the summer in which they occur (e.g., baseball season might always run into mid-June, restricting family activities for those early weekends; the availability of a cabin), and the actual wishes and plans of each parent. Because the content might change each year, the procedure should focus on how the decisions will be made each year, following the axiomatic standards. For example, the procedure might include something like the following:

1. Each parent will gather information that might affect his and her summer weekend plans (non-vacation).
2. The parents meet by April 30, share the information, and divide up the weekends according to the axiomatic standards.
3. This procedure might presume that the parents have already provided notice of and scheduled summer vacation times.

The summer weekday residential schedule game might be tied into the weekend game, but usually includes other content issues. These might include summer camp programs, daycare issues if both parents work, summer school, visits to extended family, and so on. Because this is largely procedural, since the content changes every year, the parties should first establish axioms—both general axioms, such as the share of time is approximately equal, and specific, based on the objective and subjective goals of the parents, such as the children will be able to attend Bible camp every summer.

Once axioms are established, the parties focus on the cooperative bargaining process of deciding the next summer, compromise bargaining if there is still a point of disagreement, and then win-win-plus bargaining; that is, looking at the payoff package of the summer agreement and determining whether the plan can be improved for both parties, or at least one party without diminishing the payoff for the other party. Through the entire bargaining process, multiple games are divided into single games and mixed games are divided into simple games. Also, effective information management facilitates the convergence of expectations by making information public, verifiable, perfect, and complete. For example, if one of the parents would like to invite her boyfriend on vacation with the children, making that information public can lead to a discussion of objective and subjective goals (e.g., her wanting to see how he handles that kind of time with the children), additional axioms (e.g., not sleeping together when the children are present until married or living together), and additional agreements. Rather than having a blow-up after the vacation that the boyfriend was on, the parents will have prepared a plan for their children. Instead of a trial, the father might simply ask how the vacation went.

School Year Weekend Game
Game theory principles focus on axioms, procedures, and the decision-making process. By now, the reader is likely to have picked up on how designing a residential schedule using game theory focuses on procedures and teaches a decision-making process that the parents can take with them after their divorce. We are now, however, approaching the content that often gives parents the most difficulty: the school year. But by following the above approach, they are more prepared to apply those same procedures to this difficult set of decisions.

Start with weekends during the school year. A good starting point is the weekends during the school year. If we subtract holidays and holiday breaks from school, which have already been decided, there are somewhere between twenty-five and thirty weekends involved, depending on the family and the jurisdiction (e.g., in Wisconsin, the last week of November includes no school on Thursday or Friday for teacher continuing education and many parents treat that as a holiday weekend). The approach to school year weekends should not be formulaic. The parents should take the time to think through the weekends in terms of the content (e.g., one parent works on weekends or most weekends include volley ball games for one of the children) and again develop axioms based on their goals. For example, they might agree as an axiom that they each get one-half of the weekend time. However, in one family, that might be better if one parent gets every Saturday and the other every Sunday (e.g., if one of the parties is a doctor on call every Saturday). In another family, there might be two teens who love to ski, a mother who loves to ski, and a father who does not. In that family, the father might get the bulk of the non–ski season weekends, and the mother might get the bulk of the ski season weekends. One family might have young children, and both parents want one weekend day with them to fortify their attachments. Another family might do a lot of weekend traveling (e.g., to see family or to camp) and want full weekends, including overnight Sunday. The parents might end up agreeing on a formulaic every-other-weekend plan, but only if this truly best fits the facts of the family at the time. This type of thinking and planning is essential, even if both parents start the process wishing for every other weekend. The professional sometimes has to insist that they go through this tedious planning process, even if they end up at the same point, because it is important that they be satisfied *based on this type of thinking,* establishing a pattern of constructive negotiation.

School Days off Game

Next step: school days off. A good next step can be to examine how to handle days the children have off from school. Each year, school calendars come out with days that are half-days, days off for various reasons, including some school holidays that the parents might not have planned, parent-teacher conference days, and so on. To plan for these days, parents might consider child-care arrangements if they both work or automatic default positions if one parent is available. For example, if one of the parents is a teacher and typically has the same days off, there might be a default position that that parent has the children on those days, independent of the principal schedule. Or, the parents might decide that the most fair and most enjoyable plan would be to rotate taking days off work to spend with the children when they are off school. In the end, the parents might decide to just follow the principal schedule, but thinking this through has value.

School Days Schedule

Then proceed to school days. One of the remarkable benefits of this approach to residential schedule design is that by the time the parents get to the most difficult issue, they have planned most of the year and have developed a planning process that redirects them from what they want and seems fair to what is likely to be best for everyone in the family. Most school districts have somewhere between 165 and 180 school days each year. That means the parties have already set up schedules for between 185 and 200 of the days of the year. This was accomplished largely by breaking a multiple game—residential placement—into subgames.

Often, the parties will have already decided on one of these school days/nights. There are five school days in most weeks, for example, which also means there are five school evenings and nights. If the parties have already agreed on Friday evening and night as the beginning of the weekend and on Sunday evening and night as the end of the weekend, then they have reduced the total number of school evenings and nights by 20 percent. Now we are down to between 132 and 148 days each year left to decide.

Work on axioms next. Again, we turn to establishing axioms first. What are the parents' goals for the children for school days and what does social science tell us that might serve as good axioms? One axiom from the research is that school-age children do best if they have at least some school days with both parents. If the parents concede to this axiom, then the difference in position between the parents will be between at least one of the four remaining school days with each parent and two with each parent. In other words, the positions of the parties might be either three days with one parent and one with the other *or* two days with each parent. This is a total difference between these two positions of between 33 and 36 days per year. Other axioms might include access to peers (e.g., riding a school bus), setting similar homework routines, after-school parental availability and so on.

Remaining Dispute Game

There might be only a minor dispute remaining (thirty-three to thirty-six days). What we have done, using game theory principles, therefore, is change the character of a major dispute into a relatively minor dispute over a few days per year. For example, assume that the mother started with a position of wanting to be primary parent (a purely subjective goal) with a 9/5 schedule (alternating three-day weekends and one school day each week) and the father started with a position of wanting equal residential placement (a purely subjective goal). This would suggest that the parties are at the front end of a bitter dispute in which one will win and one will lose, or they will both lose with an 8/6 split. Our bargaining model has narrowed the issue to a simple single game involving between 33 and 36 days each year in dispute.

If we further examine the nature of this remaining dispute using game theory principles, we might see that the parties are even closer to an agreement. Exploring the subjective goals for these few days each year, for example, might yield a point of agreement. Consider this situation: the mother really believes that the children will do better in school if the bulk of school nights are in one house, or believes that the children really benefit from riding the school bus from her house with their friends more days than not. The father is very interested in participating in the schoolwork with the children or being more involved in after-school activities. We actually could play two games here: the after-school/evening game and the school night and morning game. If the subjective value the father places on "equal" is extremely high, and he cannot be discouraged from this meaningless position (relative to the needs and interests of the children), then perhaps those thirty-three to thirty-six days could be made up elsewhere in the year, or perhaps he would trade those days for a "win" on some other issue (e.g., he gets impasse-breaking authority on enrollment in extracurricular activities). Other options might be a procedural ones. For example, the father might be given the option of twelve additional school days each year if he can get off work early and agrees to drop the children at the bus stop near the mother's residence. In other words, the parties made agreements through the cooperative bargaining process for all but about thirty-five days each year and then have to look for solutions to those thirty-five days through compromise bargaining. If both are worried about child support implications, the child support game could be played independently of the schedule, if it is already this close to equal.

By using a planning approach, limiting the most difficult part of residential scheduling to last, playing it as a single simple game, reducing the days that might be in dispute to just a few each year, and peeling away other complicating payoffs, what might have started as an insurmountable dispute can be narrowed to a minor compromise.

The other advantage to this bargaining approach is that it helps amicable parents design a child-focused schedule. It might be easy for high-functioning parents simply to agree to an alternating-week schedule, for example, without really thinking through their goals, without understanding the guidance of social science research, without setting axiomatic standards, and without a close examination of the fact situation. By going through this more tedious bargaining process, they might end up with a residential schedule that is very different from alternating weeks, perhaps one that is not equal but that which better fits the needs and interests of all family members.

GOAL-BASED PLANNING—RESIDENTIAL SCHEDULES:

1. Break the residential schedule game into simple and single games by playing separate games for each part of the residential schedule and by separating out the payoffs for each game into separate games.

2. Analyze the positions of the parties by determining their objective and subjective goals and payoffs for which they are playing the games-not only what each of them wants, but also why they want it or what they hope to accomplish with those payoffs.

3. Subjective payoffs are determined in two ways: First, by setting axioms, where the parties disclose their outcome goals. Second, when the parties run into a dispute, they shift (on their own or with the assistance of an attorney or mediator) to what they are trying to accomplish with their positions.

4. By revealing the objective and subjective goals of the parties, we create conditions of perfect, complete, public, and, to the degree possible, verifiable information, which facilitates best possible outcomes for both parties.

5. This goal-based planning process accomplishes two important outcomes: First, it focuses the parties on the design of a schedule that works best for everyone involved, and it moves the entire process in the direction of win-win-win (a win for the mother, for the father, and for the children). Second, it models and practices an axiomatic, procedurally based approach to decision-making in an extensive repeated form game format, which can be used in the future by the parties to adjust the residential schedule to fit the facts of the family and the needs of the children.

Child-Planning Game (Co-parenting Tasks)

At the time the parents are playing the complicated legal game, they are also beginning to play the child planning game. The earlier that they understand this and understand what the game entails, the less likely they are to get off on the wrong foot, have misunderstandings, believe myths about raising children separately, and begin a conflict-oriented approach to this game. It is difficult to play the child planning game well early in the divorce process, because of the intense emotions and possible disagreements in the legal game, regardless of whether the conflicts are about children, money, or both. The paradox is that social science research tells us that the earlier in the process parents begin to play the child planning game well, the more likely they are to do so in the future. If they at least understand the child planning game at the beginning, even if they delay playing it well, they may be less likely to make as many mistakes as they would otherwise.

Child-Planning Tasks

Researchers have studied families with children who turned out well even though the parents separated and divorced. They do five things well. We have further analyzed these five dynamics using game theory principles and modified them to some extent.[11]

1. They establish *rules of conduct*—that is, they decide and plan how to treat each other well. These include general rules but also specific rules (e.g., how they will conduct themselves at a school play). The rules of conduct might also include rules for the children (e.g., how to handle complaints about one of the homes).

2. They *communicate effectively.* There are two facets to communicating because there are two functions of communicating: sharing information and taking action. They *share information* about the children and have effective ways of *taking action*—that is, making decisions, solving problems, raising and resolving parenting concerns, and resolving scheduling conflicts.

3. They establish *parent-child access* arrangements, including ways to be flexible with the residential schedule.

4. They design smooth *child-focused transitions* between residences.

---

11. A companion Co-parenting Workbook from Unhooked Books is available to be given to clients of the attorneys and mediator.

5. They *coordinate parenting and similarize both homes* as closely as possible and work on parenting tasks together.

These five child-planning tasks are not the "feel-good" opinions of a couple of psychologists. These are summaries of a great deal of social science research, including necessary conditions for success. One of those conditions, for example, is that successful parents are able to separate the issues and problems of their marital relationship from their rights and responsibilities as parents. They understand that their feelings about and problems with one another as spouses are not the same as their job as parents. Parents who do not separate the dynamics of their spousal relationship from their teamwork as parents often end up arguing about the same issues after a divorce that they argued about when they were married. In a sense, they foolishly terminated the good parts of the marriage but retained the bad.

Establish Rules of Conduct

From the child's perspective, there is still one family, but now its members live in two residences. For the parents to work well with one another, it is important that they not only follow general rules of conduct but also design rules of conduct that are important to each of the parents and that protect the co-parenting relationship. In a sense, they are modeling social maturity to their children. General rules of conduct might include the following:

A. For successful co-parenting, parents must expect to be treated with *courtesy and respect*. They should keep each other informed, be on time, make requests in a respectful manner, and talk to each other with courtesy.

B. Parents should exercise *self-control*. This includes withholding blame and criticisms, refraining from inappropriate language and tones, and express anger and frustration in a respectful manner.

C. *Communication should have a purpose*—something to do with the children. Information and comments should relate to the children and be limited to child-related issues.

D. *Agreements should be explicit and specific*, formal, detailed, and in many instances put in writing. Details should be confirmed.

E. Parents should be *respectful of each other's privacy* by keeping conversations to child-related issues. Often, it is helpful for parents to have a mutually agreed-upon method to get back on track if they "slip" and get personal.

F. When sharing information, the *information must be honest*. Parents need to rely on the information they receive from each other and can only work as a team if they are honest with one another.

G. Parents must *honor their agreements*. Trust is built when agreements are kept; distrust is fostered when agreements are broken.

H. Once parents have a list of which decisions are to be made jointly, they must *honor the joint decision list*. Unilateral decisions lead to conflict and distrust.

I. For children to feel emotionally safe in their family, the *parents must feel emotionally safe* with one another. Therefore, as they go, parents should raise any issues that make the parents feel unsafe with one another and establish additional rules of conduct.

In game theory terms, these are the axiomatic standards for conduct between the parents. When the parents interact (e.g., attend a parent-teacher conference together), they make choices of behavior. These axioms are the standards for those choices. In addition to these general axioms, separating parents should add additional axioms specific to their situation. For example, in a case we had, a stepfather called the father "bud" in a friendly way, but the father found this demeaning. He proposed adding a rule regarding this.

Communicate Effectively

"Communication" can sound like a vague principle and mean different things to different people. We define communication in a much more concrete and practical manner. Communication is composed of two parts or functions:

A. Sharing information

B. Taking action

Sharing Information

In the child-planning game, we will further define several different ways in which parents can share information about the children. There are four types of information sharing:

1. Weekly contacts

2. Paperwork

3. Transition information

4. Emergency contacts

Each of these plays an essential role in parents having sufficient information for the child planning game to be played well. In game theory language, we are creating an open information system in which information in the family is public, available to both parents, verifiable by a commitment to honesty, complete, and where appropriate perfect.

First, by having a shared body of information, many *misunderstandings can be avoided.* Many of the conflicts that arise between separated parents are based on inferences (guesses) made by the parents because they lack information. For example, if parents do not communicate directly and a parent relies on information solely from the children, that parent might get the impression that the other parent is very permissive. If the parents communicate information about rules, chores and responsibilities, and discipline, that same parent is unlikely to fall into this inferential trap. Then, when that same child misrepresents or exaggerates, the parent can teach the child to report more accurately rather than jumping to negative conclusions about the other home.

Second, sharing information provides a sense of *participation* in all aspects of the children's lives, reducing the amount of loss that the parents experience. Much conflict between parents emanates from a sense of loss. If parents do not effectively share information, when the children go to the other house, it is like they are going into a black hole—no information escapes.

Third, sharing information allows each of the parents to *coordinate the parenting* across homes. For example, if a parent knows that the children will be going away for an upcoming weekend with the other parent, some planning can be done with regard to a school project.

Fourth, informed parents can *identify issues* that need to be resolved between one another or on behalf of the children. For example, if a parent knows that the other parent plans to introduce a new romantic interest to the children, that parent can have some input on how this is done and even help prepare the children. Or, for a child-related example, by being informed, one parent can caution the other parent about a particular group of friends the child might spend time with in the other home.

The cornerstone of this information sharing is the *weekly meeting.* Parents should contract to have a specific information-sharing meeting once per week. This can be by telephone or in person. Some parents try to do this in writing, either in a journal or by email, but this rarely works well. If parents simply cannot talk with one another, email comes much closer to working than does passing a journal back and forth.

1. Weekly Contact

Step one: The parents establish a weekly information-sharing meeting—in person or by telephone. They set a day and time and determine who will be responsible for making the call, if by telephone.
Step two: The parents make a list of information to share.

Sample List of Weekly Information

- past events of importance or interest to one another, including extracurricular activities
- upcoming appointments, events, and plans in which the other parent might be interested or like to participate in
- current information about the children's health and well-being, including any major life events that might affect them
- occurrences during times that the children are in each parent's home
- school progress, ongoing schoolwork, and school events
- social involvement with friends, social plans, and other social events
- positive experiences the children have had
- any special schedules for the week
- important conversations in which the children might have commented about the other home
- behavior of the children
- life experiences that might have affected the child's general well-being
- keeping each other informed about chores, rules, expectations, routines, and discipline in each of the homes
- asking and answering questions each parent has about the children

2. Paperwork

Step one: The parents make a list of the paperwork to share.
Step two: Then, they set up the manner in which paperwork will be shared.

Sample Procedure for Sharing Paperwork

"There is to be a 9"x12" 'Parent Envelope' in Jack's school backpack. Each parent will place either the original or a copy of the agreed-upon paperwork in that envelope for the other parent to see. If the parent wants the paper back, he or she will include a note on it requesting this."

3. Transition Information

The parents provide a way of sharing information at transitions so the parent to whom the children are returning is informed. If the transition is directly from parent to parent, parents can spend five minutes or so providing transition information. If the transition goes through school or daycare, there could be a telephone call/message on the transition day, a note in the "parent folder," or an email.

4. Emergency Contacts

Step one: The parents make a list of immediate "need to know" generating events.

Sample List of Immediate Need-to-Know/Generating Events

- Medical emergencies—illnesses or injuries that require treatment or that interfere with the child's regular activities
- Last-minute changes in the child's schedule (e.g., a change in the date of a soccer match)
- Unexpected contacts from the school (e.g., principal calls regarding a problem)
- Particularly positive events (e.g., child wins an award at school)
- Life events that have or are likely to greatly affect the child (e.g., death of a pet)

Step two: The parents set up the procedures for contacting each other.

Taking Action

In the child planning game, the second function of communication is to take action. This should be treated as a separate task from sharing information. It is a mistake to share information and then launch into taking action on some information. For example, it would be a mistake for the father to tell the mother that he received a note from the school that the children were late three times and then launch into telling the mother that she should get them there on time. This likely will lead to an argument, not to solving the problem. In all of the taking-action procedures listed in chapter 7, the first step is to make an appointment. Thus, in our example, after telling the mother about the school contact, the father should ask the mother when she has time for a problem-solving meeting and set an appointment to deal with the problem of the children being late for school.

The procedures for each of these types of taking action are distinct, although there are parallels and overlap. For example, with a decision-making process, parents might arrive at a conflict and need to apply the principles of conflict resolution before being able to complete the decision-making process. We have presented each of these types of taking action first by defining the action and, second, by providing a specific six-step procedure for taking the action. Those procedures are in chapter 7 of this book and, in parent language, in the Co-parenting Workbook available from Unhooked Books.

We cannot give due credit to all of the authors who have developed these procedures over the past fifty years, other than to mention that we have borrowed much from scientifically proven methods developed by others. The formulation of these procedures as presented in this book, however, is our own.

There are four types of action that separated parents must be prepared to take:

1. Making a decision
2. Solving a problem
3. Raising and resolving a concern
4. Resolving a conflict

1. Making Decisions

The first type of action parents might need to take is making a decision. We have already introduced the concept of decision-making and referred to the six-step procedure in chapter 7 for doing so. As a review, parents have made a list of joint decisions, which involve taking action in the future, understanding the importance of including both parents from the beginning in making those decisions and having a decision-making procedure for doing so.

2. Solving Problems

Solving a "problem" is different from addressing a "concern," though both need to be addressed. A second type of action that parents might need to take with one another is solving a problem. A problem is a pattern, which is occurring and is expected to continue to occur unless solved, that is adversely affecting the life of one or both parents and/or the child. Let us look carefully at each part of this definition. We will use two examples, one that is adversely affecting the life of a parent and one that is adversely affecting the life of a child.

Many separated parents waste much time and energy, often creating a good deal of ill will, trying to address a single instance that may or may not occur again. This occurs because of habits established during the marriage. In a marriage, if our spouse upsets us, we have an emotional obligation to express those feelings and achieve a resolution. This is not necessarily to solve a problem, because there might be no problem, but to reestablish *emotional equilibrium*. Thus, spouses get into a habit of addressing single instances and trying to "work out" their feelings. However, a single instance does not need a solution and therefore is not a problem as we are defining it. To illustrate this, let us introduce our example. If a wife is reliably on time, but in one instance is very late, the husband has a right to be upset, to express this, and to expect either a solid explanation or an apology. To reestablish emotional equilibrium, the wife "owes" her husband an opportunity to vent as well as an explanation or an apology. Once this is done, the emotional equilibrium is reestablished, with hugs all around. However, at no point do the husband and wife need to address a problem of the wife being late, because there is no pattern of her being late. Only if she were consistently late would they address the problem; that is, if there were a pattern of troubling behavior, there would be a problem to solve.

When parents are separated (divorced or in paternity cases separated), they no longer have an emotional equilibrium to balance. Emotional equilibrium is a facet of intimacy, an intimacy that they no longer share. There is no need to vent, no need to explain, and no need to apologize. This sounds harsh, but part of the emotional detachment that leads to successful child planning includes no longer being emotionally dependent on one another. If there is a single instance of an otherwise reliable parent being late, there is no problem to solve. It is a mistake to try to treat this the way one would with a friend or spouse. The late parent may provide either an explanation or apology, but should not be expected to do so. There is no interpersonal goal here of having emotional equilibrium. Using our example with divorced parents, if the dad is upset because the mother's lateness interfered with some of his plans, he should keep it to himself or "work it out" by venting to a friend. With regard to the mother, he should assume that there is a good reason, because otherwise she would have been on time as she usually is. As the Dalai Lama might put it, the dad should let this single instance "pass by like a warm wind behind his ears."

The second part of our definition reiterates that the problem is defined as a pattern, but adds that the pattern is likely to continue unless solved. This is the foundation for *cooperation*. Parents have a mutual obligation to work together as a team for the future of their children. They do not have an obligation to the emotional welfare of the other parent as they did in the past; that is, they do not have an obligation to soothe, comfort, apologize, defend themselves, and so on, relative to past occurrences. If the mother is consistently late, and this is adversely affecting the life of the father and/or the child, this is a negative pattern that is likely to continue into the future and thus should be addressed. The mother has an obligation to cooperate with the father in solving the problem so that her pattern of behavior will have less adverse impact *in the future*. She does not have an obligation to make the father feel better about the past, nor should the father expect her to. Again, this might sound harsh, but it is a necessary distinction if parents want to child plan successfully. The "payoff" is a solution to the problem, not emotional equilibrium.

The third part of our definition specifically identifies the negative impact of the pattern as a necessary condition for cooperation. If the dad cannot show a negative impact on his life or on the life of the children of the mom being consistently late, then there is no problem to be solved. That the dad might just not like this about mom is insufficient reason to address this issue as a problem. If mom is consistently somewhere between five and fifteen minutes late, for example, and the dad can accommodate this pattern by simply never making plans that would be disrupted by this pattern, and if the children are "used to" mom's pattern and untroubled by it, the dad should not address this as a problem. It is something he can solve without requiring the mom's cooperation in a problem-solving process. If, however, the mom is more unreliable than this—sometimes being as much as forty-five minutes late—and the dad either can never make plans on transition days or is repeatedly having his plans disrupted, then there is a problem. Or if the child sits by the window and tearfully keeps asking, "When is Mom going to get here?" then there is a problem.

To reiterate, *a problem is a pattern*, which is occurring and is *expected to continue* to occur unless solved, that is *adversely affecting* the life of one or both parents and/or the child. The parent raising the problem should first ask, "Is this a single or occasional instance, or a pattern that is likely to continue if not addressed?" The second question to ask is, "Is this adversely affecting my life or the life of our child?" Third, the parent must ask, "Is this a problem that I can solve without the cooperation of the other parent?" If it is, a better approach is usually just to solve the problem. If the solution requires the cooperation of the other parent, or if the cooperation of the other parent will significantly enhance the quality of the solution, then the parent should address the problem using the a problem-solving procedure, such as the one in chapter 7 of this book.

To further illustrate our point, let's consider another example of a problem that is adversely affecting the child and that will be best solved if addressed by both parents. A child is particularly introverted, and by third grade is already fairly socially isolated. The mom recognizes this pattern and is concerned about how the child will do socially in the future. She is also concerned about how well the child will do in school, since for many children, the "glue" that holds a child to the school process is the social context. The mom recognizes that she can provide some solutions, but because the child is in a shared residential schedule with the dad, the solutions will be superior if both parents cooperate. Here is a problem that has no adverse impact on the parent, except as the parents might be concerned about how well the child will do in the future. The problem is solely an issue of adverse effect on the child. The mom decides that the solution must be a long-term plan, followed in both homes, and decides to treat this as a problem and address it with the other parent. The issue meets the definition of a problem because it is a pattern that is likely to continue into the future and it is likely to have an adverse effect on the child.

A "concern" is a special type of problem. One might notice that problems and concerns are similar. In fact, a concern, as we have defined it, is really a special type of problem. However, we have separated problems and concerns for three reasons. First, concerns specifically have to do with the parenting in the other home and, as such, carry with them especially charged emotions. Concerns are, after all, criticisms of the other parent, for decisions, for lack of action, and so on. In game theory terms, we are dividing problem solving into two single games. By giving them special treatment, therefore, we minimize the negative impact on the child-planning relationship. Second, we have distinguished between major and minor concerns, and have proffered different methods for resolving these, which is not true of problems. Problems can be addressed with the same method, whether major or minor. Lastly, failure to resolve parenting concerns is a key obstacle to establishing and maintaining successful child-planning relationships. These concerns come up more frequently and cause more ill will than does solving or not solving problems. By pulling parenting concerns out of the rubric of solving problems, and giving it special treatment, we utilize methods that improve the child planning relationship.

3. Raising and Solving Parenting Concerns

There are two types of parenting concerns: a major concern and a minor concern.

• Defining a Major Concern

Raising and resolving concerns is important. Most parents develop concerns about the parenting taking place in the other home. Even happily married parents usually have concerns about the approach that the other parent takes with the child at times. When parents live in separate houses, the likelihood of having concerns increases simply because each parent has less information and often has less confidence or trust in the other parent. Raising and resolving concerns is important. Often, this is contrary to advice parents receive during a separation and divorce. Parents will often be told to ignore what goes on in the other home. This is contrary to parenting instincts, and the failure to raise and resolve concerns leads to increased distrust and conflict.

At the same time, not all concerns are equally serious. Neither parent should try to control everything that the other parent does or does not do simply because he or she does not like it. An effective method of resolving concerns begins by determining whether a concern is major or minor. Because the definition of "minor concern" is simply a concern that is not a major concern, we must first define a major concern. A major concern is a concern about the *safety* of a child or about an *ongoing pattern* that is likely to harm the child over the long run. Let us take a closer look at each of these.

Safety concerns include issues of health and risk of injury or death. This might include eating patterns if a child is overweight or a long-term health risk (e.g., a female child needing to ingest sufficient calcium to ensure long-term bone strength). This might include recreation, such as wearing a helmet when riding a bicycle or pads when Rollerblading. In essence, it includes concerns that one parent has about the immediate or long- term potential of physical risk to the child.

An "ongoing pattern" major concern must meet two standards: a pattern of damaging behavior and a likelihood that the behavior will affect long-term adjustment. Another type of "safety" has to do with the emotional safety of the child. Here we are talking about patterns, not single events, which a parent believes threatens the long-term adjustment of the child. Because nearly all parents occasionally make mistakes, this must involve a pattern of behavior that is out of character or is somehow harmful to a child. Children usually recover from these single incidents with little or no harm. Thus, if the other parent yells something demeaning at the child, but this is not a pattern, the behavior does not constitute a major concern. Only if there is a pattern of the other parent yelling demeaning comments at the child does it become a major concern. To qualify as a major concern relative to emotional damage, two basic standards must exist: there is a pattern of behavior perceived by one parent as damaging to the child, and the damage is likely to affect the child's long-term adjustment. Making a child cry one time is not major; making the child cry every day is.

Because it is important that the concern over emotional safety meets both standards, we will examine this a little further. An example of a concern that might not be "major" because it does not include both parts of the standard is when a child has no supervision over homework at the other house. If this occurs only occasionally, but there is a general pattern of providing supervision, then this concern does not meet the first standard. If this occurs regularly, thereby meeting the standard of being a pattern, but the child is very self-motivated and does her homework regularly without supervision, then this concern does not meet the second standard. If, however, there is a pattern of inadequate supervision of homework *and* the child is not self-motivated *and* is not doing her schoolwork when at the other house *and* the parent can reasonably predict that the long-term interests of the child will therefore be damaged, this would qualify as a major concern.

Major concerns deserve special treatment because a successful child planning relationship requires that both parents are confident that the child is safe, both physically and emotionally, when with the other parent. Therefore, separated parents who want to raise their child successfully must agree to share control of those aspects of parenting that include major concerns. In order to do so, both parents must assume that if one parent believes that some behavior or pattern in the other home meets the standards of a major concern, then the concern will be treated as a major concern, even if the other parent does not believe that the issue is major. Let us illustrate this with our example. Assume that the dad raises what he believes is a major concern with the mom that is a pattern of low supervision of their daughter's homework time. The mother disagrees that this is major because she believes two things. First, she believes that what is at risk is their daughter's quality of the life and that the daughter needs to learn to take responsibility for how it turns out. She might even believe that the father is overly controlling in his supervision. Second, the mom does not think it is so harmful to that do poorly in school because she did poorly in school and has done very well in life. Therefore, when the dad brings this issue up, the mom might be thinking that this does not qualify as a major concern.

However, if the mom is committed to having a successful child planning relationship, she must respond to the dad's major concern by following the format for resolving major concerns. She will agree to do so, not because she agrees that this issue is a major concern, but because she agrees that the dad should feel their daughter is "safe" in the mom's home. We should note here that the mom is agreeing to follow the format for resolving the concern; she is not automatically agreeing to provide more supervision of homework. The eventual solution to the concern might be very different from what either parent was thinking at the beginning of the process.

The goals and payoffs for each of the parents in this example are different and cannot be compared. The dad's goal is for the daughter to do well, and the payoff is a plan that enables her to do well in school. Note that his goal is not to have the mom supervise homework. The mom's goal, on the other hand, is for the dad to believe that their daughter is safe in her home, and the payoff is the maintenance of a functional co-parenting relationship. Note that the mom is not required in this example to agree with the dad that there is a problem in her home.

Also note that both parents agree on the goal of their daughter doing well in school; they simply disagree about how to accomplish this. When discussing this concern, the mom can express her concern about their daughter becoming too dependent on her parents' help and not showing independent initiative by taking care of her responsibilities. If both parents express their objective and subjective goals, they can arrive at an optimal agreement that provides a payoff or value to both of them. The point of their interaction is not a power struggle over whether or not the mom supervises homework time; the point is to have a plan to help the child become an independent worker who does well in school. They might, for example, decide that the dad should do less hands-on supervising and both set up an incentive system for the child to complete her homework every day.

Parents need to remember to cooperate in resolving major concerns. Blame does not resolve concerns. It is crucial for parents to remember to work together to resolve *major concerns*, no matter in which setting they occur. Sometimes parents will say to each other, "That is your problem. That does not happen in my home," without reflecting on how silly this is. If a teacher called and said that their son is acting up in school, they would not say to the teacher, "That is your problem; he does fine at home." Parents want their children to do well in all settings. When one parent says this to the other parent, it is just a subtle form of blame. Blame doesn't resolve concerns, even if the person doing the blaming is correct. What if part of the reason the child is not doing her homework is because the mom is not consistent enough with her and lets her have privileges without expecting her to do her work? In a sense, the dad would be correct to blame the mom, but it wouldn't solve the girl's problem of not being responsible. In fact, by blaming the mom, the dad teaches the child to blame others for her problems; i.e., it is Mom's fault she is not doing her homework. Cooperative parents learn to "borrow" each other's strengths and cover for each other's weaknesses. To resolve the homework problem, both parents might need to work together to make sure their child not only doesn't blame other people for being lazy but learns to take care of her responsibilities and has parental guidance and incentives for doing so.

• Defining a Minor Concern

A *minor concern* is a concern that is not a *major concern*. If a concern is "minor," the parent still needs to express this concern to the other parent in order to keep information public, perfect, and complete.

While all parents need some independence to make decisions on minor issues, input from the other parent can nevertheless be invaluable. It is a mistake to try to control the manner in which the other parent deals with the children on minor issues, but it is also a mistake to fail to give that other parent input. This kind of feedback loop helps both parents reflect on parenting decisions and, in many cases, modify them for the better. A specific procedure for resolving minor concerns is included in chapter 7 and in the Coparenting Workbook available from Unhooked Books, which not only recognizes the independence of the parents in their homes but also keeps the information system open.

4. Resolving Conflicts

The fourth type of action that parents sometimes need to take is to resolve a conflict. Here we use the technical definition of a conflict, not the more general term which refers to a disagreement.

• Defining a Conflict

The term "conflict" often is viewed with negative connotations. However, a conflict is not a dispute, an argument, or an ongoing pattern of disagreement. Technically, a conflict is a situation in which individuals have interests that are incompatible and mutually exclusive of one another. Two individuals can address a conflict in a calm and amicable manner. Let us break this definition down into its parts to understand what a conflict really is.

First of all, a conflict occurs in the *context of a situation*. The situation might be one in which a decision has to be made, such as a choice of school for the child. It might be one in which there are different scheduling needs, such as when both parents want the child on the same weekend. It might be one of differing values, such as whether or not the child should be put on medication for a medical or psychological problem. A conflict then occurs regarding an individual situation that has arisen and needs resolution.

Second, in order for a conflict to exist, both parents must have an *interest in the outcome*. If the dad wants the children on a particular weekend and the mom really does not care one way or another, there is no conflict. It is only when the mom also wants the children that same weekend that both parents have an interest in the outcome. Now we have a conflict.

Next, the interests of the parents must be *incompatibly exclusive* of one another, meaning that there is no "win-win" solution. Both parents cannot prevail in the conflict; one must "lose" or give in. If the conflict is choice of school, with the mom wanting the child to go to a private school and the dad wanting the child to go to public school, the child can only go to one school, so one of the parents will "lose" in the conflict. If the mom wants the child to play basketball and the dad wants the child to learn dance, this is not necessarily a conflict because through careful discussion and planning, both parents might prevail. A conflict exists only when one individual will not prevail and the other will.

Many situations have the initial appearance of a conflict, but are not. For example, assume that the dad calls the mom and asks to have the children on a weekend he is not scheduled to have them. He explains that his family has organized a family reunion, and he had no control over the choice of weekend. Assume that the mom had plans to take the children camping with her sister and brother-in-law. On the face of it, this might appear to be a conflict. However, the mom might be able to easily rearrange the camping weekend and thus, there is no conflict. The children get to do both activities. Most residential schedule disputes are really decision-making issues because they entail planning. However, within a residential schedule discussion, a conflict might arise. For example, assume that the mom is devoutly Catholic and the dad is neutral on religious training and will not take the children to church on Sundays. However, the dad wants full weekends with the children so that he can, at least on occasion, take weekend trips with them. The mom wants the children every Sunday, to take them to church. Both parties cannot prevail and thus, we have a conflict.

It is not always easy at first to tell if what appears to be a conflict really is one. Thus, we have built into the conflict-resolution procedures in chapter 7 and the Co-parenting Workbook a means to further explore the situation and determine if the interests of the parents really are incompatibly exclusive of one another.

Communication: Summary There are two parts to communication (sharing information and taking action). There are four types of information sharing (weekly contact, paperwork, transition information, and emergency contacts). There are four types of taking action (making decisions, solving problems, resolving major and minor parenting concerns, and resolving conflicts). We have suggested a method for each type of taking action—methods that have been proven successful by good research—which are presented in Chapter 7 and the Co-parenting Workbook. The methods rely both on good research and on game theory principles.

Parent-Child Access Arrangements

The quality of the co-parenting relationship and flexibility are key. Access is a special type of parent-child contact. One type of contact is that afforded by the residential schedule, a legal task. This is the blueprint for the child's residential life. Access is the "off-schedule" contact that provides flow and flexibility to the child's life. Access breaks down the barriers that the residential placement schedule appears to impose on the relationships between the child and each of his or her parents. In an important study, adults who were raised by separated parents were asked what they liked and did not like about the experience. The number one focus was on the *quality of the co-parenting relationship.* Those children whose parents got along well talked very positively about this and those whose parents did not wished that they had. The second most important issue identified by these children was *flexibility in the schedule* (i.e., access). Those who had it, loved it, and those who did not have it wished that they had. Thus, after being most concerned about how well their parents got along, children with separated parents were concerned with the access arrangements in the family.

Access not only serves the interests of the children; good access arrangements also benefit the parents as well. Access allows parents to see their children during the residential time with the other parent and allows for schedule changes that accommodate plans. While too much access can create chaos, some access is wonderful for all concerned. Following a rigid residential schedule without access can divide the family in half for the child and prevent the child and the parents from having many enriching experiences, simply because the schedule does not allow for them.

At the same time, parents are living separate lives about which the other parent might not be informed all of the time. Additionally, separated parents can easily regress into conflict and a negative tit-for-tat game, in which one parent will deny an access request, and to get even, the other parent denies the next request, and so on.

Rules and procedures create the access blueprint. The solution is to develop and agree upon a clear set of rules and procedures that allow all involved to cross the lines set forth by the residential schedule. The residential schedule and access run parallel to one another; the residential schedule provides the blueprint and access provides the flexibility.

Here are some types of access:

- telephone contact between parents and children
- visits with extended family
- child-initiated off-schedule contact
- parent-initiated off-schedule contact
- parental attendance at children's activities outside of the homes

Structured flexibility is a good guideline. Successful coparents will design access rules and procedures that fit the circumstances of their family. As examples, telephone access will vary depending on the residential schedule, and off-schedule access will depend on geographic distance between homes. Successful access rules and procedures will create a general atmosphere of structured flexibility in the family; will allow the child to feel like both parents are available to him or her most of the time, independent of the residential schedule; and will allow both the parents and the child to have opportunities that would be lost if parents rigidly upheld the residential schedule.

Telephone Access

Parents set up the rules and expectations for successful telephone access. It might be acceptable to have no limits (e.g., the parents can call the children at any time, and the children can call the parents at any time), but there is nothing wrong with a few rules. For example, one parent might not want calls coming in, from anyone, during the dinner hour. Another might not want calls after 8:00 p.m. because of the bedtime routines. One call a day is reasonable, but not if it is for one hour every time. Parents need to think this through and design reasonable but non-interfering telephone contact. Once agreed upon, the telephone access arrangements should be openly discussed with the children, so that they are not confused. The parents could apply this same thinking to other forms of electronic communication.

Extended Family Access

Children in many situations are likely to do better with a parental separation if they can maintain their involvement with extended family members. Parents need to decide if extended family members can contact the children in the home of the other parent (e.g., the dad's parents contacting the children at the mom's home). Extended family members often do not know what to do, so they back off, when even the parents might not want them to do so. Parents should advise extended families and the children regarding the extended family access procedures.

There is no right or wrong way to do this. A procedure for the mom's parents might be to initiate contact through her, for example, and then she and the dad will make the arrangements, or it might be that the grandparents can contact the dad directly. The point is not to have a right way; the point is to have rules and procedures so that everyone knows what to do.

Child-Initiated Off-Schedule Access

Although less frequent than parent-initiated schedule changes, sometimes children request to go "off schedule." It is important for parents to have a procedure in place for such schedule changes but also to acknowledge that the residential placement parent is in the decision-making role, because that is the parent who has the most information about the request. Points of discussion include who the child should ask first, whether the child is to talk with both parents or whether the parents will talk to one another and so on.

Parent-Initiated Off-Schedule Access

The residential placement schedule is somewhat artificial in a child's life. Because it divides the child's life into "Mom's house/Dad's house" time, the child has the potential of missing important opportunities. One way to correct for this is to allow parents to go "off schedule"— that is, to be able to change the schedule temporarily so the child can take advantage of opportunities when they arise.

If the amount of time needed off schedule is short, no make-up time might make sense. If the time needed off schedule is long (e.g., includes an overnight), the parents can have a trade-off procedure.

To prevent a negative tit-for-tat game from getting started, the parent to whom the request is being made should always try to say "yes." For example, if the dad requests a change, but the mom has plans, before saying "no," she should consider changing her plans. If she can, she should. If she cannot, then at least the dad will appreciate that she considered doing so. If both parents understand that the other parent will try to say "yes," an occasional "no" is easier to take. This is how to get a positive tit-for-tat game going.

Access to Activities Outside of the Homes

Access to the children's activities outside of the homes can be awkward for parents and for children. However, children should be able to count on having both parents at important events without conflict or embarrassment. Parents should make agreements about how they will conduct themselves at such events. They should also anticipate questions children might have and answer them beforehand. Decide, for example, if it is okay for the child to greet the other parent, and then tell the child before the event what it is that you decided. Before each event, parents should think through difficulties that the child might encounter and develop solutions for them..

Having a general set of rules for such activities is very helpful. For example, the parents might decide it is fine for the children to choose with whom to sit as long as they ask the residential parent first. Or they might decide that the children can go greet the other parent but sit with the residential parent. Parents might decide it is best for the children if the parents at least greet each other in a courteous manner (e.g., wave when they see each other or say "hi" if close enough). Once the general rules are established, the children should be told the applicable general rules. However, prior to each event, there might be some modifications to the general rules that need to be discussed. A quick phone call can accomplish this.

Some parents have particularly difficult problems with this form of access. For example, if the mom had an affair and is now living with the man, the dad might find it particularly provoking or awkward for that man to be at events with him and the mom. Or, there might be some "bad blood" between a parent and the extended family of the other parent. While these might seem insurmountable, they are simply problems to be solved, using the problem-solving method discussed earlier.

Essentially, the parents are playing the mutual-attendance-of-events game:

- setting goals that include objective and subjective values of the parents
- establishing axioms to use as standards against which to measure proposals and agreements
- moving first through the cooperative bargaining phase, then, if they must, through the compromise bargaining phase, and then finally reviewing their agreements to see if they meet the axiomatic standards and if they can be improved

Summary

Access runs parallel to the residential schedule and provides the additional contact and flexibility that children need and from which parents benefit. Rules and procedures are designed by successful child planners for telephone access (and perhaps email and other electronic communication), extended family access, child-initiated access, parent-initiated access, and attendance of activities outside of the homes.

Design Child-Focused Transitions

Transitions are difficult for children. Transitioning from the home of one parent to that of the other parent is difficult for children. Children list transitions—that is, "going back and forth"— as the biggest drawback to having separated parents. However, children must have transitions in any residential placement schedule. A "transition" is defined as the child moving from one residence to the other for a period that includes at least one overnight. Just spending time with the other parent is not a transition and is not inherently stressful. However, parents can make daytime contact stressful by engaging in arguments in front of the child, but the contact itself is not as stressful as moving to stay at the other residence for at least one overnight. While stressful, transitions are an inherent part of the reality of being raised in two residences.

The task for separated parents is to minimize the stressful aspects of a transition and to do everything possible not to add to the inherent stress of a transition by getting sidetracked with adult issues. Successful coparents do not put transition burdens on their children like clothing, but rather work out the logistics between them.

We list some basic "do not's" and "do's" below, but the real task for parents is to give transitions the attention they deserve and to design them as well and as stress free for the child as possible.

The "Do-Not's" of Transition Management

- Never have open conflict at a transition.

- Never conduct other adult business at a transition—the transition is about the children.

- Never design a transition that has drop-offs and pick-ups at the curb—the walk from the car to the house alone is very stressful and is a form of exposure to conflict between the parents. Think of this type of transition as through a demilitarized zone.

- Never have transitions occur at public parking lots in order to control conflict. First, it does not control conflict, and second, it models social immaturity to the child. If a public parking lot is a convenience, it may be okay.

Location of Transitions: The "Do's" of Transition Management

- If transitioning directly from parent to parent, make the location sensible (e.g., a porch or inside the front door).

- If transitioning directly from parent to parent, be prepared for normal questions (e.g., "Can Dad come in and see my new room?").

- If too much tension and conflict exists between parents, or if it is more convenient, have transitions go through a neutral zone, such as school or daycare.

- If transitioning directly from parent to parent, spend a few minutes giving need-to-know information so that the child can spend a few moments with both parents. This makes the transition for the child easier and gives the parent useful information.

Personal Belongings: More "Do's" of Transition Management

- Make transitions easier by having sets of clothing, toys, and other personal items at both homes.

- In weekly contacts, discuss which clothes and other items need to be exchanged between the parents.

- Let the child take his or her personal belongings back and forth.

- If the transition is at a neutral zone, work out the transfer of clothing and other personal items directly between the parents. (Do not have the child toting suitcases or big bags to school.)

Hellos and Good-byes: Even More "Do's" of Transition Management

- Have routine hello rituals.
- Have routine good-bye rituals.
- The parent who dropped off the child sometimes may want to make a call to the children the day of a transition just to let them know he or she is thinking about them.

Summary: The "Do's" of Transition Management

- Have conflict-free transitions.
- Concentrate on saying hello and good-bye to the children.
- Let the children take toys, clothes, etc. back and forth and have a plan for getting children's belongings from one home to another.
- Determine a sensible location for the transitions.
- Model social maturity by controlling oneself and concentrating on a smooth transition for the children.

Summary

Transitions are a difficult time for children. Keeping the number of transitions low is helpful, but not always possible. Children will do best if they have transitions that are planned well and child focused. Occasionally parents should ask their children if there is anything hard about transitions that perhaps the parents can fix. The children are the experts about their transitions.

Coordinate Parenting and Similarize Homes

Children have a difficult time adjusting to major differences in how each parent runs his and her home. The younger the child, the more difficult this adjustment can be. At young ages under five or six years old, these differences can disrupt important developmental tasks and cause serious long-term damage to the child. The older the child, the more likely the child can adapt to differences in how the two homes are run, without any serious damage. Nonetheless, it is still difficult for an older child and would be easier if the parents made an effort to *similarize the two homes*.

Communication to coordinate adjustments in the two homes is important. Successful coparents attempt to make the two homes as similar as possible and keep communicating in order to coordinate adjustments in their homes. For example, if a parent adds some important chores as the child gets older, it would be very helpful for the other parent to consider assigning the same in order for the child to learn lessons about being a responsible, contributing member of a group of people living together. When this occurs in one home and not the other, the lessons learned by the child are often unhealthy. A child might see the parent with more chores as too strict, for example, and might learn to maneuver and rebel, rather than how to be a responsible person.

The task facing separating parents is twofold. First, parents must begin with a baseline of doing things as similarly as possible. This involves establishing similar routines, a similar focus on schoolwork and other outside commitments and responsibilities, having similar expectations and rules, using similar forms of discipline, and setting up similar chores and responsibilities. Second, parents must continue to communicate about these areas in order to continue to similarize them as circumstances change and the child gets older.

Parents do not have to be perfect at this to be successful. All parents have different styles. If parents decide on an 8:00 p.m. bedtime, one can be rigid about this and the other can be a little less organized. As long as both are aiming at 8:00 p.m., it will likely work out well. Both could have a mealtime chore for the child, but in one home, it might be putting the dishes in the dishwasher, and in the other it might be setting the table. The point is to have the two homes be similar, not exactly the same.

Making this effort has several secondary benefits. First, having the two homes be fairly similar reduces the stress of transitions, because the children have fewer differences to which they must adjust, fewer things they have to remember, and fewer consequences for failing to remember. Second, having this information prevents some of the manipulations children will sometimes use with parents, playing one parent off against the other. Finally, and perhaps most important, the child will learn the lessons that the parents are trying to teach, rather than simply learning to maneuver in different settings. If the parents want the child to learn good self-discipline, having the same expectations in both homes accomplishes this. Having major differences only teaches the child how to read cues and maneuver, doing the minimum to get by.

Task of Similarizing Two Homes

Although it might be understandable for separating parents to avoid this task, successful child planners address this task head-on and do the work necessary for their children. Successful child planners similarize their two homes and continue to do so throughout the children's lives. The following are some initial ideas to focus on when trying to similarize the two homes.

Routines

- Parents should discuss bedtimes, morning routines, meal routines, and so on.
- If the routines are already similar, set this issue aside and move on.
- If major differences are identified in routines, come to agreement on making them more alike.
- If either parent wants to make a major change in the routines, discuss it first with the other parent and work out a similar change in both homes.

Schoolwork

- Establish similar expectations for homework—e.g., will there be a specific homework time and will the parent check the work afterward?
- Be clear with the child about what kind of success both parents expect in school.

Standards and Expectations

- One of the five characteristics of quality parenting is having high expectations for children. Set high expectations.
- Set clear and similar expectations in both homes.
- A corollary to expectations is the rules in each home. Set similar rules.

Discipline

- Support each other as authorities with the children. Never take a child's side against the other parent.
- With older children, set up ways to carry discipline across homes.
- Do not rely on personal discipline; that is, persuasion, yelling, the power of personality, nagging, and so on. With all children, have structural discipline—that is, built-in incentives for meeting

expectations and punishments for not meeting expectations or breaking rules.

Chores and Responsibilities

- Children learn skills and are trained to be industrious by having chores and responsibilities in the home. They also learn to be contributing roommates.
- Set similar sets of chores in both homes.

Summary

Children have a much easier time going back and forth between two homes when the rules, routines, expectations, chores, and discipline are similar. It is helpful to the children for parents to coordinate this across homes. The first step is to set a starting point; namely, how things will be at the point of the separation. The second step is to keep each other informed of changes, and, if there is a disparity between the homes, spend some time closing the gap to make both home situations more alike. If there is a disagreement, the "Taking Action" steps provided in the "Communication" section above can be used.

The Child Game: Conclusion

Establishing decision-making responsibilities and establishing a residential placement schedule are the two primary legal tasks addressed at the time of the divorce. Decision-making includes both a normal form game and a repeated form game. Thus, there is a focus on the content at the time of the separation, such as making a list of joint and/or unilateral decisions, for the normal form game, but also on procedures, for the repeated form game—that is, how those decisions will be made when they arise. The second legal task is establishing the multiple game of a residential schedule. By now, the reader should have a good idea how to design a residential placement schedule using game theory principles, which focus on procedures and teach a decision-making process based on the parents' objective and subjective goals. The legal game is not the goal; it is the means by which parents try to accomplish long-term goals.

Game theory principles also apply to the extensive repeated form game of child planning that will last the rest of the parents' lives. We have divided this multiple mixed game into the five subgames social science research tells us successful coparents play. We have provided research-based procedures for each of the child planning games and have included in chapter 7 procedures for the most difficult game, taking action. This information is also presented in the Co-parenting Workbooks, written for parents, available from Unhooked Books.

CHAPTER 5

Game Theory:
Applied to Property Division
and Support

Introduction

A number of the principles, definitions, and even some of the examples used in this chapter can also be found in chapter 4, regarding children, and in Chapter 2, regarding game theory. The repetition and restatement of this information has the drawback of some redundancy, but the advantage of enhancing learning, with the intent to illustrate the application game theory bargaining to the financial issues of divorce. In this chapter, we repeat many game theory principles, but explicitly apply them to financial issues and provide financial examples.

Similar to the child games discussed in chapter 4, divorcing spouses often play two parallel games simultaneously relative to the financial aspects of their divorce. Remember that there are two legal tasks facing divorcing spouses with regard to financial issues: property division and support determination. These are parts of the legal game, which are generally normal form games, where the focus is on content—that is, a focus on the facts at the time of the divorce. In addition to dividing property, debts and income, issues such as dollar values, dates certain, appraisals, and future value amounts are also part of the legal game.

Most of the financial issues involve playing only the legal game, because once the issues are resolved, the agreements become part of the Marital Settlement Agreement and the Judgment of Divorce, in which the issues are final and not modifiable in the future. These are generally normal form games, although there are advantages to playing the game as a goal-based planning process rather than a strictly competitive normal form game.

However, there are some financial issues where the parties play the financial planning game. These involve issues that, while settled at the time of the divorce, involve *repeated form* games. In the financial planning game, attention is on *procedures,* such as conditions for modifications and exchanges of tax returns.

Game Theory Bargaining Principles

In this chapter, when we discuss negotiating and settling the financial issues in divorce, we will be applying many game theory bargaining principles. (See also Chapter 8, which sets forth these Bargaining Principles in a Checklist format.) As a reminder:

1. Assume that the parties' interests are more in concert than in dispute. This is our working assumption.

2. Recognize that the parties are playing multiple games in the divorce process and that the demands of each game might conflict. The legal game and the financial planning game are two of the important games played, but individual financial games might conflict. For example, owning real estate might conflict with retirement security. Thus, optimal solutions to one game might adversely affect the solution to a different game.

3. A determination must be made in each game as to whether it is a normal form game (focusing on content), a repeated form game (focusing on procedures), or both (focusing first on content and next on procedures).

4. Manage information by making it public, verifiable, perfect, and complete. Managing the disclosure of information will optimize the likelihood of and quality of the settlement. Take advantage of Bayes rule by taking turns making proposals and include the subjective goals of the parties in those proposals.

5. Spend time learning about the objective and subjective goals of the parties for every major financial issue. This might seem cumbersome (which is true), but doing so is at the heart of getting an optimal settlement and having the parties experience satisfaction with the process.

6. Set axiomatic standards for every agreement based on the objective and subjective goals of the parties for that issue. Measure every

agreement against those standards, and either revisit an item if it does not or balance that issue with another issue. Measure the entire settlement of all of the financial issues, including the payoff structure, against the Five E's: educated, equitable, effective, equilibrant, and envy free.

7. Identify the parties' shared interests and, on every issue, bargain through the three bargaining phases in sequence: cooperative bargaining, compromise bargaining, and win-win-plus bargaining.

8. During bargaining, separate multiple games into single games and mixed games into simple games. Play a subgame for each game and payoff.

Basic Assumptions in Traditional Divorce

As a reminder, the basic assumptions in game theory bargaining are fundamentally different from those in traditional divorce. Ironically, traditional divorce fits the emotional states of divorcing parties in many ways, even though the fit often leads to rational, but self-defeating behavior and agreements.

As discussed in detail in chapter 3, from the beginning of the divorce process, spouses are traditionally viewed as people having conflicting interests, who need *opposing* lawyers to *argue* their positions in a *dispute*. The attorneys therefore *argue* the case in an effort to *resolve the dispute* and, failing settlement, *argue* their clients' cases before a judge (or jury in a few states). Even experienced attorneys will often advise their clients accordingly, operating under this basic assumption that positions needed to be "argued," making the "wants" of the client seem paramount.

Divorcing spouses often engage in arguments with one another, trying to "win" on their points of financial management, who should get the kids and the house, how much money one party should pay another, whether the stay-at-home parent should get a job, and so on. The idea of having a "tough guy" professional arguer (the attorney) is emotionally appealing. Additionally, the fear and anxiety about their future might make a professional "protector" seem reassuring. However, five years later, when the anger, fear, and anxiety have diminished, will this aggressively competitive battle against "the other side" really lead to optimal outcomes?

Another manifestation of the assumption that the parties' interests are adverse is how people are described. For example, if attorney A is talking about attorney B, attorney B is likely to be referred to as "*opposing* counsel." Therefore, there is an assumption that the parties are "opposed" to one another and a further assumption that the attorneys are "opposed" to one another.

Are these fundamental assumptions really true? Can the focus of the parties be changed? Perhaps the financial interests of most divorcing spouses are not really in conflict! In traditional family law, from the very beginning of the bargaining process, there is an assumption of conflicting, and perhaps even incompatible, interests because the focus is on the *legal outcome* (who must pay child support, who gets what property and which debt, and how will the income-sharing affect each party's financial condition), not on the *underlying long-term goals* of the parties. Because this is the focus of the traditional legal system, even parties whose long-term goals might be much more similar than different are quickly thrust into viewing themselves as at odds with one another.

Applying game theory, your authors submit that this traditional approach has a high likelihood of promoting the grim strategy (sometimes referred to as the "battle to the death" game) and/or a "war of attrition." Essentially, the parties end up using continuous antagonistic strategies until the transaction costs wear them out or they simply have nothing left to argue about.

What if we assume as a starting point that the interests of the parties are shared or similar across the board, that they each want the best outcome for each other, that they are willing to make personal sacrifices to accomplish this, and that they both want each spouse eventually to be doing as well as possible financially, independent of one another? What if the legal outcomes for child support, property division, allocation of debt, and spousal support are seen as tools or means to be used in achieving financial goals—not as goals themselves? What if by playing the divorce game rationally, the parties can optimize the outcome for both of them down the road when they are not quite so angry, fearful, or anxious?

Playing the Game Rationally

Each Team Needs an Attorney

We know that a game is a strategic interaction between two or more players, with rules, payoffs, and choices that affect the outcome of the game. It is important that parties have attorneys in this model so each player is made up of a team composed of a spouse and an attorney. One team member, the client, knows his or her objective and subjective goals, as well as many of those of the other spouse. These will serve as axiomatic standards for decisions and many of the payoffs involved. The attorney understands the rules of the game, the other players in the game (the other attorney and the judge), the local standards, and parts of the payoff structure (the legal and tax implications of certain decisions). Additionally, the presence of each attorney helps make each team rational, with each attorney informing the client of the objective and subjective payoffs, so that the client is not making poor choices based on temporary emotions.

For example, assume both spouses assert that they want the homestead. If the marital home is viewed by the parties as "ours" and "I want it," they are looking at the homestead through emotional lenses. The attorney can tell the client:

Examples

One scenario: "The marriage owns the house and is selling it for $X. If you want it, you have to buy it from the marriage for $X. If your spouse also wants the house, and wants to buy it from the marriage, he or she may have to offer more than $X. If you still want it, you may have to offer more. Do you think before getting into a bidding war over that house, you should look at some other houses and see how much they might cost or at least what you could get for $X?"

Or

Another scenario: "The equity in the house is about $100,000. Houses are currently appreciating at about 2 percent per year, and the house is valued at $180,000. Most investment managers average between 6 percent and 10 percent over time. So, we are comparing $100,000 invested in a house worth $180,000 with an annual appreciation rate of about 2 percent versus that same $100,000 in a retirement account at 8 percent (tax deferred until retirement). Assume that you sell the house when you retire *in fifteen years. Let's look at what you would have in these two scenarios, getting the house or getting the money in retirement." The attorney does the future value calculations, and it becomes apparent that having the money in a retirement account may lead to a much more comfortable retirement.*

Now, no matter which scenario the spouse chooses, it is at least a rational choice. The spouse might still choose the house, because the house has additional subjective value (neighbors, neighborhood, friends, and so on) that is worth the difference in dollars, but this is also a rational choice, made possible by the attorney remaining rational.

Mediation is another forum in which the mediator assists parties and/or their attorneys in remaining rational players, not only by setting up rules and payoffs in the mediation that promote rational play but also by helping shape payoffs in a more creative manner to promote reaching the subjective goals of the parties. The mediator can ensure that the game stays rational by keeping the focus on the process and on the standards for making good decisions.

Both attorneys and mediators are often an effective line of defense against parties employing the grim strategy or battle-to-the-death strategy with one another.

Solutions and the Nash Equilibrium

John Nash is responsible for the combined concepts of cooperative and compromise bargaining (although Raifa contributed heavily to the concept). The Nash equilibrium is reached by combining a process of improving the outcome for both parties until it can no longer be improved and then looking for the compromise point. We assume that there is a point of equilibrium for each subgame of the divorce game, which can be reached by following the three phases of bargaining and employing game theory principles.

Financial Game Forms: Normal Form and Repeated Form

There   are basically two forms that a financial game can take: normal form or repeated form. A normal form game is played one time and then it is over. The focus is on the *content* of the issue. Most of the legal financial tasks of a divorce are normal form games; that is, they are played one time, ordered by the court, and then the game is over. Property division is usually a normal form game.

A repeated form game is played over and over. The focus is on the *procedures.* Spousal support is an example of a simple repeated form game, because it is played over and over, might be changed if support is adjusted, but also, in many (perhaps most) divorces, has an end point (i.e., death, remarriage, or a certain term of years).

Extensive repeated form games are played without an end point. Few divorces have issues that fit this type of game.

Because many of the financial issues are normal form games, there is a temptation to compete and "win" by playing dirty. One good reason to resist doing so is the spill-over effect of playing a financial legal game "dirty" when the parties also have children and must interact in an *extensive* repeated form game as coparents. Another is that the payoffs of the normal form games at the time of the divorce are not goals; they are planning tools for the future economic conditions of both spouses. When long-term goals are the focus, optimal outcomes are best achieved through application of game theory principles.

If the parties have no children, and there is no financial planning game, the argument could be made that it does not matter if the normal form game of divorce is played dirty. However, even in this type of case, many parties, if asked, would rather have an outcome that seems fair and assists each of them to do well independent of one another in the future. In a sense, there is a *subjective game* being played, with each party seeing themselves as having been fair, perhaps even generous, to accomplish mutual goals. We remind the reader of the subjective goal of being fair illustrated in the "split-the-dollar ultimatum game."

When people, especially those involved in the legal system, assert that the court system seems to make matters worse for divorcing parents, there is at least one fundamental reason: the legal system emphasizes the normal form games and the strategies that work best for those cases. However, most parties are going to be playing extensive repeated form games for the rest of their lives, if only subjectively, and do not learn or adopt the strategies that work best for those games.

Discovery and Disclosure

The first step in the divorce process is called "discovery and disclosure." This is essentially the process of getting all of the information on the table and shared between spouses. The attorneys generally guide this process because they know what information is needed and the best ways to get it. In mediation, the mediator may also guide the spouses through this process. Discovery and disclosure begins the process of making information public, perfect, complete, and to the degree possible, verifiable.

Often not included in this step are the subjective goals and values of the parties, which are an essential part of reaching optimal solutions. Not all of the subjective values and goals will be made public at this early stage, possibly because the parties themselves might not know what they are or because they want to hold back at the outset of the case. Subjective values and goals sometimes become more apparent as specific issues are addressed in the process, but if the attorney is an adept interviewer, many of the subjective values and goals can be elicited early in the process. Disclosure of the subjective interests of the parties at the beginning of the negotiations can facilitate optimal outcomes. For example, disclosing that the wife is particularly anxious about her retirement can set the stage for optimal proposals.

Unguided parties often make a major mistake by going immediately to bargaining, without having done full discovery or received complete disclosure. In a goal-based planning process, discovery and disclosure are essential, because they establish the current situation, "point A." A goal-based planning process requires a full description of point A, before describing "Point B," the objective and subjective goals of the parties. The "problem" in this model is how to get from Point A to Point B, which is an impossible task without knowing the resources, obligations, and obstacles at point A. Point A is the starting point, the current situation. Point B can be an arbitrary time in the future. For example, the parties might agree that Point B is the objective and subjective goals for the parties five years hence.

Bargaining Basics

Once all of the information is on the table, Point A, and Point B have been defined. The long-term objective and subjective goals of the parties should also be known. Now *axioms* are developed and the bargaining process can begin. Everyone is ready to move from Point A to Point B. Bargaining can have a negative connotation, that it is necessarily an adversarial process, but this is unnecessarily prejudicial. Bargaining is really a goal-oriented planning process. Carefully and creatively planning how to use the resources available to maximize the long-term financial outcome for both spouses *is* a "bargaining" process, but is not adversarial. Within the process, the parties might reach points of disagreement, as with any type of planning, but these can be resolved without digressing into an antagonistic competitive process.

The bargaining process is really one of making a series of mini-decisions—that is, playing a series of simple and single games—and then slowly and carefully putting those decisions into a complete package—that is, the payoff structure—which is presented to the court in a written Marital Settlement Agreement.

As the parties go through the process of bargaining, each issue should be identified as either a normal form game or a repeated form game, or both. If normal form, the focus is on the *content* of the issue; if repeated form, the focus is on *procedures*; if both, there should be a focus on content *and* on procedures. For example, child support is both normal form and repeated form. The content includes the current incomes of the parties, the residential schedule, the number of children, and ultimately the amount of child support paid by one to the other. Paying for variable expenses (e.g., extracurricular activities) and adjusting child support in the future are repeated form games, so the focus is on procedures. The procedures might include how the variable expenses will be shared, in what ratio, and a reimbursement timeline or procedures for sharing income information for the purposes of adjusting child support and how to adjust it.

Many of the legal issues involving finances can be both types of games, and the question should at least be asked, "Do we need a procedure in case the circumstances change?" For example, if the parties are managing college IRA's or trust funds on behalf of the children, they might need to make a decision at the time of the divorce, a normal form game, but also they might need to make decisions in the future, such as to transfer money for one child to another child with higher expenses, a repeated form game. Attending to both forms of games, normal form and repeated form, at the time of the divorce can substantially assist the parties in the restructuring of their financial relationship.

Information Management

The four characteristics of information generally managed by the attorneys are reiterated below:

i. Public or private

ii Verifiable or non-verifiable

iii Perfect or imperfect: Information is perfect if both parties know the complete history of the game prior to making a choice. Part of that history is the subjective goals and values undergirding proposals.

iv Complete or incomplete: Information is complete if both parties know all of the rules and the payoff structure. Attorneys are particularly helpful at this point because there are elements to the rules and payoffs of which clients are unaware.

The best bargains are those based on public, verifiable, perfect, and complete information, to the degree possible. Another benefit of handling information in this manner is that complete, perfect, and public information includes the subjective goals of the parties. By understanding each other's goals, especially the subjective goals, the parties can identify and create solutions that are win-win.

Bargaining to Optimal Solutions

Expanding the Pie

By considering both the objective and subjective goals of the parties, the separating spouses can expand the pie and both receive more than one-half. An objective goal is the "what" someone wants; the subjective goal is the "why" he or she wants it—that is, what is the party trying to accomplish with a proposal. Everything has both an objective and a subjective value.

As a reminder, when both objective and subjective goals are incorporated into the bargaining process, the pie expands and players both gain value.

Example

When both spouses initially want the homestead, the one party may want the homestead chiefly because he or she believes that by getting it, there is a better chance of getting more time with the children, when compared to moving out of the homestead. That same party is also concerned that the children will want to spend more time with the other party, if awarded the homestead, because that party is in the familiar residence, near neighborhood friends and activities, and the like. In other words, one party may not really not want the house (the objective goal), and in fact considers the house too large and/or expensive, but wants it as a means of accomplishing several tangential objective goals and subjective goals. The other party may want the homestead because he or she (1) is not handy and the homestead has already been fixed up in a perfect way going forward; (2) wants the children to go through as few changes as possible; (3) likes the children's current school district; (4) two of the neighbors are best friends and has easy access to them; and (5) one of the neighbors watches the children after school, which has worked out nicely because they will continue to need after-school child care. One party therefore wants the homestead (objective goal) for important and difficult-to-replicate subjective reasons.

The house has a market value, which would typically be the value used in settlement. However, as can be seen, the house has a higher total objective and subjective value to one party than the market value. If that party agrees to "pay" more than market value in a settlement offer, which allows the other party to buy a residence in the same basic neighborhood, and agrees to a residential schedule that provides that party sufficient time with the children, conditioned on continuing to use the same after-school daycare provider, we can see that both parties would consider this a better than 50 percent agreement.

By determining the combined objective and subjective goals of the parties, a skillful set of attorneys or a mediator can assist parties in accomplishing more than one-half of what they want to accomplish. This leads us to a very important conclusion discussed below.

Divorce Is Not a Zero-Sum Game

In a zero-sum game, the payoff is absolutely limited. If we view settling property division and support as the "problem," then it is a zero-sum game. On the other hand, if we view property, income, and debt as the description of the current situation at the time of a divorce (point A), and if we view the objective and subjective goals of the parties as the future (point B), then we can define and reframe the "problem" as how to get from the current situation to the future. In other words, instead of a property, debt, and income "problem", we can view the situation as a goal-based planning process. Those same assets and debts are not "objects" to be divided in a zero-sum game; they are "tools" to be used to help the parties reach goals.

Example

Assume that divorcing spouses have defined their future objective and subjective goals. The husband's goals involve less interest in the short-term and more interest in the long-term (e.g., retirement). The wife is more interested in the short-term (e.g., owning the homestead) and less in the long-term. They develop two settlement packages. Package 1 provides 55 percent of the net worth of the marital estate for the wife, including the house, with a reasonable prediction that growth in that estate will be at about 3 percent per year for five years. Package 2 provides 45 percent of the net worth of the estate to the husband, but with a reasonable prediction of growth in the estate of about 7 percent per year for five years. If we convert percentage to dollars, wife is getting $55 and husband is getting $45. Package 2 looks like a loss in a zero-sum game, but in the goal-based planning game, it is actually a win. Both parties receive more than one-half of the estate, when measured against the goal-based standards, and this settlement meets the axiomatic standards of the Five E's. The wife receives more money to work with in the short-term, but has a slower growth rate (e.g., the appreciation of the homestead is 3 percent), but this is what she values subjectively. The husband receives less in the short-term, but with the expected annual return, will actually have a greater net worth in the long-term at time of retirement, which is what he values subjectively. Both are winners because both achieve their long-term goals. Neither would trade his or her outcome with the other party (i.e., the solution is envy free).

It is therefore important to note that the best solutions in divorce settlements occur when both parties understand that divorce is not a zero-sum game. By understanding the objective and subjective goals of the parties, each can achieve more than one-half of the payoffs available. If the parties truly understand this, they will no longer compete for the current resources, but rather will cooperate and have the current resources assist them in meeting their goals.

Separate Mixed Games and Turn Them into Simple Games

A mixed game is a game played for multiple payoffs, and a simple game is a game played for just one payoff. Simple games are much easier to solve than mixed games. Having multiple payoffs often adds suspicion and deceptive bargaining to the game. Simple games reduce suspicions and emphasize making private motives public, because optimal solutions are more likely to be achieved when the objective and subjective goals of the parties are public.

Strategy

Turn mixed games into simple games whenever possible. The first step is to identify the parties' objective and subjective goals for every payoff. The next step is to play a separate game for each payoff. With good information management, the issues are more easily resolved in separate games.

Example, Continued

In our prior example, if the husband discloses his retirement plan and the wife discloses her financial plan and needs (e.g., a sufficient portion of the marital estate to own the homestead outright), engaging in a cooperative bargaining process might well solve both plans. If the wife ends up with the house, owned outright, and the husband ends up with sufficient retirement income to pursue his dreams, both parties receive more than one-half of the pot.

Separate Multiple Games and Turn Them into Single Games

Multiple games are made up of more than one game but played as if they were one game. Single games are those that cannot be divided into more than that one game. Support is a financial example of a multiple game. Although the game appears to have a singular goal of reaching a specific dollar amount, the subjective goals of the parties are multiple; that is, what is each of the parties trying to accomplish for their futures when addressing support. Separating multiple games into single games shrinks the "dispute." By the time the parties got to the "nub," if the objective and subjective goals and process standards are used, the solutions are usually fairly simple.

Example

Assume Spouse A resists paying spousal support that Spouse B believes is well deserved. Assume that the court is likely to award $1,000 per month in spousal support for a period of eight years, and both attorneys know this. Spouse A begins with the position of paying $500 for five years, and Spouse B begins with the position of receiving $2,000 for twelve years. We could calculate the present value of such an obligation for both parties and examine the impact on both of them, and perhaps consider an unequal division of property as a support buyout. This is the traditional bargaining approach.

However, those dollars really make up a number of single games, especially for Spouse B, who will use the money to accomplish a number of different goals. Spouse A is also playing several games because the lost income actually has an opportunity cost; that is, limitations on some of his or her goals because of lost wealth. Each party is playing multiple games; one for each of their objective and subjective goals for how they will use the money. Assume that one of Spouse B's goals is to obtain more education so that when the support stops, Spouse B will be better able to maintain the marital standard of living. Because the parties have agreed to an equal residential schedule, child support will not be sufficient to reach Spouse B's goals. Spouse B understands that he or she will have to go to school very part time in order to continue to work the current thirty-hour-per-week job and in order to have time to care for the children during the stipulated placement time. Thus, Spouse B is trying to achieve multiple goals through what appears to be a single game for spousal support.

Without getting into the numbers, assume that Spouse A also knows that this is the game being played by Spouse B. Assume Spouse A proposes paying enough family support for enough time to allow Spouse B to go to school full time to obtain a degree as a teacher (his or her goal), conditioned on a waiver of spousal support after that time. In this scenario, Spouse A would be paying more in spousal support in total dollars than would have been paid at $1,000 per month for eight years. However, Spouse A also projects that child support will be lower if Spouse B is earning more sooner, likely balancing (or approaching) the total dollars paid over time. This might better accomplish Spouse A's goals of being relieved of spousal support sooner, ensuring that the children will not have to move in eight years, and supporting Spouse B to reach the goal of becoming a teacher. In other words, even if Spouse A pays more dollars than a judge would have likely decreed, the subjective goals accomplished might be more than worth that difference. This also expedites case settlement, promotes family stability, ensures better communication and cooperation going forward and saves transaction costs if not litigated.

Strategy
Notice that playing simple single games is only likely to work well

when the objective and subjective goals of the parties are included in the planning process. Surfacing the parties' subjective goals allows for a creative plan that both parties are likely to see as a "win."

Use Bayes Rule

Information is helpful (generally critical) in the bargaining process. Bayes rule is a complex math principle, but for our purposes, simply means that as a player receives additional information, the player updates his or her beliefs and uses these updated beliefs to bargain more effectively to optimal payoffs.

Strategy

When a proposal is made, information should be volunteered as to why the proposal was structured in a certain way. Likewise, the response should include information, such as how a rejected proposal does not accomplish certain subjective goals of the rejecting party. This flow of new information in both directions causes a dynamic that in game theory is called a "convergence of expectations," meaning that by its very nature, the process moves the parties closer and closer to an agreement, sometimes very creative, as their beliefs are updated.

For example, Spouse A proposes paying twice the expected amount of spousal support, but for one-half the expected period of time, including the information that Spouse A plans to travel to work in Africa after completing the support obligation (i.e., the reason he gives for wanting the term shorter). Spouse B and his or her attorney now know that Spouse A has a subjective goal and can not only tailor a counterproposal taking that goal into consideration, but also provide more information. In our example, Spouse B might respond that the shortened term is acceptable, but that it would work even better if the term was shorter still but the amount higher, so Spouse B can attend school full time to become a teacher. One can see that by including subjective information, the beliefs of both parties can be updated, and there is a convergence of expectations toward a solution that is optimal for both parties.

• •

Side note: This is one of the advantages of using mediation in dealing with divorce disputes, when they do occur. The mediator, perhaps in private meetings with the parties and their attorneys, can update and enhance his or her information in such a way that the mediator can more easily see a solution. By protecting that additional information, however, the parties' positions have not been compromised, should they not settle.

• •

Bayes rule also has another implication that has been proven in game theory research. The most effective way to reach ideal solutions (agreements) is by taking turns making proposals. This is because each proposal provides information to the other party, and thus, according to Bayes rule, updates the beliefs of the parties. This approach is particularly successful if each proposal includes additional perfect and complete information.

Example

Spouse A makes a proposal on real estate owned by the couple. In the proposal, he or she gives his or her objective and subjective values and goals and a best estimate of Spouse B's objective and subjective values and goals. Now, Spouse B and the attorney not only have a proposal in hand, but also can update opinions based on this information. Spouse B and the attorney take a turn and make a counterproposal, including information about his or her objective and subjective values and goals. We will soon see a *convergence of expectations* in this process, providing numerous opportunities to continue with this cooperative bargaining phase. Assume, for example, Spouse A really wants to keep a vacation property and proposes this. Assume Spouse B also wants to keep the vacation property, and the counterproposal includes this information. The attorneys explore the subjective value placed on this by each party (i.e., the "why" of keeping the vacation property). Assume that the long-term goals of each of the parties for the vacation property are not only to pass it on to their children but also for each of them to use it with the children, for weekends and some vacations. Because they will only be using the property when they have the children and because they each eventually want the property to go to the children, one can see several win-win solutions (e.g., the parties could jointly own the property under a property-sharing agreement or put it into a living trust that includes rules on use).

Summary

While most attorneys understand that proposals include new information that can inform the bargaining process, more explicit focus on making public additional information in the bargaining process, especially with regard to the objective and subjective goals of the parties, can lead to a convergence of expectations and creative settlement solutions. The notion that keeping subjective goals private provides a strong hand in the bargaining process does not bear up under the scrutiny of research. Research on bargaining concludes that with only few exceptions, the more information becomes public, the better the bargaining outcomes for both parties. The impact of *hardball* bargaining approaches with private information can lead to resentment and distrust over settlement outcomes, which, when children are involved, can be destructive.

Client's Objective and Subjective Goals as Standards for Settlement

Without standards, there is simply no way to plan successfully and maximize the resources available to accomplish the parties' goals. In addition to "goals" as standards, there are "axiomatic" standards, sometimes thought of as "process" standards.

The legal questions or outcomes might be:

- "Do you want to end up with the homestead?"
- "Do you want a maintenance waiver?"
- "How much support do you think you need and for how long?"

Unintentionally, these questions set up a conflict, unless the case has the good fortune of both parties wanting the exact same thing.

- If Spouse A replies: "I want the house," the lawyer has a position to fight for, if the other spouse does not agree.
- If Spouse B replies, "I want at least half of the marital income for life," the lawyer also has a position to fight for, if the other spouse does not agree.

Goal-oriented questions might include:

- "Tell me what you would like your financial position to be in five years?
- When are you thinking of retiring? or,
- Do you see yourself marrying again?"

With the responses to these questions, the lawyer no longer has a position to win, but instead has client *goals* to achieve, using legal outcomes as tools to reach those goals.

The "goal" standards will reflect both the objective goals *and* the subjective goals of the parties. Focusing only on the parties' short-term objective goals not only limits the solutions to a less-than-optimal outcome but also turns the divorce into a competitive process.

Example

If both parties want the homestead in the property settlement, and the focus stays solely on this objective goal, one of them will end up with the homestead and the other will not, making it a competitive process. Worse yet, this might not actually be the best solution in this particular case for either of them.

Strategy

By carefully identifying the subjective goals of the parties, the bargaining process has a much better chance of achieving an optimal solution in a cooperative process rather than a competitive one.

Five E's Axiomatic Goals as Standards for Settlement

Focusing on the parties' goals represents one set of standards for settlement. The other set of standards are the *axiomatic or process axioms* defined as the "Five E's," which answer the following question: how well do the final agreements accomplish the client's goals? These axioms are as follows:

Educated

The parties have a much better chance at achieving an optimal agreement if both have all the information relevant to their agreement. By being educated regarding the objective and subjective goals of both parties, each of the parties can contemplate and offer solutions (proposals) that are optimal for each of them.

Equitable

People have a fundamental belief that a strategic relationship should be equitable. In social science research, this is called the "principle of reciprocity." When a situation is not equitable, people feel "coerced" and are fundamentally unhappy with the outcome. People do not mind making compromises, for example, if they feel that the other person has also made compromises of a similar cost. Equitable does not mean equal; it means fair. When we look at the issue of "fairness," we again find ourselves including the subjective meaning of the outcome as well as the objective meaning. Each individual agreement might not be equitable, but the total package of agreements, incorporated into the Marital Settlement Agreement, should be equitable.

Effective
Attorneys usually are very proficient regarding this standard, especially with regard to financial issues. An effective agreement might also include procedures for the parties to modify certain financial arrangements, if that is appropriate in the case.

Equilibrant
The final deal is as good as it can be for both parties. If an agreement can be improved so that at least one party gains, as long as the other party does not lose, then it is not yet equilibrant. Only when the agreement can no longer be improved for at least one party, without hurting the position of the other party, does an agreement meet this standard.

Envy Free
Divorcing parties usually understand that they will leave the marriage with losses. If, however, at the end of the settlement process, neither of them would trade their package for the package of the other party (ergo, envy free), then this standard has been met.

Summary

BARGAINING TO OPTIMAL SOLUTIONS:

1. Legal outcomes are not goals. They are means to accomplishing the parties' long-term objective and subjective interests and goals.
2. The interests of the parties usually are more similar than different, and they can achieve optimal outcomes for both of them.
3. Solutions to financial games are optimal when achieved first through cooperative bargaining and then through compromise bargaining.
4. Even in very complex negotiations, as each of the simple and

single games are solved, there is a "saddle point"—that is, a point at which there is equilibrium, where all of the issues are balanced, even if some of the agreements favor one of the parties and some the other.

5. The win-win-plus bargaining phase is a bonus round, which might provide added value to at least one if not both of the parties' payoff structures. This is the third and final phase of the game theory bargaining model.

6. Usually there is more "front" time required with this approach (e.g., taking the time to thoroughly explore the objective and subjective goals of the parties), but this effort will likely generate clients who feel listened to and understood, where their interests and goals were well considered in the bargaining process. It might also reduce "back" time associated with costly litigation.

7. Optimal solutions require considering both the objective and subjective goals of the parties as standards for individual agreements, as well as the Five E's axiomatic process standards: educated, equilibrant, effective, equitable, and envy free, for the payoff structure for all of the agreements.

8. Rather than angry client rejoinders to angry responses to proposals, posing questions such as, "Is there anything in the current proposal that fails to accomplish your goals?" can turn the confrontational competitive approach into a cooperative bargaining process.

Playing the Normal Form Games with Complex Financial Issues: Examples

Most attorneys and mediators will have little difficulty applying game theory principles to most divorces and, in fact, might do so intuitively when there are only a few assets and debts to handle and the Nash equilibrium is obvious from the outset in the case.

Example: Assume the parties each keep their vehicles, one gets the homestead, the other gets equal value in retirement money, other liquid assets are split, household items are distributed, and spousal support is minimal or agreed upon as a certain amount for a certain duration. These cases might benefit from a more thorough examination of the objective and subjective goals of the parties and some creative bargaining, but the transaction costs might outweigh devoting too much time to this task. Spending a few minutes exploring objective and subjective goals and a little creative bargaining might well be worth the transaction costs, but if there are few assets and few disagreements, a more time-consuming bargaining process might lead to a net loss for the parties.

Where game theory bargaining can be particularly valuable is in dealing with more complex legal issues. In order to explore this assertion, four examples of cases with difficult financial issues are presented to illustrate the application of game theory principles. The four examples present four different *difficult case* issues:

1. A large complicated estate with disparate incomes, Spouse B in need of support, and Spouse A does not want to pay support. (Example 1)
2. A closely held key-employee business, where it is difficult to determine if it should be treated as income or as a business with value. (Example 2)
3. A support case confounded by child-related issues, including a relocation issue. (Example 3)
4. A Prenuptial Agreement with intervening variables before the divorce. (Example 4)

Example 1

The spouses have a marriage of twelve years and have accumulated a marital estate worth approximately $1.2 million, including the following:

1. A homestead worth approximately $475,000 and a mortgage of $343,000, with a net value of $132,000. Payments are $3,100 (PITI) per month for twenty-two years of the remaining thirty-year loan.
2. $386,000 in a 401(k).
3. $129,000 in a Roth IRA.
4. Vehicles worth $28,000 and $14,000, with a net value of about $7,000 and $9,000, respectively.
5. A boat worth about $82,000 and debt of about $50,000, with a

net value of about $32,000.

6. A real estate limited partnership share with a current value of about $212,000, which is not liquid and is expected to terminate in six years, with a projected future value of $400,000.

7. Twenty-five percent interest in an insurance agency partnership where the Spouse A works, with a net value of about $280,000.

8. About $15,000 in household and other personal assets.

Spouse A earns $145,000 per year in commissions and about $12,000 in residuals from the insurance partnership. Spouse B earns $68,000 per year as a teacher. The parties have two children and have already agreed to an equal residential time schedule.

Spouse A would like a settlement with no continuing financial obligations to Spouse B, aside from child support, and is willing to have an unequal division of property to accomplish this settlement. Spouse A wants the current share of the ownership of the insurance partnership. Spouse B would like the homestead but cannot afford the payments, even with child support, and believes that spousal support is needed to keep the homestead and to afford the marital lifestyle with the children.

Solution: First, the objective and subjective goals of the parties must be identified, for each of the simple and single games:

- What is Spouse B attempting to accomplish for him or herself and the children by retaining the homestead?
- Does Spouse A have any objective or subjective goals regarding the homestead?
- How far away are each of the parties from retirement, and what are their retirement goals, and therefore, what resources would they like to have for retirement?
- Do either or both of them have goals that include the boat?
- What are those goals and what do they hope to accomplish with those goals?
- Does Spouse B have subjective goals associated with the insurance business? What are Spouse A's objective and subjective goals relative to remaining a business partner with Spouse B without active involvement?
- What are long-term goals that each of the parties have that might

be facilitated by terminating the limited partnership in six years?

- What does Spouse B expect his or her lifestyle to be like with spousal support, and why does he or she want that lifestyle?

- In what ways will Spouse A paying the spousal support hinder Spouse A's lifestyle?

- What is Spouse A trying to accomplish by not paying spousal support?

A thorough examination of the clients' goals should also lead to a listing or determination of their *priorities*. How important are Spouse B's subjective goals in leaving the marriage with the homestead, compared to receiving support payments, and compared to having a retirement nest egg?

A game theory technique to determine priorities is the auction. The attorney tells Spouse A that he or she has 100 points and a list of nine goals. Spouse A's "homework" is to divide the 100 points among those nine goals according to their relative value. In other words, he or she is to give the most points to the goal that is most important. This not only organizes the list of goals by priority, but also the number of points demonstrates the gap between goals. For example, if 80 of the points are given to the first two priorities and 20 to the remaining goals, achieving the first two goals are substantially more important than the others.

The next step is to separate the single and simple games from the multiple and mixed games. Following this step, the attorneys can start bargaining for each of the single and simple games by alternating proposals. Each proposal can include the objective and subjective goals of each of the spouses, allowing information to become increasingly public, perfect, and complete, thus allowing Bayes rule to influence beliefs and creating a convergence of expectations on solutions.

Attorneys will help define the parameters of the game by providing their clients the best-case and worst-case scenarios should the case go to trial. This helps the clients better understand the range within which solutions are to be found and the transaction costs should they not settle. The attorneys should also tell their clients some of the options available through settlement that are not available through litigation, such as Section 71 support payments, college support, and the like.

Game Theory aficionados will recognize two solution concepts in this case, both of which are worth mentioning, even if no one does the mathematics. First, payoff values can be assigned to all of the dollars in this case, and a matrix can be developed listing the relative value of the many different divisions possible. For example, every dollar of the boat's value might actually be worth $1.10 to Spouse A, and every dollar of the homestead's value might be worth $1.15 to Spouse B, because of subjective values. The subjective value of these assets can also be recalculated. For example, Spouse A might assign a subjective value of $1.25 to every dollar paid in support, but only $0.95 if that same dollar is applied to the mortgage. The subjective value, in dollar amounts, of not paying support directly to Spouse B is $0.30. Second, a grid with all of the values could be constructed, and if completed, we would find that there are actually several "saddle points" or Nash equilibria in this game, meaning that there are several possible optimal solutions. A game theorist could actually do calculations and find those saddle points, reducing the "art" of settlement to a science. However, this is not necessary. What is necessary is to understand that in complex games, there are likely several different solutions of relatively equal value to the players, and that by taking the subjective payoff values into consideration, the apparent objective values change. A dollar is no longer a dollar; it is more or less than a dollar!

The bottom line is simple: the attorney's recognition that the parties are bargaining over assets and debts that have subjective values beyond the objective values. For example, in this case, the subjective value of the mortgage is high for Spouse B but low for Spouse A. Having no mortgage on a homestead worth $475,000 might well be worth more than $343,000 to Spouse B, because of all the subjective values assigned to having the homestead for him or herself and the children and the lifestyle issues in being able to continue to live there without having to make the monthly payments. The $343,000 mortgage might be of lesser value to Spouse A than the same dollars in the ownership of the insurance company and/or the need to pay spousal support.

The solutions to this game lie in solving the simple single games associated with the parties' objective and subjective goals, with a likely outcome that Spouse B will have the homestead, mortgage free, with sufficient assets and income to live at the marital lifestyle, and Spouse A will have fewer assets but no spousal support payments. Perhaps Spouse B will receive or share in some of the insurance company residuals as additional income/support, or perhaps the real estate limited partnership will be used to pay off the mortgage in the future, with Spouse A paying the monthly mortgage for six years while this is pending. Whether the trade-offs will be the boat or retirement funds depends on the subjective goals and priorities of the parties. The ultimate settlement might be an unequal division of the objective dollar values of the assets, but both of the parties are likely to end up with more than 50 percent of the subjective value of the estate- or perhaps more. For example, if Spouse B is able to accomplish all of his or her objective and subjective goals *and* not have monthly spousal support payments and any accompanying resentments or feelings of dependence to deal with, he or she might consider this a major win. Likewise, Spouse A might also consider it a major win to preserve the homestead for the children and have his or her full income to use for his or her own life choices.

An illustrative exercise is to go through this case as if representing one of the parties and do a Marital Balance Sheet, but make assumptions about the subjective values of the assets and debts, relative to what little the reader knows about the case. In other words, imagine representing Spouse B and place a subjective value on the homestead (e.g., $525,000 rather than $475,000), the mortgage (e.g., $380,000 instead of $343,000), and so on, based on what these actually mean subjectively to Spouse B. Do all of the assets and debts this way for each spouse. It will begin to become clear where the possible solutions lie, because this experiment makes the Nash equilibria more apparent.

There is a third stage of bargaining, the win-win-plus stage, and this case illustrates the potential benefit of this stage. If an accountant looked at the final "deal," he or she might have several suggestions for improving the deal for at least one of the parties, if not both, without harming either. This presumes that the accountant is familiar with the subjective values of both of the parties, because a small tax benefit in one game might not be "worth" the subjective payoff of a trade-off in a different game. Because there are multiple Nash equilibria in this game, however, an astute accountant might find other solutions that are better for at least one of the parties, if not for both of them.

Example 2

The parties have a nine-year marriage. Spouse A works in a closely held business, owned by Spouse A, which has blossomed in the past year into a major moneymaker. Spouse A meets with schools and procures materials, mostly of a decorative nature. Spouse A built the business largely with his or her own efforts, developing relationships with schools in a five-state region. The business has four employees, but Spouse A is the key employee for developing business relationships and sales. The employees do office and delivery work. The business is producing a projected annual profit of $420,000 and could grow. An initial appraisal suggests that this is a key-employee business, with a very low barrier to entry and with relatively little value separate from the cash flow. Spouse B is a school principal and earns $86,000/year. The parties have three children, who will live primarily with Spouse B, because of flexible work hours and Spouse B's travel schedule. The parties parent amicably, and Spouse A will have the children about 30 percent of the time. Separate from the business, the marital estate is approximately $480,000.

The starting point in the case is that Spouse A feels that the "business" is his or hers, the result of individual efforts, and does not wish to pay Spouse B for any value of the business (if it has any value) or share the income produced. Spouse A believes that Spouse B earns enough to be self-supporting.

Solution: Again, the first step, after the initial discovery steps, is to analyze the case, including a determination of the objective and subjective values and goals of the parties. Key to this case is the subjective value of child support to both of the parties. Spouse A is getting a great deal of access and flexibility that complements a career in relation to the children, while also ensuring that the children get the stability of a primary home, an available parent, and open access to Spouse A in a way that does not present any major obstacles to a very exciting career path. Spouse B gets the dominant parenting role, has sufficient income and, if constructed well (owns the home outright) and the freedom to live a comfortable lifestyle.

After analyzing the objective and subjective payoffs for both of the parties, the aim should be an arrangement in which Spouse A does not pay spousal support (this is the only normal form game with an obvious objective goal). So, where does the payoff value come for Spouse B? That depends on his or her goals and the ability of his or her attorney to explore them. If rather than simply pursuing support, the attorney asks questions like, "What would it take for you to agree to no spousal support?" then a deal is more likely to be made. For example, Spouse B, as a principal, has most of the summer off. He or she might be willing to forgo support if Spouse A agrees to finance a major vacation each summer for Spouse B and the children worth a certain amount. For example, assume that Spouse B, knowing Spouse A does not want to pay support, proposes that Spouse A finance a $3,000 vacation for him or her and the children each summer with input into what that vacation will be, with the focus being on their joint goal of enhancing the children's lives. Spouse A might find this acceptable because of the benefit to the children, especially if they know who paid for it (i.e., the children get to have the vacation with Spouse B, but know that the vacation is a gift from Spouse A). Or, they both might be able to agree to a higher-than-usual child support amount to enhance Spouse B's ability to take care of the children and be satisfied with the necessary flexibility. A lump-sum payment into a retirement account at a date certain in the future might be the perfect trade-off. Spouse A could offer to pay additional support to Spouse B for the children's expenses or pay those expenses directly on their behalf. Spouse A funding college accounts for the children might be a trade-off. It depends on the objective and subjective goals of the parties. The cooperative bargaining game encourages Spouse B to disclose willingness to forgo support if there is a payoff of equal or greater subjective value in the trade.

Thus, rather than simply telling Spouse A that he or she is going to have to pay some spousal support because this is the likely outcome of litigation and that the task at hand is to negotiate the amount, Game Theory bargaining allows for creative solutions that enhance the payoff structure for both parties and improves their subjective satisfaction with the deal.

Example 3

The parties have an eleven-year marriage and a marital estate worth about $465,000, most of which is the combination of net real estate value in the homestead and retirement accounts. Spouse A earns about $82,000/year, and Spouse B has been a stay-at-home parent. Employment opportunities are sparse for Spouse, who has an offer to move to Kansas City and work for family, at $72,000/year. Independent of the job, Spouse B would like to move closer to family, in part for the sake of the couple's two children, ages nine and six years.

The starting point in the case is that Spouse B wants to relocate to Kansas City, and Spouse A does not want to be away from the children.

However, Spouse A also wants Spouse B to work, recognizing that finding employment in the area where they live might be difficult, and if working in this area, is more likely to earn close to $45,000/year rather than the $72,000 to be earned in Kansas City. Thus, Spouse A has conflicting goals, each of which has an objective and a subjective value. For example, Spouse A wants to be near the children, but also agrees that the involvement of Spouse B's extended family would be good for the children, including the in-law's offer to provide after-school care, which has subjective value to him or her, never mind the objective value of child-care savings.

Solution: This case has some obvious simple and single games that have to be played separately from one another. Two of those games involve the residential schedule game if Spouse B does not move and the game if Spouse B does move. In other words, in order for the parties to compare what would happen if Spouse B does not move and what would happen if Spouse B does move, both options should be fully explored. Playing both of these games requires both players to explore their objective and subjective goals for the children. This game also illustrates the importance of having the outcome of one game, if it favors one of the parties, balance with the outcome of another game that favors the other party. By playing both games, the parties can examine the payoff value of both outcomes before making decisions about which game they are going to play. If they simply play the "I want to move" and the "I object" game before playing both "move" and "doesn't move" games, they do not have complete information; that is, they have not examined the outcome payoff values. In describing game theory earlier in this book, we illustrated two types of analyses: the normal form grid (e.g., the four-square box for the prisoner's dilemma) and the repeated form game tree. In the normal form game, with simultaneous choices, the rational choice for the players can be self-defeating. The advantage of the game tree is that by rolling back the choices, one can see which strategy optimizes outcomes.

If the spouses in this example play the relocation game in a four-square grid, which is "I want to move" and "I object," they are going to compete and make rational choices that might be self-defeating. By playing both the "move" and "doesn't move" games, they can roll back and see the optimal payoff outcomes for each of them. The "move" game presumes that Spouse B is moving and the bargaining process assumes this outcome. Then the parties bargain regarding the residential placement schedule and the division of property and income, again, presuming Spouse B moves. The "doesn't move" game presumes that Spouse B does not move and assumes this outcome and bargains on all of the issues. In a sense, both parties bargain for both games.

Playing this game in this way is undergirded by giving value to the subjective goals of the parties. For example, by playing both games, Spouse A can assign subjective value to the two types of involvement with the children. In the "move" game, he or she can look at the best schedule available for that game and give that subjective value. For example, he or she might highly value having two months of uninterrupted time with the children every summer, to organize the children's time without interference from Spouse B. In the "doesn't move" game, he or she can look at the type of involvement with the children he or she is likely to have and assign values. Spouse A can then add the other values for the other parts of the game, such as Spouse B earning nearly an identical income, resulting in no spousal support, and the availability of Spouse B's extended family as a support system for the children, what is commonly called the "social capital" for the family. By playing both games, Spouse A can better analyze his or her conflicting goals.

In addition, Spouse B can also better analyze his or her objective and subjective payoffs with each game. He or she might assign a great deal of value to being near extended family, but might reduce some of that value when assigning value to the children being away for two months in the summer or by taking on sole responsibility for schoolwork and medical care. Assume Spouse B raises the objection of not wanting to go two months each summer without contact with the children. The parties can now play the summer game. By making public each of their subjective values and goals, they might arrive at an agreement that Spouse B gets a one-week vacation with the children in the middle of the two months, but Spouse A gets to pick the week so that time with the children does not interrupt his or his ability to make plans for them. Working for family gives Spouse B this flexibility. Assume that Spouse A raises the objection that with the move, he or she will be too far removed from the children's schooling. The parties can now play the cooperative game of long-distance school involvement by Spouse

A. This could include an agreement that Spouse A is involved in school choices, gets a weekly package of schoolwork by the children, and will travel to Spouse B's area for parent-teacher conferences.

Similarly, the parties can continue to play the "doesn't move" game, refining and improving the payoff value to both parents. The point is that by maximizing the payoff value of both games, the parties are likely to have a convergence of expectations as to which game they should play in real life. This game also promotes cooperation as the best strategy rather than competition or even dirty fighting. If done carefully, we end up with "values" assigned to the outcomes of both games based on the long-term goals of the parties.

Although not yet playing the child support game, both parties are aware that the family, as a whole, will have more total family income to work with if Spouse B does move, which shapes part of their planning. Assume that the parties actually assign payoff points to each part of the two games and at the end of this exercise, Spouse B has a total of 380 points and Spouse A has a total of 290 points if there is a move, and the numbers total 180 for Spouse B and 320 for Spouse A if there is no move. Spouse B's numbers are substantially lower if there is no move, because she or he will have to work in a non-flexible, lower-paying, lower-satisfaction job, and both numbers are also lower because of the need for child care compared to grandparents caring for the children when Spouse B works. Spouse A's point total for the "moves" game are high because of the values assigns to blocks of time with the children compared to a blended schedule, the impact of the move on the children's involvement with extended family, including after-school care, the points assigned to the flexibility in Spouse B's work schedule in Kansas City, and the impact of her his or her income on the family wealth and Spouse A's support obligations.

Assume that after comparing the points, they decide to allow the move. They could now enter the win-win-plus phase of bargaining. Assume that they hire a psychologist with good knowledge of the social science research on relocation, and they present the parties' objective and subjective goals with regard to the residential schedule upon which they have agreed. The psychologist reviews the schedule and provides information on the risk factors to the children with the relocation and suggestions for improving the schedule to reduce those risks. This could improve the payoff value to one or both of the parties without diminishing the payoff value to either of them.

Example 4

Assume the same facts as in Example 1, except the parties signed a Prenuptial Agreement fifteen days before the wedding. The parties have a marriage of twelve years and have accumulated a total estate worth approximately $1.2 million. The net estate cannot be determined without knowing whether the Prenuptial Agreement will be enforced. The total marital/divisible estate includes the following, with certain items covered by the Prenuptial Agreement and thereby potentially excluded from the marital/divisible estate:

1. A homestead worth approximately $475,000 and a mortgage of $343,000, with a net value of $132,000. Payments are $3,100 (PITI) per month for twenty-two years of the remaining thirty-year loan.
2. $386,000 in a 401(k) (excluded as a marital asset by the Prenuptial Agreement).
3. $129,000 in a Roth IRA.
4. Vehicles worth $28,000 and $14,000, with a net value of about $7,000 and $9,000, respectively.
5. A boat worth about $82,000 and debt of about $50,000, with a net value of about $32,000.
6. A real estate limited partnership share with a current value of about $212,000, which is not liquid and is expected to terminate in six years, with a projected future value of $400,000 (excluded as a marital asset by the Prenuptial Agreement).
7. Twenty-five percent interest in a real estate partnership, where Spouse A works, and with a net value of about $280,000.
8. About $15,000 in household and other personal assets.

Spouse A earns $145,000 per year in commissions and about $12,000 in residuals from the insurance partnership. Spouse B earns $68,000 per year as a teacher. The parties have two children and have already agreed to an equal residential time schedule.

Solution: In this case, the first step is to review the prenuptial agreement to find out what were the objective and subjective goals for making the agreement and then assess the degree to which the agreement accomplished those goals. The next step is to analyze which of those goals are still relevant. For example, the 401(k) was excluded, because at the time they both considered this an issue of "fairness." In analyzing a Prenuptial Agreement, four legal standards are typically used:

1. Was the agreement voluntary when made?
2. Was there full financial disclosure when made?
3. Was the agreement fair at the time it was made?
4. Is the agreement fair now?

These standards are weighed relative to whatever state laws apply to allocations of property at the time of a divorce. We are assuming that the agreement was voluntary, that there was full financial disclosure, and that it was fair at the time the agreement was made. The question of fairness now is a subjective determination, and only makes sense in terms of the degree to which the agreement accomplished the spouses' original goals and continues to accomplish those same goals.

There is one more standard to include, and that is whether there were intervening variables during the marriage that could not have been anticipated. For our purposes, assume that the unanticipated variable it that Spouse A has been substantially more successful than either party anticipated. Assume that the 401(k) and the real estate partnership are both titled to Spouse A. In a traditional bargaining model, the focus would be on whether Spouse A can retain those as excluded property or whether Spouse B can have them classified as divisible marital property, or at least get some portion of the value in settlement. Spouse B no longer considers the Prenuptial Agreement "fair" because, in her mind, good fortune in terms of career has been more rewarding for Spouse A compared to Spouse B (e.g., there has been a local real estate boom). In other words, this game could be played as a normal form game promoting competition, litigation, and potentially high transaction costs.

Game theory bargaining views assets as resources at the time of the divorce, with the potential of helping the parties achieve their objective and subjective goals. At this point, therefore, the attorneys should focus on those goals, as they apply to the need for resources.

Both parties need a place to live, so there is the residential game. There is the children's lifestyle game to be played. There is the time-available-to-be-with-the-children game; the vacations-I-would-like-to-take game; and so on. As the parties map out their goals (payoffs), and play the games for those payoffs, the resources needed become more apparent. Spouse A might propose, for example, that the real estate partnership payout be used to accomplish three of the goals, two in favor of Spouse A and one in favor of Spouse B. Spouse A is viewing the payout, not as whether or not it should be his or shared, but as a tool to help both of them achieve their goals. Spouse B's portion might be smaller, but is thinking of it as a means to an end, not as an end in itself. In a sense, they signed a Prenuptial Agreement because they wanted to accomplish something. Using the same process, they are making divorce agreements to accomplish something, independent of what could have been a costly power struggle over whether or not the Prenuptial Agreement would be enforced.

This might rankle some people, because they get distracted by the question of "Is it fair to do it this way?" Determinations of "fair" when it comes to prenuptial agreements in dispute pare down to what a judge thinks is fair. Viewing resources as tools to be used to reach goals does not settle the issue of fairness; it simply makes the issue of fairness irrelevant. Spouse B might begin this process believing that he or she should get one-half of the value of an item that Spouse A thinks should be excluded. By bargaining with game theory principles, Spouse B's focus changes to whether or not he she will be able to accomplish goals. If able to accomplish stated goals, he or she might not care about receiving only 22 percent of that item's value. Spouse A might begin the process believing 100 percent is fair, but in the end, be very satisfied with 78 percent because both parties were able to put together a plan that accomplishes their long-term goals.

Summary

In the "difficult issues" examples above, we have focused on the process more than the content, particularly the process of identifying the objective and subjective goals of the parties and making those a public part of the negotiations. Making information public, perfect, complete, and, to the degree possible, verifiable enhances the bargaining process because of Bayes rule. Focusing first on cooperative bargaining to achieve win-win solutions, then on compromise bargaining when necessary, and finally on trying to add value to the settlement with win-win-plus bargaining, keeps the focus on achieving the objective and subjective goals of the parties, steering clear of making divorce a normal form zero-sum game, even when dealing with financial issues. Breaking the multiple games into single games and the mixed games into simple games facilitates the process by playing games that are easier to solve.

Financial Planning Issues: The Financial Planning Game

"Financial planning" in the context of Game Theory has a very specific meaning; namely, the use of procedures to resolve issues when the parties play repeated form games. This definition is also used in Chapters 2 and 4, so that there are parallel principles when discussing the Child Planning and the Financial Planning games.

In some divorces, only the Legal Game will be played, because no continuing obligations or need for future decisions exist. However, if there are continuing financial obligations or future financial decisions that call for the parties to negotiate procedures, such as modifications in spousal support or child support, then the Financial Planning Game is played.

Repeated Form Games Are Played in the Financial Planning Game
Child support is a good example of a simple repeated form game because it is played over and over, may be changed if support is adjusted, but always has an end point (e.g., the child reaching the age of majority or the child changing primary residential placement). Spousal support is another good example of a simple repeated form game because it is played over and over, may be changed if support is adjusted, but also, in many divorces, has an end point (i.e., death, remarriage, or the end of a set term of years).

Extensive repeated form games are played without an end point. For example, if the parties retain some financial connection to one another post-divorce with regard to a certain asset, such as owning recreational property that they wish to keep in the family. They might or might not establish a property partnership or some form or a trust, but they will need procedures for the management of the property and their separate uses of the property. The end point may be the death of the parties and the assumption of ownership by the children.

Each time the parties play a game within the repeated form game, it is called a "node." For example, one of the types of repeated form games played by parties would be maintenance/spousal support paid for an indefinite term. Each time the parties change the support (perhaps annually), they play a game, and once completed, that is a game node. The game is setting the support for the coming year.

Traditional divorce tends to focus on the normal form games and not so much on the repeated form games, although most attorneys do focus on repeated form games when it comes to simple issues like adjusting child support. If the game is keeping recreational property in the family, the parties might have to deal with unpredicted changes of circumstances (e.g., one of the parties temporarily loses a job), which might require playing the game again. If there are no repeated form games, the divorce is a normal form game only.

Example

If the spouses have no children, a short marriage, and comparable incomes and are only going to divide property, there is no repeated form game involved. It does not really matter if they hurt each other's feelings or let each other down, except for whatever sense of character and kindness they might have.

Team Conflict

A paradox between the games the spouses are playing and the games the attorneys are playing is that each attorney is playing a normal form game, at least with the other spouse. After the divorce is over, the attorney has little vested interest in how satisfied the other spouse is with the final agreements or outcome of litigation, other than perhaps reputation. However, the reputation game can go either way. The attorney might gain a better reputation in some communities to be a "winner" for one party, compared to being an attorney focused on the outcome for both parties. Mitigating this paradox is another matter. Engaging in cooperative bargaining is also self-serving and optimizes the payoff value to the represented spouse. Thus, engaging in cooperative bargaining often produces the best deal for the attorney's client.

Many times, attorneys might include some procedures (e.g., exchanging tax returns annually) in the Marital Settlement Agreement, but there may be other events that warrant a change in the financial support structure. One of the parties might wish to shift the structure of child support or spousal support because of a tax opportunity, or a party might want to buy a house and would do better if the other party bought out the remainder of the spousal support in a lump sum. Making these changes requires procedures.

Simply stated, the financial planning game involves designing a financial settlement in which there are repeated form games. When playing the financial planning game, the parties focus on setting up procedures; that is, when a decision comes up, what axioms will apply, *how* will the decision be made, and what steps will the parties need take in order to make decisions successfully?

Examples

There are a number of financial issues which are settled at the time of the divorce but that may involve repeated form games going forward. Here are a few examples:

1. Child support
2. Family support
3. Maintenance
4. Children's variable expenses
5. Use of a family credit card for child-related expenses
6. Use and sale of the family home
7. Filing a future joint tax return
8. Contempt
9. Enforcement of judgment

The common denominator regarding all of these issues is the possible need for financial planning and decision-making over time, including the need for procedures to assist the parties in making these future decisions.

Components of Procedure-Based Planning

As was discussed in Chapter 4 regarding the design of a residential schedule, etc., all procedure-based planning has three components: axioms, content, and actual procedure.

Axioms are the basic unchanging standards that will be applied to the decision and against which decisions are measured.

i. **Example:** In designing a spousal support schedule, one axiom might be that an effort will be made for the dependent spouse to be self-sufficient at the end of a specific term. Another axiom might be for one spouse to remain in the family home until the market improves, until the youngest child goes off to college, or the like. Thus, when various settlement alternatives are considered, some will be eliminated because they do not meet these axiomatic standards.

ii   In order to design an extensive repeated form game for determining any of these issues, therefore, the first task for the parties is not only to make a list of the axioms on which they will make their current decision, but also to set axiomatic standards with regard to making all future decisions. These axioms should be based on the parties' short- and long-term goals and priorities.

iii Having these axioms frames each node, thus providing some structure and reassurance to the parties.

Content is the fact situation at the time a decision is being made.

i.   At the time of a divorce, both parties might be working single parents living two miles from one another.

ii. Two years later, one of the parties might be remarried, one might have gotten a degree and moved to another community, etc. After another two years, both might be remarried, one may have another child and be a stay-at-home parent, one might be traveling for work, and so on.

Procedure is the agreed-upon manner in which a desired change in the existing agreement is handled. Procedures for cooperative parties will differ from procedures for non-cooperative parties.

Procedures for Cooperative Parties

Agreed-upon procedures at the time of the divorce can prevent re-litigation. What the procedure should be depends on the relative level of communication and cooperation between the parents. In a highly cooperative co-parenting relationship, the procedure might be a simple decision-making model, as is presented in chapter 7.

Procedures for Non-cooperative Parties

In a more problematic relationship, the following three steps are likely more formal:

1.   Exchanging proposals and the rationale for each proposal

2. Involving professionals to provide input and to help mediate disputes if any

3. Having the arbitrator make a final decision if the parties reach an impasse

If there is a mediator or arbitrator, the professional should be guided by the same axiomatic standards set at the time of the divorce, consider the content (current fact situation), and follow an agreed-upon procedure for making the decision.

On a practical level, attorneys or mediators can greatly assist the parties to a divorce by focusing primarily on developing a repeated form game procedure for making future decisions regarding support, the house, variable child-related expenses, and so on:

1. This involves establishing the *axioms,* based on the parties' long-term goals.

2. The *content* or current facts at the time of the decision are disclosed.

3. A *procedure* for making the decision is designed that can be used at the time of the divorce and also later as the facts change.

Thus, the Marital Settlement Agreement will not only include the agreement at the time of the divorce, but also the axioms and procedures for making changes or decisions in the future. Engaging in this process at the time of the divorce provides the parties with guided practice that they perhaps can repeat in the future without guidance.

One caveat: Parties in high-conflict relationships are unlikely to benefit from any approach that uses the procedures for cooperative parties. The goal in a high-conflict relationship is not to design procedures for continuing contact per se, but to design a settlement that provides for *disengagement* and *protects* the parties from future conduct problems and conflict.

Summary

THE FINANCIAL PLANNING GAME:

1. As we stated previously, divorcing spouses play two parallel games simultaneously relative to the financial aspects of their divorce—the Legal Game and the Financial Planning Game

2. There are two major financial tasks in the Legal Game: (1) property division and (2) support determinations.

3. In the Legal Game, attention is mainly on content. Most of the financial issues involve playing only the legal game, because once the issue is resolved, the agreements become part of the final Marital Settlement Agreement and Judgment of Divorce, where the issue is final and not modifiable in the future. These are the Normal Form Games played as a goal-based planning process rather than a strictly competitive normal form game. .

4. There are some financial issues that may call for the divorcing spouses to play the Financial Planning Game. These issues, while settled at the time of the divorce, involve repeated form games. In the Financial Planning Game, attention is on procedures, such as conditions for modifications, exchanges of tax returns, or meeting with experts.

5. It is important to remember that parties who have continuing repeated form games to play should begin to play the Financial Planning Game at the time of separation. Often, people with repeated form games have children involved, and developing cooperative bargaining habits with regard to money often has the positive effect of supporting a cooperative relationship with regard to the children. While it is difficult to play the Financial Planning Game well shortly after a separation, parties will be grateful down the road if and when they at least start the process.

6. Game Theory principles also apply to the extensive repeated form game of child planning that will last for the rest of the parents' lives.

7. The Legal Game is not the goal. It is the means by which parties try to accomplish long-term goals.

8. When designing both the settlement of the property and support issues, and in designing procedures for any repeated form games facing the parties, a final step is to measure the payoff packages against the Five E's axiomatic standards. Is the package educated, equitable, effective, equilibrant, and envy free? If the package does not meet these standards, it will (in most cases) be worth revisiting issues and bargaining again. Sometimes attorneys see a settlement as "fragile" and are

frightened of the whole settlement coming apart if revisited. However, if the settlement is fragile, perhaps it should come apart. Only when both spouses can look at a financial settlement and agree that it meets the Five E's standards is it no longer fragile. The parties can then walk away from the settlement feeling the losses involved, but knowing that their payoff package is as good as could be accomplished within the limits of the fact situation.

CHAPTER 6

Game Theory: Advanced Topics

In earlier chapters, we introduced basic game theory principles that are sufficient for an attorney, mediator, or parties to apply the bargaining model we are proposing. This model is applied to children and finances in chapters 4 and 5, respectively. Chapter 6 assumes a familiarity with the game theory principles in this book and provides additional tips.

Definition of a Game

A game is defined by its four ingredients:
- players
- rules
- payoffs
- choices/strategies

Players: Multiple Players; Multiple Games

As others have pointed out, the divorce game is really a game played among a number of players, depending on how complex the case. In *Beyond Winning*, Mnookin, Peppet, and Tulumello (The Belknap Press of Harvard University, 2001), for example, identify six games (which they call the six relationships) actually being played, when one simply includes the two parties and the two attorneys: client-client, attorney-attorney, attorney-client, attorney-client, attorney-other party, and attorney-other party. When one adds a mediator, child specialist, or a CPA on one or both sides, we can see how complex this can become.

Each of the parties is playing a game with one another, and this is the primary game being played. The attorneys are also playing a game with one another. In most communities, the number of attorneys who specialize in family law is relatively small, and most of them know each other, some very well. They likely will have had cases with one another in the past, might well be good friends or perhaps competitive foes, likely will have attended conferences together, learned the same material, have reputations in the professional community, and perhaps even practiced together in the past. They are playing a game with one another with its own rules and payoff structures, about which the parties might know little or nothing. Like the spouse-spouse game, the behavior, choices, and strategies of the attorneys in this game will be largely controlled by the rules and payoff structure for them.

There is another player in the divorce game who is often little more than a specter early in the case, the judge. The attorneys most likely know the judge and his or her inclinations on issues, and because all bargaining in the legal system is generally done "in the shadow of the law," this will to some extent shape the attorneys' choices and strategies.

Typically, attorneys measure agreements reached through bargaining (or mediation) against what would likely happen if the issue were litigated. The judge might also be the type who plays a much more active role in the process, which changes the game completely.

Other games are being played if in mediation. In theory, the mediator is "guardian of the process" rather than someone who takes sides with either party on any issue. In practice, many mediators will slip into evaluative mediation and attempt to sway the parties in a particular direction. For example, if there is administration pressure to settle cases, the mediator is playing a game with his or her organization. The mediator is also likely familiar with social science research that suggests that certain residential placement plans are better or worse for children and might incorporate this information into the mediation, putting pressure on one or both of the parents to move in a particular direction. These games have their own payoff structure, especially if the parties have attorneys either in the background or actively playing a role in the mediation process. This can become even more complex if the mediator has contracted for "med-arb," which typically means that the mediator will attempt to mediate the issues, but in the end, if the dispute is unresolved, will issue an arbitration opinion that is either binding or non-binding. The behavior, choices, and strategies of parties in med-arb versus mediation are completely different, because the rules and payoff structure are different.

The point is that in any given divorce, there are at least four or five players, and in some, even more. These games are interrelated and, to some extent, affect the spouse-spouse game.

The attorneys or mediator should not ignore these games. The professional can easily consider game theory principles when dealing with another professional. A mediator, for example, can as easily respond to an attorney as to a party by separating a mixed game into a simple game. Attorneys can do the same with one another. Bayes rule works as well when updating beliefs about opposing counsel or a judge as when working to better understand the parties. Understanding the objective and subjective goals of the professionals could be as important as understanding those of the clients.

Rules

Information Management with the Client

In family law, the "rules" are often known to the attorney and not to the client. Thus, the client is often playing a game of incomplete information, relying on the attorney to know and guide the client through the game without the client really knowing the rules.

If the attorney manages information well and educates the client regarding the hidden rules of the game (e.g., the judge tends to be very punitive toward spouses who have had an affair), the client will be a better team player with the attorney.

Payoffs

Subgames and Nodes

"Nodes" are an important concept in game theory because divorce is rarely played in an all-or-nothing manner where all of the payoffs are received at once. It is rare that one party will propose an entire marital settlement agreement to the other party and have it accepted *en todo*.

An attorney can apply the basic principles of game theory and respond to a multiple mixed game with a focus on one simple single game.

For example, the response to "My client wants a 50/50 residential schedule" could be, "My client would like to begin with holidays." This is a "node" in game theory. The attorney can then play the next simple single game, another node. Thus, the process is shifted to a pattern of negotiation that slowly builds a payoff structure, the MSA.

Let us consider a strategy for dealing specifically with nodes, a strategy which has an unusual and unexpected effect on players in game theory research. At each node, a subgame has been completed, and the payoff structure will often favor one player over another. In parlor games, each node has a value that is accumulated into a total. Almost every card game, for example, keeps track after every hand of points, chips, or some form of counting method. The players, therefore, know "where they stand" after each subgame relative to the total collection of subgames. What if two players in a divorce did this? What if the parties kept some kind of score for each subgame? What would be the effect?

Game theory research provides us with a surprising answer to these questions. In one example study, subjects were divided into two groups. In one group (the "salary" group), the subjects went through a series of aversive experiences and were told at the beginning that they would be paid a certain fixed amount of money for the entire experiment, that is a salary for participating in the study. In the second group (the "rating" group), the subjects went through exactly the same aversive experiences but were told that they would be paid according to how aversive they rated the experience. In other words, these subjects did not know how much they would earn, but at the end of each experience were able to rate the experience on a scale of 1 to 10 as to how aversive it was. They were told that the more aversive they rated the experience, the more money they would receive. The experimenters had pre-calculated how much would be paid out, but the subjects did not know this. For example, if the subject rated the first experience as a 2, they were paid $3. If they rated it an 8, they were paid $6. The amount the subjects were paid was pre-determined by the experimenters. Both the salary group and the rating group received the same total pay for the experiment; the only difference was the process of how they were paid.

The first surprising finding was that the subjects in the rating group took their responsibility for rating the experience very seriously and appear to have been very honest. This was measured by comparing the ratings across subjects, which found that most of the subjects rated the experiences very similarly. This seems counterintuitive because the subjects would be paid more money if they rated the experience higher in averseness, but there is another game being played here—called the "trust game." The subjective payoff for being honest, when trusted, was more important than the money. Later we will develop the concept of and differentiate between the "selfish game" and the "altruistic game." In this experiment, the subjects were playing the altruistic game, because the trust of the experimenter was a more important payoff than the money. If the subjects had played the selfish game, they would have artificially ranked each experience as more aversive than it was.

The second interesting finding was reflected in the post-experiment questionnaire administered to both groups. The total payoffs were exactly the same for both groups. The experimenters had predetermined the total amount that would be paid to the "rating" subjects so that it would equal the amount paid to the "salary" group. Both groups experienced the same level of aversive experience, and both were paid exactly the same; only the manner in which they were paid differed.

The key questions in the questionnaire had to do with how "fair" the subjects felt treated, how "worth it" it was to participate given how aversive were the experiences relative to the money received, and other similar items. The "salary" group on the whole did not feel that they were treated fairly, felt they were misled about how aversive the experience would be, did not think it was worth it, and reported that had they known at the beginning what they knew at the end, they would not have participated. They were disgruntled participants!

The "rating" group provided exactly the opposite responses, feeling that the experience was fair, that they felt it was worth it, and that they would participate again, knowing what they knew at the end. Both went through the exact same experiences, and both were paid the exact same amount of money. Only their internal experience of the fairness and value of playing the game (the experiment) were different. Other game theory experiments have produced similar findings.

What was being measured was the value of having a payoff value at the nodes and the degree of participation of the subjects in determining the value of that payoff. If we extrapolate to a divorce, what might we expect if spouses, at the conclusion of each subgame (e.g., the end of determining the holiday schedule), the parties rated the outcome (his and her payoff structure) on a scale of 1 to 100. If the cooperative bargaining portion went well, we might expect both to rate it reasonably high, but also we might find a difference in their ratings (e.g., Spouse A might rate the Christmas holiday schedule game as a 68 and Spouse B might rate it as an 84). If these were made public to one another, there might be a sense of proportion as the divorcing spouses entered into the next game and node. Most likely, Spouse B with the 84 will subjectively understand that Spouse A made a little more sacrifice and might be inclined to do the same on another game; that is, Spouse B might be more inclined to give in a little more to balance the scale. If at the completion of all the nodes, the total scores for each party were relatively similar, the parties might conclude that the total divorce game had an equitable payoff structure. Without that, one or both might feel shorted because of what happened in a couple of the last or key subgames.

The game theory experiment described above teaches us that while the outcome for two groups in terms of payoff structure can be exactly the same and the game that they play can be exactly the same, the subjective experience can be substantially different depending on how the game is played—that is, with a slight variation in the rules. We also note that one set of rules promoted the altruistic and trust strategies while the other promoted selfishness and dissatisfaction.

In this respect, game theory makes use of another area of mathematics called "utility theory." Every payoff has a "utile," i.e., value to the player, a value which has an *objective value* and a *subjective value*. Each type of value theoretically can be assigned an ordinal value, if somewhat arbitrary, and can be used to determine preferred outcomes to the game. Interestingly, research on successful marriages asserts the surprising finding that while the spouses might have a fair amount of success resolving some disagreements, there are times when one of the spouses simply gives in. Who gives in is most often the result of how much subjective value each of the spouses ascribes to the outcome. In a sense, successful spouses sense how important an outcome is to each of them and the person to whom the outcome is more important "wins."

Subjective values are critical considerations in game theory, and this is especially true in family law, where subjective values are often a more important consideration than objective values. Subjective values can be difficult to detect, even those of one's own client, without careful inquiry. The solution for objective values can be simple; the solution when adding in subjective values can be complex. This is particularly true in divorce, especially when the *psychological importance of prevailing* is involved!

Thoroughly exploring and in some instances quantifying the subjective values his or her client assigns to payoffs in the divorce game might prevent later conflicts and disputes and maximize the value of the payoffs for his or her client.

Summary

A Marital Settlement Agreement states the entire payoff structure of the divorce, but is comprised of many subgames, each with a game node with its own payoff structure. Subgames are best played one at a time. If attention is paid to the parties' objective and subjective goals, and bargaining is done carefully and thoughtfully, each party could rate the outcome of each subgame, share those values, and thereby positively affect future subgames and also their experience of the process. Rating each subgame might be as simple as asking both parties, at the completion of a game node, to rank their satisfaction with the outcome on a scale of 1 to 100. If a party ranks one node as 15, but later another node as 93, even though deeply dissatisfied with the first, the balance later might leave the party with an overall positive impression of the outcome.

Extrapolating from this, we suggest that if the divorce game was played with different rules, all of which can be informal without changing basic legislative or jurisdictional rules, the subjective experience of the parties could be different, and decisions and strategies that promote satisfaction, trust, and altruism could be incentivized.

Strategies/Decisions

Preferences in Game Theory

Formal game theory emphasizes the importance of the players' "preferences" as a factor to consider. In fact, the choices made by the parties make no sense unless their "preferred" outcome is understood. For example, assume Spouse B prefers flexibility in a schedule. Spouse A agrees with this. However, Spouse B's attorney "prefers" to win the legal battle and advises the Spouse B not to give Spouse A any additional time with the child because this could disadvantage the legal game. Because of the attorney's preference, Spouse B (trusting the guidance of the attorney) refuses flexibility. Facing this rigidity, Spouse A no longer agrees to Spouse B's preferred residential schedule and an expensive custody dispute follows. In other words, the preferences of the parties coincided nicely, but the preference of one attorney disrupted settlement because the attorney believed he or she was promoting her client's interests.

Chance in Game Theory

Most games have some element of chance involved that might affect the outcomes. Not all outcomes are solely the result of the choices the players make. Some games are mostly chance, and some are dominated by decisions and strategies. Divorce is a mix of the two. Probability theory in mathematics deals with chance. In divorce, the element of chance might include the following:

- Which judge is assigned to the case might be an element of chance.
- The initial choice of attorneys by the parties has elements of chance. One might be a troublemaker; the other might be an uncreative bargainer. The attorneys might be friends who work well with one another, or they might have a history of conflict with each other.
- Who is chosen to do a custody study or to act as a guardian *ad litem* might have an element of chance to it.
- Who is chosen to perform an appraisal or some other financial calculation might have an element of chance, and the person is likely relying on chance as part of the calculation (e.g., a retirement account valuation is dependent on actuarial tables with regard to when someone might die).

Many lawyers are familiar with these chance issues and even employ some game theory games to deal with it. For example, if the attorneys agree that each will submit three names of a professional for some function and a third party will pick one, this is a variation on "cut the cake" game, in which player 1 cuts the cake and player 2 gets first pick of pieces. Another common game is to have two appraisals with a prior agreement (axiom) to pick a number exactly one-half of the difference between the two.

One of the ways in which parties benefit from having attorneys is that the attorneys might have developed good strategies for dealing with the chance events in the divorce process.

Summary—Definition of a Game

There are actually many players involved in parallel games during the divorce of one set of spouses. By taking the time to assess the games and payoffs involved for all of the players, a skill set for better negotiating can be developed. Careful management of information can greatly affect outcomes, and paying close attention to the subgames and payoff nodes can help construct an ideal agreement. Finally, understanding the real preferences of the clients, recognizing and dealing with the chance issues in a divorce, and understanding mixed strategies can increase bargaining effectiveness, not only within a case but also across cases.

Game Theory Principles

Game Theory Focuses on a Solution

While professionals might "enjoy" the process of a divorce, the parties rarely do and want it to be over. Divorce is a solution to marital problems, or at least it should be. Therefore, the goals of parties who engage the services of attorneys or mediators include completing the divorce process, oftentimes the sooner the better. They want a "solution."

The central focus of game theory is the "solution" to the game. In this sense, game theory fits hand in glove with the goals of the parties. Parties usually have a *compatibility of interests* and a *conflict of interests*. There is only a "dispute" if there is a *true* conflict between the interests of the parties, not the appearance of one.

The best "solution" will be one that maximizes the utility value of the payoffs, the settlement, for both of the parties. This involves bargaining. However, bargaining between rational players only makes sense if there is some chance of improving the payoff for at least one player. For example, if player A owns a winning lottery ticket, there is no reason for him or her to bargain with player B for a share in the ownership of the ticket. The *status quo* is that player A is the winner, who gains nothing by giving a share of the winnings to another player.

This concept of "status quo" is critical to the solutions of game theory, underpinning the theories for which Nobel Prizes have been won. Shapley identified the status quo as the solution to one-half of the game. His is a complex mathematical concept, but a simple one in family law. Shapley calculates that the worst a person can do in a reasonable game is the status quo. In family law, this is the worst outcome a person can expect reasonably in court. For example, if given a particular jurisdiction, a set of case facts, and the judge involved, Spouse A can expect at least five of fourteen days with the children in a residential schedule, his status quo is 5/14. If Spouse B can expect to do no worse than 50/50, then his or her status quo is 7/14. The parties will only bargain if Spouse A expects that he or she might improve from 5/14 and Spouse B expects that he or she might improve from 7/14. Similarly, Spouse A might expect to pay a maximum of $800 per month in spousal support, his or her status quo, and Spouse B might expect no less than $300 per month, his or her status quo. They will only bargain if they both expect that they might do better. If Spouse B is perfectly satisfied with $300, he or she has no incentive to bargain. Spouse B will simply put the issue before the court and do at least as well as he or she wants—and perhaps better. Family law attorneys are generally familiar with this concept.

What Nash added was two factors: the threat factor and the cooperative bargaining factor. His status quo is not a static feature and is influenced in real life, through his famous four theorems, by the threat strategy and the cooperative bargaining strategy. The *threat strategy* is obvious. Given that all values have subjective value, one party in a bargaining situation might have more to lose than the other. For example, assume that Spouse A in our 5/14 versus 7/14 scenario above has deep pockets and Spouse B does not. Spouse B might calculate that while he or she might prevail at 6/14 or 7/14, his or her quality of life will be so diminished by the transaction costs that he or she concedes. Likewise, in our spousal support case, the transaction costs might dissuade one of the parties from seeking an outcome in court. If Spouse A spends $14,000 in transaction costs and receives a spousal support order of $600, he or she has improved on his or her status quo of $800, but it will take five years to recoup the transaction costs (without considering the present and future values of these two sets of numbers).

Far more interesting, however, is Nash's *cooperative bargaining concept*. We take this for granted today in many aspects of our lives. For example, if there are four competing coffee shops, historically they would seek locations where they could dominate. Each would look for a location away from the others but close to potential customers. After Nash's concepts filtered into the business world, however, the coffee shops were likely to locate on the four corners of the same intersection. This seems counterintuitive, but by doing so, they increase the total amount of business for all of them. They then compete for market share on the same intersection. All of them gain by making the intersection a coffee haven. This is why fast-food restaurants are almost always clustered. Nash saw the two sides of the same coin; that is, that all successful negotiation outcomes between self-interested parties include a cooperative aspect and a competitive aspect. In the cooperative aspect, the interests of all are enhanced; in the competitive aspect, each party seeks personal gain at the loss of others.

Raifa crystallized this concept and proposed that in non-zero-sum games, there is a cooperative component and a competitive component (we call this the compromise component). His contribution is that rational players will bargain first in a way as to arrive at a payoff which is jointly the largest. After assuring themselves of the maximum joint payoff, they can then compete for the largest possible shares of the payoff. Cooperative bargaining is the first phase in the game theory model as a means of reaching the objective and subjective goals of the parties.

R. B. Braithwaite has a similar idea, although he posited that parties should solve the zero-sum game first before moving on to the non-zero-sum games; that is, determine the percentage of the pot that each will receive, and then engage in the cooperative bargaining process. In this approach to a game, the parties decide on how to split the pot and then bargain to grow the pot to its largest size. We have interpolated this solution concept in the win-win-plus bargaining phase, the final phase of bargaining in which the parties have already agreed on a payoff structure (the MSA), but then attempt to improve the payoff for both of them, or at least one of them without diminishing the payoff for the other party.

In a divorce game, Braithwaite's principle could work something like this. The parties decide that they will assign points to the subjective value of all of the property and income available for support and will have an equal division. For example, the estimated market value of each car could be changed by a modifier based on the subjective value of the cars to both of both parties. Thus a car preferred by one party but about which the other party is indifferent worth $5,000 at market might be modified to be worth $6,000. The parties would continue in this process until all of the marital property has been modified by the subjective values. Then the parties would divide the modified values of the property equally. In this way, the parties decided on the zero-sum game first, the percentage of the split, and then engaged in a cooperative bargaining process to enhance the payoff value to each of them.

Returning to our opening principle, the goal of parties is to have divorce be a *solution*. Game theory provides a means of achieving a solution that maximizes the payoff value to both parties. Although elements of game theory bargaining can be tedious and time consuming, such as determining the subjective values and goals of the parties, the approach very quickly begins to provide the parties with solutions. As each of the game nodes produce subgame payoffs of value to both parties, their experience of the game becomes increasingly positive. As posited earlier, this can be enhanced by having the parties rate the payoff for each subgame and share those ratings with one another. If their best decisions and strategies in such a game promote trust and altruism, their chances at ending the process with satisfaction and a workable co-parenting relationship are improved.

Summary

GAME THEORY BARGAINING— THREE PHASES OF BARGAINING:

The Game Theory bargaining model combines solution concepts into the three phases of bargaining:

1. Cooperative Bargaining, in which the parties first try to maximize the value of the payoffs for both of them (GROWING THE POT)
2. Compromise Bargaining, in which the parties determine relative shares of the payoffs (SPLITTING THE POT)
3. Win-win-plus Bargaining, in which the parties try to improve the value of the payoff (GROWING THE TWO POTS)

Are Players Rational?

Whether or not divorcing parties are rational players in the divorce game is an important question. Following are some factors to consider in understanding whether or not divorcing spouses are rational players:

Brain Stem Thinking

Divorcing spouses are likely going through high levels of emotion that might cloud their judgment at the time of the separation. These emotions include anger, guilt, shame, sadness, and fear. When human beings are in situations of very high emotions, the brain will often trigger a survival mechanism in the central brain. The limbic system in the brain plays a key role in the modulation of emotional experience and most of the time works with the cortex, the higher centers of the brain, to interpret situations that arouse emotion and to plan responses. However, when the limbic system becomes overloaded, it switches from interacting with the cortex to interacting with the brain stem, wherein lay primitive instinctual responses. Most familiar of those responses are fight/flight/freeze, which are instinctual reactions to a perceived threat. We see these in divorcing spouses in their impulses to engage in conflict, even become physical, or to avoid one another like the plague. However, there are other features of the brain stem that play a role in how rational divorcing spouses are. Preening occurs in the brain stem, which can account for how incredibly picky spouses can be. Hypervigilance occurs in the brain stem (i.e., a heightened lookout for danger), which helps explain how touchy and paranoid divorcing spouses can sometimes seem. Mating and nesting are in the brain stem, which can account for how divorcing spouses will sometimes recklessly throw themselves into new romantic relationships, sometimes setting up house (nesting) within weeks or months of separating from a long-standing marriage. Perhaps the most important feature of the brain stem for our purposes is that it cannot tell time; it is all about the here and now. Thus, we see divorcing spouses making decisions that might make sense in the short term but that in the long term are self-defeating. The brain stem does not think long term.

Attorneys and mediators are not in states of high emotion, and thus they can lend their egos to their clients and as a team create a "rational player." The attorney can help calm the client, provide protections, provide reassuring information about the future, make the "threats" more realistic, advise the client against self-defeating strategies and choices, and think long term on behalf of the client.

Subjective Value in the Payoff Structure

Players sometimes appear irrational, but in fact are playing the game as rational players, making choices that maximize the potential payoffs. These players appear irrational because the subjective payoff values are not always obvious. Bayes rule can increasingly reveal the subjective payoff values of the other player, making it possible to adjust the bargaining strategy to better reach an optimal solution. Such a solution is not possible without including the subjective value of payoffs. However, it is important to remember that the appearance of irrational behavior does not necessarily mean that it is irrational. For example, a spouse might be willing to spend $300 on transaction costs to get a Christmas ornament worth $10 because of the subjective value of the ornament.

Narcissism versus Altruism

The dimension of Narcissism at one end of a continuum and Altruism at the other end of the continuum plays a key role in understanding how players can be rational even when they do not appear to be behaving this way. Healthy human functioning stems from a balance of self-interest (narcissism) and interest in others (altruism). Thus, a healthy divorce is one in which the parties have a balance of self-interest and interest in the other spouse. The structure of traditional bargaining promotes self-interest, having attorneys litigate solely on behalf of his or her client's positions.

Game theory assumes that players are rational; that is, are completely selfish. Narcissism, for our purposes, is pure self-interest. We earlier described a game called the "ultimatum game" that has been the subject of a fair amount of research. The game is quite simple: player A proposes to player B a division of a sum of money (e.g., $10.00); player B accepts the proposal, and the sum is split per the proposal or player B rejects the proposal, and neither player receives any money. The rational move for player A is to propose that A receives $9.99 and B receives $0.01, and the rational move for B is to accept. In this play, A is maximizing the payoff to A, while still offering a sufficient amount of money to B to make it worthwhile for B to accept. B accepts, because $0.01 is better than nothing.

However, if this game is actually played, players rarely follow this strategy. There are multiple reasons, including a sense of fairness on the part of both players. If the rule of the game is changed, and player A simply decides on a split and player B has no choice, the most rational play for A is to take the whole $10.00, but this too rarely happens in real experiments. In other words, something else comes into play so that players in real life rarely play as purely rational, if defined as purely narcissistic.

At the other end of the continuum is altruism, which for our purposes, we shall define as working toward maximum value for the other player, completely ignoring self-interest. In the "ultimatum game," for example, a purely altruistic player A would offer the $10.00

to player B. However, this too rarely happens in experiments with real people. What does tend to happen in real life is that players fall somewhere on the continuum—between pure narcissism and pure altruism. Player A, with a pure balance between narcissism and altruism in the ultimatum game, might propose an equal split of $5.00 each. This perfectly balances self-interest (narcissism) and other-interest (altruism).

This continuum is not always a definition of the player; that is, the game is not always shaped by the combination of narcissism and altruism in the player. Some games often shape whether the strategies *should be* narcissistic or altruistic. For example, in a tennis match, pure narcissism is the best strategy for both players, even if the players have generally very altruistic attitudes toward one another. Good friends can be purely self-interested in such a game and enjoy the competition. The structure of some games (i.e., the combination of rules and payoffs) better promote altruism as a strategy. For example, players on a team in basketball have a better chance of winning if they play with one another in an altruistic manner. Thus, people who neither like nor respect each other as people can work very well together on a team because altruism is in one's self-interest. In the ultimatum game, player A might offer a $6.00/$4.00 split, both for narcissistic and altruistic reasons. Player A might assume that it would be a better outcome if both players walked away with money. However, player A might also fear that if too little is offered to player B, B will reject the offer and A will get nothing. Therefore, the ultimatum game is structured to promote both narcissism and altruism, and the results of research are consistent with and supportive of this conclusion.

Thus, the narcissism versus altruism dimension is affected by the player and by the structure of the game. A highly narcissistic player, for example, might play even basketball in a self-defeating manner by failing to be altruistic (e.g., taking a low-percentage shot, for the glory, rather than passing to a player who has a better shot). Likewise, a highly altruistic player might play tennis in a self-defeating manner (e.g., serving more softly to give the other player a chance to stay in the game). One game, like tennis, might pressure a highly altruistic player to play the game in a highly narcissistic manner (e.g., in a club tournament), while another game, like basketball, might pressure a highly narcissistic player to play the game in a more altruistic manner (e.g., getting into the playoffs means higher bonuses).

In the divorce game, the players come to the table with personality traits falling somewhere on the narcissism versus altruism continuum, and the structure of the divorce game might pressure each of them to play the game in a more narcissistic or altruistic manner. If an attorney pressures his or her client to make proposals solely on the basis of the client's preferences, that attorney is promoting a narcissistic game. The other spouse is likely to respond narcissistically. If the attorney probes to find out the other spouse's objective and subjective goals and pressures his or her client to include those in proposals, the attorney is promoting a balanced narcissistic and altruistic game.

A narcissistic player believes that he or she is special—that is, that the law and likely outcomes in a trial do not apply to him or her, that he or she deserves a positive outcome and will do what is necessary to achieve that outcome, independent of the effects on others (low empathy), that personal status is on the line, and that anything short of a complete win is a failure, making compromise extremely difficult. If both parties are narcissistic, the divorce is likely to include a fair amount of conflict and a great many legal disputes.

The altruistic player is likely to want to settle the case in a manner that meets the needs and interests of the others involved, including and perhaps especially the children in the family, but also the other spouse. What is important to note in the altruistic player is that the subjective value of the payoffs is syntonic with an altruistic view of the world. An altruistic player, therefore, will see a good outcome for others as the highest payoff value and thus is likely to look like the most irrational of all players.

A legal game set up to appear as a zero-sum game establishes incentives for playing the game in a narcissistic manner.

In reality, however, the best outcomes are likely to be those in which both players have a balance of narcissism and altruism. Altruism might be fine if one is a missionary in Africa, but it is self-defeating in divorce and often lowers the payoff value for the other player. An optimal solution can only be achieved when narcissism and altruism are balanced. The mother in a case, for example, might want the children to live with her most of the time and for the father to see them every other weekend. An altruistic father might agree, not only because he views this as a good outcome for the mother, but also because he feels the arrangement will produce much less stress in the children's lives and will give them the stability of living in just one home, with all of the advantages of doing so. The father might even see the mother as the more competent parent. However, is this really the best possible outcome for the mother and the children in the long term?

Being a single parent has long been known to be a high-stress experience for mothers, for the children, and for the relationship between the children and their mother. Boys, especially, who are raised almost exclusively by a mother have well-documented and substantial adjustment problems and poor relationships with their mother. Social science research tells us that children do better if they have strong bonds and an active involvement with their father. Thus, the purely altruistic solution is actually worse when compared to having a balance of altruism and narcissism.

Inferring that there is something wrong with considering child support when designing a schedule is a mistake. Considering the financial implications of decisions is part of the narcissistic/altruistic balance. Thus, parents considering various residential schedule outcomes should be considering the financial implications and openly discussing them without negatively judging the other for doing so.

In a financial example, an altruistic Spouse A might cede most of the property and a substantial portion of the income to make sure that Spouse B has a good life and that the children enjoy a financially stable situation. However, if Spouse A is unable to provide a reasonably good setting for the children to spend time with him or her, or is so stressed keeping up with the finances that he or she is not a good support system for Spouse B and the children, has anyone really gained?

The game theory bargaining model in large part attempts to establish a game structure that promotes a balance between narcissism and altruism by seeking solutions that maximize the benefit to both parties as much as possible. Even a purely narcissistic player might be more amenable to cooperative bargaining, for example, if the ultimate payoff value increases by doing so.

Business provides good models for this in what is called "coopetition." The concept behind coopetition is that two purely self-interested businesses can increase profits for both by cooperating and competing at the same time. Earlier, we used the example of coffee businesses and fast-food restaurants. Two coffee shops will do better to locate near one another, because this increases the market size, and then each business competes for market share of a larger market rather than locating a distance from one another.

A price war between two companies is another example. By having a price war, two companies are competing, but at the same time they are both gaining market share from all of the other companies that sell the same product. A price war between Wal-Mart and Amazon. com, for example, on the price of new hardcover books is vicious competition between them, in which they might both lose money in the short term, but they both pull business away from all of the other bookstores, and so in the long term together might have increased their total market share. Here again we see the importance of narcissism in balance with altruism.

Most people will say they admire altruistic players, although some might think of them as chumps, and most people find narcissistic players distasteful. In the divorce game, both will play a role in the game. By structuring the game to promote a balance of narcissism and altruism, game theory bargaining strives to achieve best outcomes for both parties.

Bargaining Basics

Multiple Games in Divorce

Applying Game Theory principles, we define two child-related games and two financial-related games. In Chapter 2, we described these games as Legal and Planning games. Traditional approaches to divorce tend to focus on the Legal Games.

In families with children, when the emphasis is on the legal game, it is at a cost to children. Residential schedules are substantially less predictive of outcomes for children than the co-parenting relationship, what we call the child planning game. In fact, the child planning game has more influence on the experience of children and the outcomes for those children than any other factor in divorce. A high-functioning co-parenting relationship will likely produce well-adjusted children, no matter what residential schedule is in place, whereas a poorly functioning co-parenting relationship will likely lead to adjustment problems, again no matter what the residential schedule might be.

Parents play both the legal and the child planning games, independent of what attorneys or mediators do. They will play the child planning game well or poorly or somewhere in between, but they will play it.

THE GAMES PARTIES PLAY:

1. Applying Game Theory principles, we define two child-related games and two financial-related games.
2. In Chapter 2, 3 and 4, we described these games as Legal and Planning Games.
3. Traditional approaches to divorce tend to focus on the Legal Games. In families with children, when the emphasis is on the legal game, it is at a cost to children.
4. The Child Planning Game has more influence on the experience of children and the outcomes for those children than any other factor in divorce. Residential schedules are substantially less predictive of outcomes for children than the co-parenting relationship
5. A high-functioning co-parenting relationship will likely produce well-adjusted children, no matter what residential schedule is in place, whereas a poorly functioning co-parenting relationship will likely lead to adjustment problems, again no matter what the residential schedule might be.
6. Parents play both the Legal and the Child Planning Games, independent of what attorneys or mediators do. They will play the Child Planning Game well or poorly or somewhere in between, but they will play it.
7. Likewise, when the focus is on the financial legal game and there is a continuing financial relationship between the parties (e.g., adjustable child support), outcomes tend to be inferior. The parties will play the financial planning game at different nodes and by establishing procedures for doing so, attorneys help their clients play the planning game well.

Normal Form and Repeated Form Games; Simultaneous and Sequential Move Games

There are two dimensions to games that determine their type. One is whether the game is a simultaneous move game or a sequential move game. In a "simultaneous move game," both players must make a move without knowing the choice of the other party. In a "sequential move game," players take turns making moves.

The second dimension defining the type of analysis appropriate to the game is whether the game is a onetime game, that is a "normal form" game (see definitions), or is a game that will be repeated to an end point, called an "repeated form" game.

Normal form games focus on the content of the issue (e.g., a valuation), whereas repeated form games focus on procedures for making future decisions. Each node in a repeated form game not only has a payoff but also has a payoff structure over time.

The flexibility game parents play is an example of a positive payoff game structure, where a particular node might have had a negative payoff. In a family where the parents are flexible with one another on requests for schedule changes, the payoff of a particular change (node) might be negative, but if on average, the players play a positive tit-for-tat game in which most of the requests are granted, the payoff structure is positive for both the parents and the children.

A game table analysis, used to examine simultaneous choice normal form games, places each player on one side of a table, with choices listed, and with the payoff structure in the choice boxes. Below is an example of a game table:

The Game

	Player 2: Choice A	Player 2: Choice B
Player 1: Choice X	8, 6 (1)	10, 2 (2)
Player 1: Choice Y	6, 4 (3)	9, 3 (4)

Player 1 is on the left side of the table and has two choices, X and Y. Player 2 is at the top of the table and has choices A and B. Within the table are the utility (units of value) of each of the outcomes for each of the players, traditionally with player 1's values before the comma and Player 2's values after the comma. By analyzing the relative values, one can see that the most rational choice for player 1 is X because no matter what player 2 does, player 1 comes out ahead by choosing X. Likewise, player 2 will choose A, because no matter what player

1 does, this turns out better for player 2. The point of equilibrium, therefore, or the solution to the game, is box (1). This is what we mean by equilibrium, or Nash equilibrium—that in every game there is at least one likely outcome. In this case, box (1) is the Nash equilibrium, not requiring communication or cooperation between players.

However, in many simultaneous choice situations, there are multiple Nash equilibria or there is no obvious way to maximize the payoff to either player without communication and cooperation. The inherent problem of simultaneous move games is that choices can be self-defeating unless there is communication and cooperation. Communication, cooperation, and trust solve this dilemma. Make it a sequential move game, and Bayes rule solves the problem.

The point here is that simultaneous choice games have an inherent weakness that can lead to less-than-optimal payoffs—that can only be corrected with good communication and cooperation. Thus, most bargaining in divorce has a better chance of an optimal payoff structure *if the attorneys play the game as a sequential game*, taking turns making proposals, and allowing Bayes rule to inform and correct the process. Even when there is good communication and cooperation, a sequential game is superior to a simultaneous choice game for two reasons. First, the parties might not have revealed all of the subjective goals and values or might at the beginning of the game not even known their own subjective goals and values. And second, the bargaining process is inductive rather than deductive, which we will cover later in this Chapter.

A subtle but powerful strategy for optimizing solutions for both parties is to avoid establishing positions at the beginning of the game. By establishing positions, parties are playing a simultaneous choice game. A lawyer can help here in the initial meeting with a client. If the lawyer asks questions that lead to the client and the lawyer identifying outcome positions, they are stepping into the quagmire of a simultaneous choice game, potentially leading to a poor outcome for the client. But if the lawyer asks questions to identify the client's long-term objective and subjective goals and avoids establishing positions, they are in a better position to start a sequential move game with proposals.

Games can get more complicated when *probability* is introduced at each node. The future is uncertain in many cases, and we cannot say with certitude what the payoffs will be. We might be able to say that there is a 75 percent chance of a certain payoff, but in some (generally most) instances, we cannot say with certainty what the payoff will be. For example, choice A might be to "settle," and choice B might be to "litigate" on the issue of spousal support. We might be able to calculate a settlement figure, but at best we might be able to make probability statements about the outcome of litigation. More complicated mathematically, utility (i.e., calculated payoff values) can be determined even in these complex games into which probability enters. In keeping with the promise not to bog down these explanations with the mathematics, we simply assert that this theorem does have a mathematical proof.

Experienced attorneys intuitively make these calculations. For example, if a spouse asks his or her attorney whether they should settle on spousal support of $1,000, or litigate, the attorney can estimate the range of probable figures should they litigate (e.g., between $800 and $1,000) with transaction costs of about $2,500. The estimate could be wrong (i.e., the judge might decide $500 or $1,200), but this gives the client information for the choice. If they litigate, and the order is for $800 and the transaction costs are $2,200, and this client is the payer, the client breaks even at eleven months, not taking into consideration any tax implications. If the order is for $1,000, the client is out the $2,200 transaction cost. If the term of support is seven years, and the attorney's estimates are correct, the client is essentially making a $2,200 bet in a game. If he or she loses, the loss is the $2,200 bet. If he or she wins ($800), he or she makes $14,600. One could add in the probability of outcome, and one could see whether this is a good bet or not. The payee has the same bet in reverse, when looking at litigating. This analysis also suggests a compromise strategy that takes chance out of the game. By counter-offering at $900, either party takes chance out of the game, saves transaction costs, and splits the difference between the probable outcomes at trial.

CPAs and/or financial advisors can be enormously helpful to attorneys, mediators, and parties by performing some of these analyses and calculations. The results of such an analysis could help shape the final settlement in a real win-win solution to the game. By pointing out to the parties what the bet is and what the potential payoffs are when working on the financial aspects of the divorce, they can make informed choices, be less disappointed with litigated results, and often find cooperative solutions with better outcomes for both of them, or at least compromise solutions that take chance and resentment out of the game.

As we indicated, game theory research informs us that sequential move games have the best chance of maximizing the payoff structure for both parties. Thus, the process of the two parties to a divorce taking turns making offers and counteroffers, without fixed positions prior to receiving an offer, will likely produce optimal outcomes. The simultaneous move game of starting with positions is much less likely to lead to an optimal outcome.

Conclusion

In this section, we focused on the importance of attorneys being involved to keep the players (clients and attorneys) rational. Inclusion of both objective and subjective values increases the size of the pot to be divided, and balancing narcissism with altruism has the best chance of producing optimal outcomes for the parties. It is important to play the multiple games in divorce and to differentiate between normal form games and repeated form games. When possible, bargaining with sequential moves rather than simultaneous moves allows Bayes rule to inform the process and produce a convergence of expectations on solutions.

Information Management, the Game Theory Way

Public or Private

Information is public if both parties have the information or easy access to it (e.g., a valuation on the homestead); information is private if one party has the information and the other does not (e.g., a likely contract that will double the value of the privately held business). Making information public in a divorce increases the chances of an optimal outcome, even though an initial reaction might be to withhold the information in order to have a bargaining advantage. This is counterintuitive but makes complete sense when we examine the underlying assumptions of game theory bargaining relative to traditional bargaining.

In traditional bargaining, the parties are assumed to be in a dispute with different interests. In that context, private information might offer an advantage. The underlying assumption in game theory bargaining is that with good information management, the payoff structure for both spouses can be optimized. The primary reason for this is that making information public grows the size of the pot.

Verifiable or Non-verifiable

Information is verifiable when it can be proven (e.g., a paycheck stub) or, and this is important, when the information is from a trusted source.

Private information becomes a particular problem in bargaining when it is also non-verifiable. Two tactics are available in such a situation. One is to use "signals." A party can deliberately signal without providing the actual information. For example, a wife offers to buy the husband's share of the homestead, but there is no obvious means by which she can do this. This could be a signal that she has access to non-marital funds, which can now be considered in the bargaining process, although she has not revealed the private information (who might be providing the money, how much she has access to, and so on).

The second tactic for dealing with private non-verifiable information is "screening." Whereas the holder of private non-verifiable information can use signaling, if a party suspects that the other party might have private non-verifiable information, he or she can screen to prevent such information from creating harm or disadvantage. For example, if a wife suspects that the husband might receive a substantial increase in salary but has no way of verifying it, she can propose that spousal support automatically adjust as a percentage of the husband's gross income. Thus, the bargaining on spousal support will focus on the percentage of gross and be unencumbered by private non-verifiable information.

Signaling and screening are two strategies that can be used to deal with private non-verifiable information to free the bargaining process while not demanding that the information become public.

Perfect or Imperfect

Information is perfect if both parties know the complete history of the game prior to making a choice. It is imperfect if one or both of the parties do not know the complete history. An example of imperfect information is when one of the parties has had a secret valuation done prior to making a proposal. Another example is when a party has an unrevealed subjective goal. One of the advantages of perfect information is that as the bargaining proceeds, if both parties know the complete history, they can see creative solutions that benefit both parties.

There are three subtle advantages to perfect information:

1. *Inductive bargaining:* This was one of the cornerstone maxims of the first formal publication on game theory by Von Neuman and Morgenstern.[12] Game theory makes no sense unless the players are rational. If players make choices at random and have no concern with the payoff structure, or no preferences for outcomes, game theory cannot predict behavior or choices. Rational players are assumed to make decisions and choices that increase the chance of achieving the preferred payoff. What Von Neumann and Morgenstern determined was that if a bargaining process was inductive, by the time the parties make choices, they have better information for making decisions.

   When the bargaining includes perfect information, the process is inductive because it is based on actual information, not inference or theory. "Deductive bargaining" in a divorce case is when parties start with positions and argue the details from their positions, rather than building positions from the information base. One can see how deductive bargaining is likely to be irrational. Spouse A's "position" on spousal support might be, "I am not paying anything." This might be completely irrational in that it might be in direct opposition to Spouse A's real interests but also lacks important information. Inductive bargaining pressures people to build positions as they get better information, thereby becoming more rational.

   For example, assume that Spouse A has information about an early retirement option coming up in his company. Also assume that Spouse A has wanted for many years to retire from his company and pursue a very different career, that of teaching mathematics to students struggling in school with math. Assume that he has researched possibilities and has arrived at an agreement in principle

---

12. There is some controversy over this because a French author, while not calling it game theory, did publish work that really undergirds game theory, and he might well be considered the "inventor."

with a school district to teach remedial mathematics to struggling students. As a result, Spouse A realizes that a burdensome spousal support order would interfere with these plans, and so he makes a proposal to divide property unequally in exchange for no spousal support. This is both a problem of private information and imperfect information. Spouse B, without this information, might or might not take the proposal, but might end up with a less-than-optimal payoff and Spouse A also might end up with a less-than-optimal payoff, particularly if his or her private ambition is thwarted in some way or does not work out. Had he or she made this information public and perfect, so that Spouse B was aware of the desired career moves prior to the proposal, the two of them might have been able to design a payoff structure that served both of them well.

A *deductive* bargaining process might begin with a positional statement: "My client wants to alternate every Christmas." To begin an *inductive* bargaining process, one presents perfect information: "My client wants both parents to have some Christmas time and would like very much to continue with the tradition of going to midnight Mass with the children and her relatives."

2. Perfect information allows for *Bayes equilibrium*.[13] As a reminder, Bayes rule is the concept that as players reveal more information to one another through proposals and counterproposals, each player has an opportunity to increase the value and quality of his or her proposals. If Spouse A offers to pay $500 per month in spousal support, Spouse B knows the baseline; that is, the minimum the other spouse will pay. If Spouse B was thinking of proposing $400, he or she will no longer do so. If Spouse B counter proposes $600, Spouse A will know that the range of the settlement will be between $500 and $600. Spouse A offers to pay $500 now but agrees to increase it to $550 when he or she receives an anticipated raise. In addition, he or she provides financial records indicating his or her current ability to pay, based on his or her acceptance of a high level of marital debt in the property settlement. Spouse B now sees that Spouse A likely cannot pay more than $500 unless

---

13. We have talked about game theory solutions in several places, and we have discussed Bayes rule but have not focused on Bayes Equilibrium and a solution concept by itself, because it is complicated and peripheral to the game theory bargaining model.

he or she is willing to renegotiate the marital debt, which he or she does not wish to do. Spouse B sees that the debt will be paid off in one year, and he or she now knows that the other spouse will likely be getting a raise in six months. Spouse B proposes $500 now, $550 when the raise occurs, and $600 when the marital debt is paid. As we can see, with Bayes rule operating, a solution becomes increasingly clear: the Bayes equilibrium. Without this information, some of which might have been private non-verifiable (e.g., the raise), such a solution might not have been obvious. The final settlement might be different from the Spouse B's proposal as it goes through compromise bargaining.

3. Perfect information facilitates a *convergence of expectations*. This is similar to Bayes equilibrium, but also slightly different. In Bayes rule, the beliefs of the parties change as more information is revealed. As even more information is revealed through a pattern of perfect information, the parties begin to have a shared set of expectations with regard to the likely outcomes. Thus, not only do their beliefs change with regard to the other party, but they also begin to both see where the negotiations are headed. In our example, both the husband and the wife begin to expect the final settlement to be $500 now and increasing at some point as the husband has more disposable income, both as a result of an anticipated raise and debt reduction.

     Not all is rosy about perfect information. Making information perfect in the bargaining process can be a disadvantage if the case does not settle and moves to litigation. For example, assume one of the parties has a subjective goal of potentially relocating, and this is revealed in the bargaining process. This information remains "known" during the litigation phase if settlement is not reached. Had the information not been revealed during bargaining, that party's case might have been better. Likewise, assume the wife knows that a major restructuring is imminent in her workplace and that she is likely to receive a substantial raise within the next two years. If she reveals this during bargaining, she enhances the chances of achieving an optimal outcome if they settle, but she might hinder her chances of an optimal outcome for her if the case does not settle and goes to trial.

Complete or Incomplete

This is the mirror of perfect/imperfect but has to do with the future of the game, rather than the past. Information is complete if both parties know all of the rules and the payoff structure. As a divorce example, the husband is representing himself in a divorce action and is told by the wife that she needs him to let her have "primary custody" of the children in the legal agreement, with a specific schedule, so that she can qualify for certain programs (e.g., housing, job training) but that informally they will continue to share equal residential schedule time with the children, as they had since the separation. He agrees. One year later, the wife remarries and moves out of the area. He now discovers that since the divorce decree gave the wife primary custody, he has no legal recourse to object to the move or to the residential schedule since it was in the original court order, greatly reducing his time with his children. In this case, he had *incomplete information,* not knowing about the rules and payoffs of doing her a favor.

Earlier, game tables and game trees were discussed as ways to analyze but also tools to illustrate to parties the likely payoff structure from different decisions they might make. Attorneys play a pivotal role in making information complete. In our example above, had Spouse A been represented by an attorney, he or she might not have made that deal with Spouse B and been disadvantaged in relocation and subsequently on child support. For example, as part of considering a decision that Spouse B have primary physical custody, the attorney could have drawn a game tree for Spouse A with the various payoffs at the end, including the payoffs if she decides to relocate. When parties have complete information, they are much more likely to make rational decisions. Rational players increase the chances of achieving optimal solutions.

Objective and Subjective Goals: Enhanced Settlement Solutions

Zero-Sum Games

In zero-sum games, there is a limit on the payoff that must be divided between players. Is there really ever a zero-sum game? Let us look at the following challenge, incorporating subjective value into the calculations. In the "split the dollar game," which we discussed in an earlier chapter, assume that two players are told to come to an agreement on how to split $100 within a time limit or face neither party receiving any money. On its face, this appears to be a zero-sum game.

Now assume the same game, except player A is wealthy and player B is not; also assume that player A drove a car to the game and player B took a cab for $10. Player A's share of $100 is subjectively less valuable than is player B's share, whatever that share might be; $50 to a wealthy person has less subjective value than $50 to a poor person. Player A is shrewd, however, and offers a bargain to player B. She proposes that she take $60 and that player B take $40, but also that she will drive player B home after the game, saving him the transaction cost of another cab fare. Given the savings of cab fare and the subjective value of $40 to player B, he accepts.

The point is that even zero-sum games take on a different character depending on the subjective meaning of the game to the players. In the example, the players had different subjective values for the actual cash and took into consideration transaction costs (the cab fare).

We discussed earlier the game theory experiment called the "ultimatum game." In that game, player A must make a proposal to player B on how to split $10, and player B can only accept the proposal, splitting the money per player A's offer, or reject it and neither gets any money. In that experiment, subjective values about fairness and altruism dominated rational choices.

It can be shown that even this game can be changed by altering the subjective value of the money—not all dollars are the same. If player A offers player B ten cents out of a hundred pennies, player B might reject the split "on principle." Assume the exact same game, but the amount to be split is $1,000,000. If the proposal is $900,000/$100,000, might player B accept the bid, given that the amount to be lost by rejecting the split is $100,000? Suddenly, the principle of fairness becomes dominated by the size of the payoff. The point of this is that although players can appear to be irrational, and some truly are, on average players are rational but have internal subjective payoffs that are not always readily apparent—and with which we might not always agree. This is why utility theory is used in game theory; that is, that the payoffs have "utiles," because a utile can be defined as "happiness points" or, perhaps more accurately, as "an amount of satisfaction" with the outcome.

Two additional general principles are important to understand relative to the objective and subjective payoffs to the parties:

- Payoffs reflect what is important to that player.
- Payoffs for two players cannot be compared.

All this sounds simple and obvious, but is not so obvious. Two parties might appear to be in a dispute over the same payoff (e.g., time with a child), but the *payoff structure of what that time means to each player could be very different*. The father might want equal residential time in order to preserve his relationship with the children, because being with the children is fun and he wants to be close to the children when grown. The mother might want primary residential time with the children because she needs child support in order to afford the homestead, on behalf of the children and all that the home means to the children. Without understanding these subjective payoffs, the parties might not be able to solve the dispute, except by an order of the court. By understanding these different sets of payoffs, however, settlement (the equilibrium point) can become obvious. In this example, the payoffs that were important to the parties were different.

The second point is that *payoffs cannot be compared*. In the above example, which is a better payoff: fun and a close relationship, or the preservation of the homestead for the children's sake? Only in zero-sum games, and only if we focus on the objective utility, ignoring the subjective utility, can we compare payoffs. In that schema, winning a game of checkers is better than losing, but this does not explain why a grandparent would deliberately lose to a child. Only by taking into consideration the subjective value of a payoff, and by not attempting to compare the payoffs for different players, can we move to solve what appear to be unsolvable disputes. In our example above, the mother might also share the goal of having the father actively involved in all aspects of the children's lives, to have the children have fun with their father, and to have the father and the children enjoy close relationships when the children are adults. Likewise, the father might also like the idea of preserving the homestead for the children, with easy access to familiar neighbors, proximity to the school, and familiarity for the children. What appears to be a dispute over the schedule is really a *compatibility of interests* in search of a solution.

The subjective payoff structure adds a complication to the bargaining over children, and there are no *exit options*. If bargaining to buy a house, one can always pull out of the negotiations, having failed to make a final deal. This exit option is not available when bargaining over children in divorce, especially in the child planning game, unless one of the parents is willing simply to abandon the children altogether.

• •

Side note: The principle of not comparing subjective payoff values is a critical issue in divorce with children. The *best interests of the child* legal standard promotes comparing payoffs in a very destructive way and promotes conflict and competition, leading to self-defeating strategies and destroying the family experience of families. Claiming and trying to prove whose goals and values are in the *best interests of the child* is comparing. This distracts parents from the real task at hand of reorganizing the family to accomplish the values and goals of both parents.

• •

Similarly, in an intact marriage, spouses rarely compete over money or the use of certain property. They rarely view marital income as a zero-sum game, but rather as a means by which to accomplish certain goals. Additionally, the money and property, as a payoff, has different subjective meaning to the parties when they divorce. When two parties compete over a homestead in a divorce, they are not competing over a house that they both want to buy at a fixed price (objective value). If that were the case, both of them would simply buy comparable houses. Remembering that the payoff structure (the combination of objective and subjective values) for each party is different and that the two cannot be compared, exploring those values with the parties in a non-competitive manner can lead to a satisfying settlement to both parties.

Non-Zero-Sum Games

In a non-zero-sum game, the payoffs can be quantified by assigning ordinal values. A non-zero-sum game occurs when the gain of one party does not necessarily lead to a loss by the other party. As we stated above, happily married parents rarely count the percentage of time that each makes decisions for or spends with the children. In an ideal family system, if one includes providing for the financial needs of the family, the division of time and decision-making authority is based on abilities, interests, the needs of the children, and practical considerations.

One can assign value to each of these factors. For example, out of a list of twenty parenting activities, each parent could assign an ordinal value to each activity. One could arbitrarily give each parent a thousand points to spend on these activities and have them bid on each. As an example, the father might bid high on helping with homework, and the mother might bid high on reading to the child at night.

Without the formality of bidding, many parents do this naturally. A father who really enjoys and is good at helping with homework might end up doing the majority of that task, while a mother who enjoys the fun and intimacy of reading to the child might find himself or herself doing much of that task. In a sense, they have unconsciously auctioned off the tasks to one another and ended up in a natural balance. One parent gains, but this is not at the expense of the other. The father's relationship with the child has not diminished because the mother is reading a bedtime story to the child. In fact, the vicarious enjoyment that he experiences in witnessing the intimacy between the child and the mother might enhance his experience of parenting. Or he might genuinely enjoy his moment of free time to work on his hobby, a gain for both parents.

Yet, during and after a divorce, parenting often appears to become a zero-sum game, in large part because the court awards residential placement time and decision-making rights to each parent *as if it is a zero-sum game payoff*. Because the time available is limited, every hour gained by one parent is an hour lost by the other parent. This is an important concept, because zero-sum games tend to be played with competitive rather than cooperative strategies.

In a healthy intact marriage, parents see one another as additions to the child's life and engage in the non-zero-sum game of parenting in a cooperative manner. If parenting in divorce is viewed by the parents as a non-zero-sum game, they are more likely to continue to see each other, and perhaps others such as new stepparents, as additions to the child's life and parent in a cooperative manner.

It is when the court system makes or changes the rules and payoffs that parenting becomes a zero-sum game. This transforms the choices and strategies that apply to this new parenting game. Zero-sum games lead to competition, not cooperation. Competitive strategies include not only touting one's positive qualities and minimizing one's negative qualities, but also emphasizing the negative qualities of the competitor and minimizing that person's positive qualities.

Summary

The court system inadvertently transforms the non-zero-sum game of parenting during the marriage into a zero-sum game during the divorce, thus extending the "split" of the spousal relationship into a "split" of the parenting relationship. This interferes with the more natural split that might occur post-divorce if the court treated parenting as a continuation of the non-zero-sum game that existed in the marriage. While this approach means changing some of the rules, *the most profound change needs to be in the payoff structure.*

Dominant and Dominated Strategies

Okay, here we get a little technical. In game theory, strategies are categorized into four types:

1. Strictly dominant
2. Strictly dominated
3. Weakly dominant
4. Weakly dominated

A "strictly dominant strategy" is one that will lead to the highest payoff for the player using the strategy, no matter what the other player does. In poker, there is a concept called the "nut." This is a hand that is sure to win. The dominant strategy when a player has the "nut" is to bet in a way that creates the biggest pot. In divorce, if the statutes indicate that a pattern of serious domestic violence in the marriage would result in the victim receiving sole custody, and a wife can prove a pattern of serious domestic violence, then doing so is her dominant strategy.

A "strictly dominated strategy" is one that will always lead to the worst payoff, no matter what the other player does. In poker, bluffing with a hand that is a sure loser is a dominated strategy. Only a beginner would do so. In divorce, a parent who does not make an effort to see the children for the first six months following a separation is a strictly dominated strategy.

A "weakly dominant strategy" is one that has the highest probability of better payoffs, but some outcomes are worse, depending on the actions of the other player. In poker, bluffing with a hand that has a reasonable probability of improving is weakly dominant. Although the hand might not improve and the player might lose the bet, creating doubt in the other players might have a higher payoff in a later hand, and also the hand might improve even with that bet. In divorce, a wife might believe that having a custody evaluation will likely favor her and could lead to her achieving her goal of being the primary parent. If her facts are good, this is a weakly dominant strategy.

Likewise, a "weakly dominated strategy" is one that has a higher probability of poor payoffs, but not necessarily. Buying a lottery ticket is a weakly dominated strategy, because while there is a cost and the chances of winning are almost infinitely remote, there is at least some chance of winning. In divorce, having a history of alcohol abuse is a weakly dominated strategy. Although that history will likely be a disadvantage in negotiations and litigation, if certain actions are taken (e.g., treatment and sobriety), the disadvantage might be mitigated.

It is sometimes unclear to parties to a divorce just what subjective payoffs they are seeking. They might get focused on legal outcomes as goals instead of life goals. Thus, they often choose weakly or even strictly dominated strategies in the bargaining process. A parent who uses ugly tactics like fictitious police reports in order to obtain a desired residential schedule, for example, is using a weakly dominated strategy.

In a common example, assume that a mother believes she has done the majority of parenting. During the marriage, she complained that the father was less involved than the children needed and wanted, and she even argued with the father to try to get him more involved. The father was mostly focused on his career during the marriage, and he believed that seeing the children in the evening and spending some time with them on weekends was sufficient. He believed that producing an increasing level of income and enhanced lifestyle was his major and, at times unappreciated, contribution to the family. However, during the divorce, the mother now wants to have the children most of the time, and because the father was marginally involved, she wants to maintain his marginal role. The father, now facing substantial loss (e.g., not even seeing the children most evenings), reorganizes his priorities and is willing to make career sacrifices in order to play a larger role in the children's lives. They begin a negative tit-for-tat custody battle.

In other words, they each adopt a weakly dominated strategy, relative to the needs and interests of their children—that is, when one focuses on the payoff structure for the children, both parents have adopted a strategy that is likely to fail. In such a custody battle, the potential payoff structure for the children diminishes. If their mother prevails, their already insufficient time with their father will become less time and involvement. If their father prevails, time with their father will be in direct competition with time with their mother. Worse yet, the chances of the parents engaging in a good co-parenting relationship with one another after such a contest is substantially lower, meaning that whatever time the children gain or lose with either parent, the quality of their family experience will be substantially poorer. These are weakly dominated strategies for the payoff structure for the parents also, for similar reasons. If nothing else, they are likely to lose all of the benefits that come with a good co-parenting relationship and are likely to see their children have adjustment problems as a result.

Of course this is simplistic, because we are isolating only one subjective payoff (the mother's awareness that the children need and want more father involvement), but the example illustrates an important problem.[14] It is only if the parties examine and focus on their subjective values that they can choose at least weakly dominant strategies. By adopting weakly dominant strategies, they move from a zero-sum game to a non-zero-sum game, thus increasing the payoff value to both of them. More important, they increase the payoff structure for the children. A weakly dominant strategy for the mother might be to encourage more father involvement by relinquishing some of her residential time, but also looking for ways for the father to meet his goals on his time with the children. Likewise, a weakly dominant strategy for the father is to continue to provide a good lifestyle for the children, spending less time with them than he initially sought, but negotiating access to the children to foster the relationship. He could include that both parents emphasize the important parenting he is doing by providing the financial resources for the children's lifestyle.

By examining both the objective and subjective values of the payoffs in all of the subgames of divorce, many, if not all, of what appear to be

---

14. We could, for example, add many more subjective values to this same situation. The mother might also want to avoid having the children going through many transitions, whereas the father does not value the stress of transitions as much as having a residential schedule fit his work schedule.

zero-sum games can be transformed into non-zero-sum games in which the parties can both choose at least weakly, if not strictly, dominant strategies and thus both have better payoff outcomes.

We see this in some amicable divorces in which both parents focus on maintaining a non-zero-sum game of parenting after the divorce, with little focus on the zero-sum game of residential time. We see children who are shared, independent of the residential schedule (i.e., where they sleep at night).

Two examples, one child-related and one finance-related, might better illustrate the application of these principles to real-life divorce situations. Before discussing these, however, a reminder about Nash equilibrium is in order. While there are several solution concepts in game theory, the Nash equilibrium is the central solution concept. Nash demonstrated that in complex games, a player will choose mixed strategies that dominate, at least weakly, and that the other player will do the same, because both players are seeking the highest payoff value. But what is the highest payoff value? In traditional divorce, getting the most residential time with the child is often seen as having the highest payoff value. The payoff structure might look something like this:

- time with the child
- avoidance of loss of time with the child
- power to make certain decisions (e.g., choice of school)
- possible retention of the homestead or other property settlement advantages
- levels of child support and possibly spousal support
- legal power or advantage (e.g., in a relocation dispute)
- gender equity or status
- retention of pre-divorce family roles
- involvement in certain aspects of the child's life (e.g., school days)

Some of these are objective values (e.g., child support), and some are subjective values (e.g., gender equity). In this game, the dominant strategy will be any action or set of actions that increase the chances of winning the most residential time. As with politics, while no one likes to fight dirty, fighting dirty is actually the weakly dominant strategy in a winner-take-all fight. Making oneself look good and the other parent look bad generates the best chance of getting the most residential time with the child.

If we ask the parents to examine their subjective values, however, and apply some of the bargaining strategies espoused by game theory, we might discover that the dominant strategy for gaining the most residential time is actually the dominated strategy for creating the kind of family experience for the children and for themselves that they actually want. The payoff structure they really want might look something like this:

- The children have as stable and predictable a life as possible, including a stable residential schedule.

- Both parents are actively involved in the children's lives and supportive of the children's lives outside of the family (e.g., with friends).

- Parents rely first on one another for decisions and care.

- The schedule is flexible, allowing for opportunities to be involved with the children off-schedule.

- Good information is communicated about the children in both homes and parents receive opportunities to work together to solve problems for the children.

- The parenting is coordinated so that the rules, expectations, chores and responsibilities, routines, and even forms of punishment are similar in both homes.

- A minimal amount of stress is placed on the children given the logistic problem of having parents in two homes, including having transitions from home to home be as smooth as possible for the children.

The negative tit-for-tat strategy that might create the best chance of getting the most residential time may have the least chance of accomplishing these larger goals. As just one example, if parent A proposes a switch of weekends and the other says "no," the parties are likely to adopt the grim strategy, which dictates that in response to this "defection," the parent who asked for the change will "defect" and say "no" to the next request made by the other parent. The parent first saying "no" is likely to have done so because of certain strategies that were used in the battle over residential time. Thus, the payoff of having flexibility in the family is not achieved, and the parties—having "won" their residential time in a hard-fought battle—end up with a highly rigid family structure that is opposed to their and their children's interests.[15]

The grim strategy is simple: If player A defects one time, player B defects for the remainder of the game (forever). While one might intuitively think that this would prevent player A from defecting, a rollback analysis of this decision tree reveals that defecting is the best move at the very end of the game. Thus, the "end" of the game moves one move closer to the present, and then it becomes Nash equilibrium to defect at that move, and so on until the best first move is to defect. Think of this in terms of an actual number. Assume that the parties will try to switch weekends a total of ten times and that they will take turns making requests, with the father making the first request. Also assume selfish parents. The mother will have the tenth request, and since there will be no further requests, the father has nothing to lose but does have a gain by saying "no," so he says "no." However, the mother is a rational player and knows that this will happen, so she has nothing to lose but does have something to gain by saying "no" to the ninth request by the father. Rolling this back to the first request, one can see why this is called the "grim strategy."

Game theory research identifies two strategies that promote cooperation. One is positive tit-for-tat. In this strategy, one player adopts the strategy of doing what the other player did in the last subgame: cooperate or defect. Assume player B adopts this strategy. If player A cooperates, player B cooperates. If player A defects, player B defects. This punishes defection but also returns to a cooperative strategy easily, even after a defection. This is straightforward enough that Nash equilibrium of cooperation is obvious. Player A can see that he or she would do no better with any defection, so the incentive is to cooperate. The other strategy that works, according to game theory, is to have a third party punish non-cooperative moves. A form of this might involve having a parenting coordinator; that is, a third party who works with the parties but who also has the authority to

---

15. We define this as "parties" winning their residential time rather than one "party" winning because there is almost always an outcome in which both parties get residential time. Assume a mother wants a 10/4 schedule and the father wants a 7/7 schedule. Both parties will likely end up with some residential time, somewhere at or between 10/4 and 7/7. One can only view this as a win for one and a loss for the other if one accepts the premise that parenting is a zero sum game. Thus, if the mother gets a 9/5 schedule, she might view this as a "win," and the father might view this as a "loss," but in fact they each have been awarded residential time with their children, each less than they wanted (e.g., 100 percent).

punish non-cooperation. This is unrealistic in most divorce cases and by definition extends the litigation process; the third party in a sense becomes the judge.

As a financial example, assume that a wife earns a great deal more than the husband but does not want to pay spousal support. The payoff structure, both objective and subjective, might look something like this:

- She pays the least amount/he receives the most amount.
- She believes he was dependent in the marriage and does not want him to be dependent in the divorce; he has low achievement drive and has enjoyed the benefits of her drive and wants to continue to do so.
- He is an adult and should be able to support himself.
- Her income is the product of her effort, not his; why should she have to share that, now that they are going their separate ways.
- He sacrificed his career for the family and should continue to be compensated for that.
- Without income from her, he will not be able to provide the same lifestyle to the children when with him that they will enjoy with her.

In this game for this payoff structure, the parties again are likely to choose strategies that have the single goal of the wife paying the least, or nothing, and the husband receiving the most. However, is that really in each of their best interests, if they carefully examine the long-term payoff structure, especially the subjective values?

What if after exploring this in more depth, the payoff structure is reconstructed in the following ways?

- In five years, both parties will be better off financially if they agree to short-term spousal support.
- Income sharing in the form of spousal support has the highest likelihood of being least disruptive to the quality of the children's lives.
- The tax advantages to the wife in paying spousal support are substantial, compared to an unequal division of property.
- The husband will be able to work flexibility and generously with the wife on her involvement with the children, relative to her career demands, because he does not have to make a substantial

change in his employment.

- The children will continue to have an after-school-available parent because the father works from home.
- In the settlement, the husband agrees to a date certain for the termination of spousal support, sooner than likely if litigated.

Although this comparison is again somewhat simplistic and artificial, it illustrates that the choice of dominant strategies depends very much on the payoff structure that is the point of focus for the parties. A close examination of the objective and subjective values of the parties may yield a very different payoff structure, one in which the parties are much more invested and with which they will be much more satisfied. Thus, the choice of strategies adopted by the parties might be very different. The game theory bargaining model is the weakly dominant strategy, which maximizes the objective and subjective payoff value to both parties.

Optimism Model

One of the more interesting aspects of human psychology is that in situations in which the outcome is ambiguous, people tend to be unrealistically optimistic. So powerful is this trait that it will often dominate other human traits. For example, research has proven that the value people place on money is different if it is won in gambling than if it is lost. The emotional experience of winning $100 is positive, but much less intense than the negative emotional experience of losing $100. One would think, therefore, that no one would gamble, especially in games in which the odds are clearly against them. However, people gamble. We know, for example, especially now with electronics, that slot machines are programmed to pay out less than they take in. However, a slot machine is the picture of ambiguity. We think, "Maybe someone else had such high losses that the machine is now set to pay out large sums, and I will be the lucky one!" That people buy lottery tickets is perhaps the most profound example of the optimism model.

Game theory research has examined this trait and labeled it the "optimism model," which is a factor that needs to be considered when players are choosing strategies in a game that includes ambiguity as to the outcome. This translates directly to family law, because litigating a case is a gamble; that is, while a trial might have a likely outcome, there is a chance that a more favorable outcome will occur, just like the slot machine reasoning. Even experienced lawyers are subject to the optimism model and are often more optimistic about trying a case than is realistic.

Basic Bargaining Principles and Optimal Solutions

In Chapters 1 and 2, we reviewed bargaining principles:

- Recognizing the multiple games of divorce: The child game, further divided into the legal game and the child planning game and the financial game, further divided into the legal game and the financial planning game.

- The importance of learning about both the objective and subjective values and goals of the parties

- Making the bargaining process axiomatic, so that it is first a cooperative bargaining process, by setting standards: this includes the content standards of the goals of the parties and the process standards of the Five E's (educated; equitable; effective; equilibrant; and envy free)

- Assume compatible interests until a conflicting interest is discovered

- Bargain through three phases: cooperative bargaining, compromise bargaining, and win-win-plus bargaining

- Determine if it is a normal form game (focus on content) or a repeated form game (focus on procedures)

- In the child game, focus most on the cooperative strategies required in the child planning game

- Manage information by making it public, verifiable (at least by reputation), perfect, and complete

- Separate mixed games into simple games: When one game is being played for multiple payoffs, dividing the game into individual games, one for each payoff or for a closely related set of payoffs, which facilitates bargaining to optimal solutions

More about Mixed to Simple Games

Perhaps the most obvious mixed game in divorce is the residential schedule for children. The subjective payoffs are multiple (see above in "Dominant and Dominated Strategies"). Individual games can be played for some of these subjective payoffs (e.g., legal advantages in making certain choices), but some cannot be separated into simple games (e.g., gender equity). One subjective payoff, the issue of "loss," can be mitigated by playing the child planning game well, but not entirely. When parents separate, even if they are highly communicative and cooperative, there is some loss of time with children that would otherwise not occur.

The two biggest objective payoffs, however, are child support and involvement in the child's life. The manner in which child support is linked to the residential schedule is, in most jurisdictions, one of the major sources of dispute between parents. In almost every dispute over residential schedules, one or both of the parties is suspected of engaging in the dispute for the money. Often, there is a moral judgment involved in this (e.g., "He just wants equal placement so he doesn't have to pay child support."). Yet, what other major choices do parents make about children that do not consider the costs? Both parents should be considering the financial impact of the residential schedule. It should not be a hidden, somehow shameful motive; it should be an open point of discussion between responsible adults.

In some jurisdictions, the law actually promotes conflict by making the residential schedule/child support game one that discourages resolution and encourages litigation. In Wisconsin, for example, there are substantial financial advantages for a parent to get from a 5/14 to a 7/14 residential schedule (juxtaposed to financial disadvantages to the other parent going from 9/14 to 7/14) *and* the law instructs the judge to "maximize" time with both parents. The law does not define "maximize," and therefore creates a legal ambiguity which, if we remember the optimism model, leads to an interesting game table. In the introduction of this book, we provided an example of the financial implications and the reasons that people in such a situation are more rational to litigate than settle.

Most divorce professionals know that the link between residential schedules and child support is a serious problem, but it appears impossible to separate these games. The very purpose of child support is to share the costs of raising children, and whichever parent has the children is the one incurring the costs. Some of these are obvious costs (e.g., food), but some are not so obvious (e.g., increased energy use).

It is true that there must be a link between the residential schedule and child support, but could this link be formulated in a way that reduces the significant incentives for litigation? One of the problems with child support is that it does not seem "fair" to many people, and seems like money being given to the other parent, not to the children. Could child support be formulated in such way to make certain it is more obviously fair and for the benefit of the children? Could the child support game be largely separated from the residential schedule game?

Assume that children benefit from at least a minimal amount of time with both parents and that the child support game can be used to provide an incentive for that minimal amount. Assume that every other weekend, a share of holidays, and at least one small vacation equals sixty days per year. The first maxim therefore could be: If parent A has less than sixty days per year with the children, parent A pays parent B a straight percentage of gross income (e.g., 17 percent for one child; 25 percent for two children—per Wisconsin law). Assume that above sixty days, the calculation produces only a low financial incentive for increasing time for parent A above the sixty-day baseline. Thus, there is a real and obvious financial advantage of staying at least minimally involved with the children, but also no substantial financial advantage above that number. This simply means that the lower level of support is almost exactly offset by the increased cost of having the children that additional time.

What might the formula look like above sixty days such that money is sufficiently linked to the residential schedule to accomplish the task of both parents supporting the children, but also insufficiently linked to create an incentive for litigation over what to the child is largely irrelevant? Social science tells us that children benefit from having substantial involvement with both parents in all arenas of their life, but it does not show a substantial difference between a 6/14 and 7/14 schedule[16] in terms of effects on child adjustment. A formula for the remaining part of the year—that is, over the sixty days—could look

---

16 In chapter 2, we present a bargaining model that divides the multiple games of the residential schedule game into single games. In this bargaining model, the difference between a 7/14 schedule and a 5/14 schedule is about forty days per year.

something like this:

$$P^H * X = \$^H$$
$$P^W * X = \$^W$$
$$\$^h + \$^w/365 = \$^c$$
$$N^W * (\$^c * PW/PH) = H$$
$$N^H * (\$^c * PW/PH) = W$$
$$H - W = \text{Support (if negative, W pays to H)}$$

Where: P^H equals gross annual income for the husband

P^W equals gross annual income for the wife

X equals the percentage standard (e.g., 17 percent for one child, 25 percent for two children, and 29 percent for three children)

$\$^c$ equals the per day support level

N equals the number of days per year that the husband and the wife have the children

W equals the wife's support obligation

H equals the husband's support obligation

Example: Assume P^H is $80,000 and P^W is $40,000 and that the parties have one child. Annual H is $13,600 and annual W is $6,800. Combined and divided by 365 is $56 per day, of which H is allocated about $37 and W is about $19. If a day is the husband's, the wife pays him $19 and if a day is the wife's, he pays her $37. In an equal placement schedule, therefore, the husband pays the wife about $280 per month. If the husband ends up with 140 days and the wife ends up with 225, H is $8,404 and W is $2,619. The husband pays the wife $5,785 or about $482 per month. If he gains 20 days, annual W is now $3,040 and annual H is $7,585, dropping the monthly obligation to about $379. However, if the real cost of raising the child is $56 per day, he effectively is picking up about $112 in expenses and saving about $103 in support.[17]

The formula above looks complicated but can be reduced to a spreadsheet in which the calculations are automatic and easy. The point of doing this is to take the financial incentives, the support game, out of the residential schedule game.

In this scheme, the daily support level is likely to be relatively

---

17. A financial specialist could likely get these numbers to match equally by dealing with rounding errors.

minor, and thus the financial advantage of gaining or losing a single day is minimized as a payoff. Even a gain of thirty or forty days per year is unlikely to be a major incentive. Also, the "fairness" of the support agreement may be more apparent in this scheme. It becomes clear that both parents are supporting the child with the same percentage of income, and any exchange of income does nothing more than make equal the amount of money that the parties are spending on a daily basis for the child. Also, in this scheme, joint expenses must be divided at the same percentage as the income levels (in our example, the husband makes two-thirds of the family income and the wife makes one-third; thus, the husband pays two-thirds of all joint expenses). Joint expenses might include the following:

1. Reasonable and ordinary education expenses
2. Health insurance and all non-reimbursed medical and dental expenses
3. Extracurricular activities
4. Child care required for employment
5. Mutually agreed-upon major purchases (e.g., a bicycle)
6. Travel expenses required for the residential schedule (i.e., if there is substantial geographic distance between the homes

If the child support game is played separately from the residential schedule game, at least as much as possible, then the residential schedule game can be played on its own merits. In another chapter, we separated the residential schedule game into single and simple games and were able to determine that a 5/9 versus 7/7 dispute handled with game theory bargaining is actually a dispute over about thirty-eight days per year, more or less, depending on how many school days there are each year and whether or not weekends include overnight Sunday. Using the above child support formula, there are no substantial financial advantages to either party for prevailing. Thus, the focus can be on the other subjective values and goals for the parties relative to the disagreement, not on the child support implications.

In chapter 4, we introduced the child planning game as another means by which the mixed game of the residential schedule game can be separated into simple games. The resolution of other financial issues can also be complicated by mixed games. Spousal support can often have many different payoffs for both parties. There might be a residential placement schedule for children, where the outcome is a number (e.g., dollar amount), the payoffs associated with that number, or some of the conditions associated with that number (e.g., remarriage) might be many. As a rule, the more payoffs for each game played, the more complicated the playing and the more intense and often contentious the strategies chosen. The principle is that even complicated mixed games can often be separated into single games and simple games are substantially easier to solve.

More about Goals and Priorities

The game theory model suggests that the attorney or mediator sets about the task of learning, in some detail, about the objective goals (what the party wants) and the subjective goals (why the party wants it; what he or she is trying to accomplish by gaining that goal) of each party. Part of this step is attempting to learn about the other party's objective and subjective goals. In other words, in order to optimize solutions, proposals should serve not only one's own interests but also attempt to achieve the objective and subjective goals of the other party. A client might know the other party well enough to make educated guesses about those values and goals. In addition, Bayes rule provides valuable information during the bargaining process. It is particularly important to learn about the subjective values and goals of the other party.

Payoffs Are Almost Completely Subjective

This is one of the most difficult concepts to fully understand, and yet it is one of the most crucial to understanding the game theory bargaining model. In earlier chapters, we discussed the ultimatum game and the dictator game; in both games one player attempts to be fair while deciding how to split a certain amount of money, and when not fair, the other player would rather walk away with nothing. This is irrational if one assumes that players are rational only if they pursue their objective self-interests.

Game theorists have long struggled with explaining this; that is, that in some circumstances, people do not appear to behave in a rational manner. There is a famous analysis of the auction of airwaves conducted by the U.S. government, in which game theorists set up the auction in order to maximize the payoff for the government. What actually happened was that some of the bidders behaved in a rational manner, but some did not. In one example, a group of dentists bid and won a bandwidth for very little money, but turned around and sold it for a huge profit to a company that had not made a bid. Why did the dentists bid for something they had no use for, and why did a company that was willing to pay millions not even bid?

In divorce, we often see players who do not appear to be acting "rational." Common examples are with regard to family photographs or dividing Christmas ornaments. The players will sometimes spend substantially more in transaction costs disputing items than what those items are actually worth.

The answer lies in how we define rational. Pure game theory defines "rational" as always choosing equilibrium when there is one (some games have multiple equilibria). A more complex definition has to do with payoffs; that is, that players are rational if we take into account the subjective value of payoffs. It might be worth a $200 transaction cost to a divorcing spouse to get a particular Christmas ornament, given the subjective value of that ornament to that player. Game theorists have experimented with this and call the subjective experience of the player a "payoff modifier." By modifying the payoffs in experiments, they are able to determine what influences decisions. For example, culture influences decisions. We know this to some extent when we think about house sizes in different cultures. In the United States, a person might move from a 1,600 square foot house to a larger house because the smaller house "is not big enough," and yet the smaller home might seem wasteful in Europe and a mansion in Central America.

Neuroscience shows that in the Ultimatum Game when a low proposal is made to player B, a brain center is activated (the "insula") that generates an emotional reaction which another part of the brain interprets as the context. In brief, because the proposal seems inherently unfair, player B becomes emotional and rejects the offer. Because of the neurology involved, game theorists have even hypothesized that there is a fundamental human quality involved that might have survival value. One might picture monkeys sharing fruit. In fact, an experiment with the highly social capuchin monkeys found that "fairness" extends beyond humans. The Ultimatum Game can be modified to move players to a more purely rational strategy. If the players are anonymous to one another, for example, player A is more likely to make a low offer. If the players are of substantially different "social classes," the offer is likely to be lower. In one experiment with the Dictator Game, with six payoff modifiers in place, two-thirds of the players kept all the money.

This raises an interesting question: Does the structural anonymity of the divorce legal system spur more pure self-interest in the parties and less altruism? In the ultimatum game and the dictator games, when the players were playing against an unseen player, the subjective value of fairness dramatically decreased. By having parties play the divorce game once removed through their attorneys, perhaps the system inadvertently promotes narcissistic behavior in the parties. Might the fact that in most mediation, parties negotiate face to face with one another encourage a better balance of narcissism and altruism and might "fairness" play a more dominant role in settlement?

Culture and some inherent human qualities can affect the subjective value that players assign to payoffs. Additionally, different facets of a payoff will have different values to the players. One party might want the money in a game, but another party might want to save time. As a rule, payoffs reflect what is important to the player, and as a result, payoffs cannot be compared. In the "honeymoon game," for example, couple A might decide on a trip to a Caribbean Island resort that costs $12,000. They conclude that once they start their lives together and have children, they will not be able to do this, at least for a while. Couple B might decide to buy a Harley motorcycle and take a short road trip for $12,000. For them, after the honeymoon, they will actually have something useful for their money and can take many more short road trips, thus extending the value of their $12,000. Which choice is "rational"? They have each maximized the value of the $12,000, given their subjective payoff values.

Another important reason that players do not choose equilibrium is that they might not actually know how to play the game. This is called "bounded rationality" because it reflects a limit in human rationality. This is important to professionals working with divorcing spouses because, very often, the subjective payoff structure of the spouses is self-defeating in the long run. It might seem "worth it" to a party in the short term to "win" a particular power struggle, especially after years of frustration in losing power struggles to a controlling spouse. This is bounded rationality.

A game example might be illustrative. Assume one hundred people are each told to pick a number between 0 and 100, with the goal of picking a number that is closest to 70 percent of the average of all the numbers chosen by the other ninety-nine people. Without explaining the mathematics, the Nash equilibrium is for everyone to choose 0. But this is not what happens. The median guess is around 35, and the winning guess is around 25. The "why" of this outcome is fairly obvious. The players who are not mathematicians and have not been schooled in game theory do not know how to figure out that 0 is the "right" answer, so they figure that it is probably around 35. This is close to 70 percent of 50, which might seem like the average number if the players were picking randomly. However, the players are not picking randomly. They are all trying to win the game. The same is true in divorce; that is, the players might not have the perspective and ability to really understand the payoff structure. This is where an attorney or mediator can be of great assistance and another reason divorcing spouses are likely to do better with lawyers than on their own.

This is perhaps easy to see in regard to child issues, although in chapter 4 we provide a good deal of information about the child planning game that might not be obvious or understood by parties. Harder to see is the subjective value issues with the financial part of the divorce. As was demonstrated in some of the earlier games, not all dollars are the same to all people. A starving man finding a $5 bill will assign a different value to that money than will a wealthy man finding that same amount of money. Which is worth more, $10,000 equity in a house or $10,000 invested in a retirement account? Does a wife do better to keep the 2002 Toyota in settlement or the 2008 Cadillac? Do two parties do better for one of the parties to retain the homestead in settlement, or do they together do better to sell it? Does the wife do better to accept a lower spousal support amount for a longer period of time, or a higher amount for a shorter period of time, or even a buyout of support at the time of the divorce if the total value of all three are the same dollar amount?

Assume for this last example that the interest rate used to determine future value of support is 7 percent and assume that the wife considers herself a savvy investor who historically has an average rate of return of 15 percent. Also assume the total support amount is $240,000 over ten years, reduced to a lower value over five years, and again reduced if a buyout to present-day value. Without doing the math, one can see that this wife is likely to do substantially better by taking the buyout if she, in fact, does get an average 15 percent return on the money.

Assume differently in terms of the subjective value to a wife, and a different arrangement might yield a better payoff structure for her. For example, assume that a wife is not a savvy investor and is risk aversive. She might value having a predictable support income for a lengthy period of time. A different wife might want the guarantee of support income to qualify for a house loan. In this example, the same dollar value in spousal support has very different subjective payoff values, or in the case of the savvy investor, a substantially different objective value.

Professionals can help parties explore these various choices, choices that the parties might not even know exist and might not know how to calculate the relative objective and subjective values. By doing so, professionals help parties get past emotionally driven choices or choices based on bounded rationality.

Two additional financial examples further illustrate how professionals can help the parties explore objective and subjective values, using the game theory principle of the auction. Studies on auctions have found that open bid auctions lead to what is called the "winner's curse." For all but very savvy buyers, open auctions tend to produce winning bids higher than the winner wanted to pay. Sealed bid auctions tend to better reflect the real value to parties. Add to this that the items being auctioned often have no objective value, or very little. A painting that is nice to look at might cost on average $800, but a painting by Monet might go for millions in an open auction. Appreciation for the Monet painting is almost all subjective.

In a divorce, assume both parties want the homestead. After both see an appraisal of fair market value, each party submits a sealed bid for the homestead, winner take all, but the settlement price is the winning bid. Winner gets the house for the value he or she placed on it, a "win." Loser does not get the house, but would not have paid higher, so the difference between the losing bid and the winning bid is "profit" in the settlement, a "win." In this way, both the objective value (i.e., price at which the house is likely to sell to a third party) and the subjective value (i.e., the differences between the appraised value and the value set by each of the parties and the difference between the parties) are taken into account.

Another use of auction is for household property. Assume the parties have divided three-fourths of the valuable household property and all of the property with minor values, assigned values, and agreed on that division. However, they dispute one-fourth of the property, twenty items of value. Assign to each party 1,000 points. Tell each to assign as many points as he and she wishes, privately, to each of the remaining household items. They can assign any number of points to an item (from 0 to 1,000), but they can use no more than 1,000 points for all of the items. After completing this task, the "bids" are compared. The party with the highest number of points on any given item wins that item. If there are any ties, those remain in the pot, and all of the decided-upon items are now assigned. For all ties, the game is played again. All items will be divided, and if the parties were sincere (i.e., the points assigned reflected real value), with both obtaining the largest piece of the pie possible. There could be one last tie for one last item. For that last item, a closed bid auction using money can be held, similar to the house game above. This type of auction requires the parties to each give an ordinal value to their "I want that" dispute reflecting his and her subjective values.

By using game theory techniques, and by taking the time to explore objective and subjective values to the parties, each party can end up with more than one-half of the pie. The dollar amount of a settlement might be close to a 50/50 split, but each of the parties might have received a 70/70 split when the subjective value is included.

· ·

Side note: An interesting new development in game theory is called "evolutionary game theory," following some of the other newer extensions of evolutionary thinking in the sciences. The basic idea is that over time people learn to use more adaptive bargaining or decision-making strategies. As a result, this solves the problem of irrational players, both by allowing for irrationality, recognizing that people have phenotypes (built-in bargaining tendencies) that can adapt to new situations, and that people will ultimately find a mixed strategy versus a pure strategy, which works well over time. Many experienced attorneys will have "evolved" in their bargaining approaches, perhaps understanding intuitively many of the game theory principles described in this book, without realizing that they have a foundation in a major branch of mathematics.

· ·

The Three Phases of Bargaining – Cooperative Bargaining; Compromise Bargaining; and Win-Win-Plus Bargaining

By way of review, traditional bargaining has inherent weaknesses:

- An assumption that the interests of the parties are adverse to each other permeates the process.

- Legal outcomes are treated as goals, rather than as means to accomplish long-term goals for the parties and their children.

- The rules and payoff structure for the attorneys are often different from that of the spouses (clients) and at times adverse to the interests of the parties.

- Information management is limited to the objective values and goals and largely ignores the subjective values and goals of the parties.

- There are no clear value propositions or axioms that provide clients with an understanding of what a divorce is supposed to accomplish.

- Without axioms, the parties have no way to judge the outcome.

- The legal system treats the major legal tasks in a divorce as normal form zero-sum games, promoting competitive strategies that disrupt the children's lives, locking the family into patterns inconsistent with a healthy family.

- Traditional divorce treats major divorce tasks as multiple and mixed games, promoting conflict, disputes, confusion, and a failure to address the objective and subjective goals of the divorcing spouses.

- Incomplete information, hindering the creative problem-solving possibility in a divorce.

- There is often a paucity of procedures for dealing with the repeated form games in a family with divorced spouses.

Game theory bargaining corrects many of these weaknesses, particularly assuming that the interests of the parties are more in concert with than adverse to each other, that they have a compatibility of interests, and that disputes are really disagreements about the best way to achieve common goals.

Game theory principles are applied at each phase of bargaining:

- discovering the objective and subjective goals of the parties, without comparing the subjective payoffs
- setting content and process axioms for each issue that reflect those goals
- separating single and simple games from multiple and mixed games
- focusing on content with normal form games and on setting procedures for repeated form games
- maximizing the management of information to produce optimal agreements, measuring the payoff structure of the entire agreement (the MSA) against axiomatic standards that focus on an optimal outcome for both parties

Cooperative Bargaining and Nash's Best Alternative to Negotiated Agreements (BATNAS)

Recalling a basic assumption of game theory bargaining, parties to a divorce have compatible interests, until reaching a real conflict. As we described elsewhere, there is a game theory concept in business called "coopetition," which recognizes the Nash equilibrium for cooperative games when some element of conflict is also present. For example, the best four coffee cafés might locate very near one another, because this will increase the number of potential customers for all. Getting 25 percent market share of a customer base of 6,000 people is better than getting 60 percent of 600 people in an isolated shop. Similarly, in divorce bargaining, the parties must understand that they will both do better if they begin the bargaining process by increasing the size of the pie to be divided through cooperative bargaining. This concept has been named the "best alternative to a negotiated agreement" or BATNA for short, joining cooperative bargaining to compromise bargaining in order to maximize outcomes for two or more parties. First, players are shown what the BATNA is for any agreement (e.g., the likely outcome in trial on an issue of spousal support, property division, or residential schedule). They are told that this is the baseline for negotiating; that is, they are told that they will not have to accept an agreement that is worse than their BATNA. In a phrase, they have "nothing to lose" by entering into a cooperative bargaining process. If there are gains in the bargaining process, this produces two surpluses: first, the amount of gain over the BATNA; and second, the surplus of transaction costs relative to obtaining the BATNA (i.e., trial expenses). Thus, they will do no worse than their BATNA, they might create surplus value, and the surplus value will be distributed to the parties, either as increased value or lower transaction costs. The bottom line, then, is the gamble of the transaction costs for the bargaining process against the transaction costs of litigation.

This is literally why poker games have an ante, to create a stake in the game even before the game is played. This is also why mediation has become a legal requirement in most jurisdictions—because the transaction costs are substantially lower and the parties are likely to reach agreements better than their BATNAs. The fact that mediation is successful about 85 percent of the time attests to this being a rational way to play the game.

Summary

In this chapter, we have expanded principles presented earlier in the book, providing more proofs, examples, and additional concepts for the professional wishing for more facility with game theory and its use in the divorce game. Clients typically enter the divorce process with a set of goals of what they want to accomplish, only to get tutored by their attorneys by what the law can accomplish. The thesis of this book is that through a new style of lawyering, attorneys can bring the two schema closer together. The fundamental notion is that divorce is one mega-game with four major subgames; and within each major subgame, there are numerous simple and single games, with different forms (normal form versus repeated form), and which require different points of focus (content versus procedures).

Information can be managed to produce the best outcomes for parties by making it public, verifiable, perfect, and complete. Recognizing that there are game theory strategies that increase the payoff structures for both parties, by including the *objective and subjective values* of each party, both parties do better, first to *bargain cooperatively*, and only then resolve any real conflict that arises through *compromise bargaining*. At the completion of the first two bargaining phases, a *win-win-plus bargaining procedure* is used to improve value for at least one of the parties, if possible, and in some instances for both parties. Finally, the settlement is measured against two standards: the content goals (the objective and subjective values of the parties) and the procedural goals (the Five E's axioms).

In the divorce game, two parties are strategically engaged, have rules (e.g., laws, local rules, and procedures) and payoffs (e.g., custody or a financial award), and have available decisions and strategies that affect outcomes. By understanding how to play the game, and how to modify it, attorneys and mediators can help parties plan their futures, increase the chances of resolving disputes should they have them, and prevent escalation of the divorce conflict.

> **By redefining the rules and payoff structure, the professional can create a game in which the most rational strategy is cooperative behavior.**

This will create a balance between narcissism and altruism. In most jurisdictions, the majority of these changes in the game can be accomplished in the context of existing laws and local rules. Only one thing is needed to make this happen: the professionals need to learn how game theory can transform the practice of family law.

CHAPTER 7

Game Theory: Procedures for Decision Making, Solving Problems and Concerns, and Resolving Conflicts

Overview

The parents (regarding children) and the parties (regarding finances) will take action post-divorce regarding the following procedures, all of which are discussed in this Chapter:

- joint decision-making
- solving problems
- solving parenting concerns (both major and minor); and
- solving parenting conflicts

Financial games do not typically include solving concerns or resolving conflicts, so the focus in those procedures is on Child Planning Games.

These are not the only procedures that have been studied in research, but they are the procedures that fit best for the types of post-judgment decisions separated parents/parties make.

In Chapter 4, in the "Legal Custody" section of the Legal Game and in the "Taking Action" section of the Child Planning Game, reference is made to a procedure for taking action. Communication is made up of two tasks:

- sharing information; and
- taking action.

In a repeated form game, action is required at each node.

Designing procedures regarding the above issues, which are set forth in the Marital Settlement Agreement substantially increases the likelihood of things going well (or at least much better), compared to a situation where there are no applicable provisions agreed to in advance. Designing these procedures, undergirded with Game Theory principles increases the chances of a **positive** tit-for-tat approach to the Repeated Form Game. Although borrowed from various sources and undergirded with Game Theory principles, we have tried to keep these procedures "user friendly" for parents/parties.

Companion co-parenting workbooks are available to be given to clients with children. Although based on game theory principles, game theory and game theory jargon are not mentioned in the workbook. **The following procedures are presented in language directed at the parents, rather than the lawyer or mediator, to demonstrate how they look to the client.**

Joint Decision-Making

Joint decision-making requires the performance of three tasks:
1. making a list of joint decisions
2. understanding the two levels of interaction and the three phases of decision-making
3. making the joint decision using the Six-Step Procedure.

Task One: Making a List of Joint Decisions

A parenting decision usually involves some action that must be taken in the future on behalf of a child. Separated parents face a special problem in determining which decisions will be jointly made, which require the active participation of *both parents*, and which decisions each parent may make *unilaterally*. State law, local rules, and specific stipulations and orders will define which decisions are required to be made jointly when there is joint legal custody. At the time of the divorce, parents might want to add to the statutory list joint decisions.

A joint custody decisions List might include the following:

- residential and child care—e.g., after-school care, daycare, common list of approved babysitters
- education—e.g., choice of school or preschool, educational programming within a school
- religious training—choice of religion, but also enrollment in

religious training programs, church camps, and so on

- discipline—some forms of discipline work best if carried across households; children also do best and learn the fastest when both households use similar discipline methods with similar rules
- basic routines, rules, expectations, and chores and responsibilities, particularly for young children
- moral/values formation
- non-emergency medical and dental care
- social/extracurricular activities—especially activities that include time (or money) with both parents
- recreational activities—e.g., planning summer enrollments and rules about movie ratings
- legal issues—e.g., driver's license, curfews, and alcohol and drug use
- financial issues—e.g., paying for extracurricular activities, optional medical and dental procedures, and ordinary school costs
- travel/transportation—especially if there is long geographic distance between homes
- how and when to introduce children to new romantic partners of the parents
- certain types of activities or changes in appearance (body piercing or tattoos)

A joint financial decisions List might include the following:

- selling a jointly titled home
- operating a business
- owning a property together
- paying for college expenses
- supporting a special needs child
- sharing expenses for minor children
- purchasing items for minor children

The first task for separated parents is to list the specific decisions that they want to be joint decisions. The sample list provided above might facilitate the discussion. Parents might check some of these items off the list as being cumbersome (e.g., babysitters, if they trust each other's judgment) or they might add to this list. Once the list is completed, when one of those issues on the list comes up, they know they have to employ the Six-Step Procedure recommended below. They will always know when they have to contact the other parent *before* making the decision. If a parent feels left out of an important decision, but the decision is not on the list, that parent should not be angry or disappointed with the other parent. He or she can only propose adding that type of decision to the list so he or she will be included the next time the issue comes up.

Task Two: Understanding the Two Levels of Interaction and the Three Phases of Decision- Making

Making a decision requires consideration of two levels of interaction:

1. The first is *emotional.*
2. The second is *rational.*

On the emotional level, it is critical that both parents feel important (by being *included* in the whole decision-making process) and feel they have some *influence* over the outcome.

On the rational level, decision-making occurs in three phases:

1. Gathering information (phase 1)
2. Brainstorming options (phase 2)
3. Choosing and enacting an option (phase 3)

Parents Make Two Big Mistakes

Divorced parents frequently make two big mistakes in decision-making, both of which can have disastrous effects on the family. The first big mistake is that they often continue with the same decision-making process used in the marriage. In a marriage, roles and responsibilities for different areas of decisions usually end up divided. For example, in the marriage, the mother might have been in charge of all the medical decisions and care. After the divorce, she may simply continue to take care of this, only to find herself surprised by the angry feelings of the father at having been left out. She might get defensive (e.g., "He never wanted to be involved before; why should he get to be involved now?"). Parents need to come to terms with the changed nature of their relationship as parents and the importance of actively including each other in joint decisions.

The second big mistake occurs when one parent goes through the three phases of making the decision before including the other parent. For example, a teacher tells a father that their child qualifies for a gifted students program that would fast-track the child for college preparation. He does all of the investigating (talks to other teachers and parents of children in the program, and reads all of the materials) and gets all of the information. He thinks about the options and makes a decision—that the child should be in the program. He then announces this to the mother ("Mr. McDonald said Sammy qualifies . . . I talked to . . . and I think we should sign him up"). The mother only has the option of agreeing or disagreeing because the emotional level of decision- making has been ignored. Disagreement and power struggles are the most likely outcome, regardless of what is the best decision.

In order to help parents make decisions effectively, we have included a six-step procedure developed from many years of research on how people and groups effectively make joint decisions. This will likely be a novel way of communicating for many separated parents, not simply a refinement of a prior style. Making decisions when divorced is not influenced by intimacy issues and past problems with control.

Task 3: Making the Joint Decision Using the Six-Step Procedure

A decision usually involves some action that must be taken in the future. Decisions occur on both an emotional and a rational level. Successful decision-making requires consideration of both levels. Both parties need to be involved in all three phases of gathering information, looking at options, and picking an option, to satisfy the emotional level.

The rational level of joint decision-making is presented in the following Six-Step Procedure:

The Six-Step Procedure for Joint Decision-Making

Step One: Make an Appointment with the Other Parent

One party becomes aware, or realizes, that a joint decision will soon be required. The first step, before gathering any information, is to contact the other party and make an appointment. When setting the appointment, it may be helpful to describe the decision, lay out any timelines involved, and estimate the amount of time required for the meeting. As a general rule, parties should not gather information independent of one another before the initial appointment. It is essential that parties not arrive at a personal decision before meeting.

Example: A teacher mentions to the mother that Sarah should go to a special program for gifted children run by the local college. The program meets on Saturdays for ten weeks. The mother knows that this is on the list of joint decisions (both for extracurricular activities that run across placement time in both homes and for special education programming). She calls up the father and makes an appointment and then does nothing else about this decision until the initial appointment.

Step Two: Discuss the Information Needed to Make a Responsible Decision

Share information each party may already know. Decide what additional information will be helpful. Make a plan to get the additional information. Make an appointment to discuss the information gathered. Note: Each party can gather the information independently or can go together and gather the information.

Example: The mother shares what the teacher said. Each party shares initial reactions to the idea to see if it is worth further investigation. They decide it is. They make a list of additional information needed (e.g., the cost, the schedule, what happens if Sarah misses one of the sessions), talk to other parents whose children have been in the program, find out specifically how the program might increase Sarah's abilities or chances for college, etc. The mother and father divide up the information to be gathered and set a second appointment in a week to share the information.

Step Three: Share the Information

At the next appointment, talk about what is known. If additional information is required, repeat step 2. Once there appears to be sufficient information, go on to the next step.

Example: The mother and father share information. They are leaning in the direction of enrolling their daughter in the program, but decide they need more information. They also decide they need to ask Sarah about her interest level in the program. They decide to meet with Sarah together, share the information, and get her input. The father also wants to check into other programs that might accomplish the same goals but might be better, less expensive, etc. They schedule another meeting.

Step Four: Brainstorm Options

This meeting might include expressing opinions, but most important is that the values, interests, and resistance the parents feel get expressed. By discussing the decision at the level of interests, values, and concerns, parents might think of options that better encompass what both parents think is important. This could avoid getting stuck arguing over just one or two opinions. In our example, the goal is to enhance Sarah's educational experience and chances of going to college, not the program. There might be better ways to reach that goal.

Example: The father did some checking, and he reports that this looks like the best program. Both parents are leaning in the direction of having Sarah enroll in this program. She seems a little reluctant but interested. The father mentions, though, that he cannot get her to the program on one of the Saturdays; the mother says she could pick her up and take her.

Step Five: Choose an Option

In most instances, when parents follow these steps, they will agree on an option without much difficulty.

Example: The parents decide to enroll Sarah in the gifted program. They work out the details of transportation and cost. They agree that the father will get the enrollment papers, fill them out, show them to the mother, and then submit them.

Note: When the underlying emotional issues are respected, the best option is usually obvious. But sometimes parents get stuck. This can occur for several reasons:

- Having insufficient information: If arguing options, it may be helpful to stop and consider, "Is there any information that would help us get over the hump here?" Perhaps getting an *expert opinion* might help.

- Differing values or goals for the children: Try not to compromise at the outset and instead, explore win-win solutions. Rather, try to think of other options that include both parties' goals and values. If out of ideas, ask someone else you both trust. Describe the issue to that person, list what each of your goals and values are, and see if the person can think of some options that would include both. Only as a last resort, compromise.

Step Six: Recap

After the option has been chosen, it is important to decide how the decision will be enacted, including who will be responsible for which part and a time when everything will be done. A businesslike attitude will help make this work.

If parties follow this Six-Step Procedure for Joint Decision Making, most of the time they will be successful making decisions together. There will always be an occasional decision on which parties just cannot agree. This is true for even happily married parents. When this happens, go to the *Procedure for Solving Conflicts*.

Solving Problems

Solving problems also occurs on an emotional level and on a rational level.

There are two important emotional issues. The first can be summarized as follows: believing that one is "right" and that if the other party disagrees, then *they* are wrong. It is in essence blaming someone else for *your* problems; doing so not only makes you helpless but also has the potential of making it impossible to solve the problem.

Taking responsibility for one's own problems (not for causing them), but for the *solution*, puts the person with the problem in control and takes the pressure off the other party. If a party feels blamed and responsible for changing in order to make the other parent's life go better, he or she is more likely to get defensive, stonewall, or cut off communication. However, if that same person is approached for cooperation, but not blamed, then he or she will more likely participate in this Six-Step Procedure.

Successful problem solving recognizes that the task is not to prove who is right, but rather how to solve a problem when both parties believe they are right.

The second important emotional issue can be summarized as follows: both parties being willing to help solve each other's parenting problems since, when children are involved, this helps avoid demonstrable negative effects on the children. Successful child planners are committed to working cooperatively to improve the lives of their children. Successful problem solving accomplishes three important goals: reduces conflict, models social maturity and teaches and models successful problem solving to children.

The rational level of solving parenting problems is presented in the following Six-Step Procedure:

The Six-Step Procedure for Solving Parenting Problems

Step One: Make an Appointment

Parties should not impulsively and spontaneously thrust the other parent into a problem-solving session. It is a courtesy to ask the other parent to find a time to help you solve a problem. The *person with the problem* should make the appointment and describe about how long it will take. It is not necessary, and perhaps in many instances unwise, to say before the appointment what the problem is, but this might depend on the nature of the problem. Keep this step as simple as it sounds. Do not use this step to vent; do not be intrusive. In brief, do not make this simple task into a dramatic encounter. It is as simple as, "I have a problem to discuss. It should take about twenty minutes. When are you available?"

Step Two: Describe the Problem

This is an important step. Avoid making accusations; instead use "I messages." State the problem in observable terms, not in vague criticisms. State in very concrete terms how the issue is making your life, or your child's life, difficult.

Parenting example: "The last four times you came to transitions, you were more than fifteen minutes late. The children are jumpy and sometimes tearful when they first come, and two times I had to cancel plans to wait for you" (not, "Why are you so irresponsible and selfish?").

Step Three: The Other Parent Responds

This is a very tricky step. First, the other parent must not make the mistake of *"stealing" the problem* (e.g., "You're right. I'll be on time from now on.") People do this out of guilt and concern, and it is a mistake. When you steal someone's problem, you make them powerless. You support the part of them that wants to blame you. You make agreements out of guilt and concern, feelings that might not always be there. You also might agree to something impulsively that you cannot really do. You feel like the other parent owes you one, which might lead to disappointment and bitterness. If you are the parent with the problem, do not let the other parent steal it.

The second major mistake people make at this step is to take on the problem, feeling criticized and blamed. When people do this, they become apologetic, defensive, angry or they stonewall, and so on. It is critical for the person listening to the problem to remember that it is the problem of the person bringing it up, even if the person hearing it agrees that it is a problem. For example, if the mom is bringing up a child's introversion, the dad might agree that it is a problem and that also wants to solve it. However, in this meeting, the dad must step back and remember that this is the mom's problem to solve. The advantage, if both people agree it is a problem, is that it will likely mean much better cooperation in the procedure.

The response should be an effort to give the other parent some information to work with.

"The reason I am often late is because we almost always go to dinner at my mom's on Sunday and the dinner is never ready at the same time. Plus, the kids are having a blast with their cousins, and I don't want it to end until everyone else is leaving. When I try, the kids practically beg me to let them stay for a while. I don't see them enough as it is, and these dinners are special, for the kids and for me."

By giving the other parent information without stealing the problem, you are helping them with the problem. The more information they have about their problem, the easier it will be for them to come up with solutions.

If you are the person with the problem and need some more information in order to come up with a proposal, ask questions. It is your responsibility to get enough information about the whole problem, including anything that the other parent knows about the problem, in order to come up with a solution that will work and that fits the facts of the problem.

Step Four: The Person with the Problem Proposes a Solution
Now that the person with the problem has all the information, a solution can be proposed. Remember, if it is your problem, then the solution is your responsibility.

"I had no idea about the dinners. I forgot how much the kids love that time with your family and how disorganized your parents are. I see your point. How about if we change the time to an hour later?" or *"Could you call from your mom's when you know when you might be able to have the kids back?"* or *"Could you talk to your mom and brother and see if the dinners could be more on time so you can get back here on time?"*

Step Five: Discussion

In this step, the other party either agrees or disagrees with the proposed solution, or with parts of the solution in complicated problems. In general, the other party should agree to the solution if he or she can do what is being asked. There are occasions when this is not the best response, but for the most part, it is the simplest and best solution.

If the mom can bring the children back one hour later from the family Sunday dinner but on time, then accept it.

Generally, a proposed solution should only be rejected if the other parent cannot do what is being proposed or if the solution is seen as harmful to the children.

If there is disagreement, the person with the problem must make other proposals. Remember, it is important that the other party not steal the problem by making proposals. It is also a mistake to believe that the first proposal is the only good proposal and try to talk the other party into it. There are always alternative solutions to problems. If stuck, or out of ideas, consider these options:

- Sleep on it.
- Make another appointment.
- Ask some friends for ideas (though this should be done with discretion and care).
- Ask the other parent if he or she has ideas, but be careful of this, because you may fall into a bad pattern of relying on the other parent to solve your problems. If you start to argue, stop and make another appointment.
- If there is doubt about a solution, try an experiment and set a review date (e.g., "Will you at least try this for one month? If it is not working, you can stop, and I'll try to think of something else").

- Stay on task. If other problems come up, make other appointments. Only solve one problem at a time.

Once there is an agreement, it is binding. However, this only works if those involved do what they have agreed to do. The other party should only agree to something if the person can and is willing to do it. If there is an agreement, and later a party is having difficulty keeping it, now that party has a problem and makes an appointment to resolve it.

Emotional level: the standard for agreeing with a proposal is *if you can do it*, not only that you think it is a good idea. Mature people let others learn from their experiences. If it was a bad idea, let the other person find that out on his or her own. If the proposed solution does not solve the problem, the other person can always make another appointment.

Step Six: Recap
Once the other party has accepted a solution, the person with the problem should recap the discussion, especially the solution. It is often helpful to write down the agreement or plan. Without this, parties might remember the outcome differently, especially if many ideas were discussed.

Summary
Blame does not solve problems, even if the person doing the blaming is correct. A problem may only involve the child, as in our example of the introverted child, or it may involve the other parent, as in our example of a parent being late. It might be a financial problem, such as not reimbursing the other party for expenses.

Problem solving occurs on an emotional and on a rational level. On the emotional level, it is important that parties take responsibility for their own problems. It is also important that the parties believe they both will work cooperatively to solve problems-- that is, they have a sense of teamwork.

The rational level of problem solving is presented in six research-based steps. The Six-Step Procedure works, if followed carefully and if the parties avoid the potential traps: blaming, stealing or giving away the problem, getting off track, or letting the old bad habits and expectations of the marriage leak into the procedure.

Solving Major Parenting Concerns

Even happily married parents develop concerns about the manner in which the other parent deals with the children at times. There are two types of concerns that parents must resolve together—"major concerns" and "minor concerns." The ways to resolve a minor concern are very different from the ways to resolve a major concern, so the first step is for the parent who has the concern to decide if the concern is major or minor. When parents are separating or divorced, a major concern is about the safety of the child or about something occurring in the other home that is likely to have a substantial negative long-term effect on the child. If a concern does not meet these standards, it is a minor concern.

If it is a minor concern, see the procedure on resolving minor concerns. As you will see in that procedure, while expressing minor concerns is important, it is not necessary to agree on a solution. The method of resolving a major concern is similar to those for solving a problem (see "Solving Problems," above), but we will reiterate those steps here. As with solving problems, raising and resolving major concerns occurs on both an emotional level and a rational level.

On the *emotional level,* it is important that a parent takes responsibility for his or her concern. Worrying about the safety of a child riding a bike without a helmet does not make you "right," even if you think that most parents would agree with you. The other parent might not worry about it, can point out that the odds of the child getting seriously hurt are extremely low, and might point out that wearing a helmet needlessly encumbers the child and is by itself a safety risk. Remember that *reasonable people can disagree about what is safe and what will damage a child.* Your goal, if you have a major concern, should never be to convince the other parent that your viewpoint is correct. Your objective is to solve the concern.

For example, look at the difference in the following assertions about a concern related to wearing a bike helmet:

"You just don't care about our son. You don't care if he gets hurt. I read a magazine article about the number of children with lifelong head injuries, and he isn't safe. Do I have to get a doctor to tell you that?" and

"I am guessing that you don't think the odds of his getting hurt are high

enough to make him wear a helmet. Lots of people might agree with you, and the statistics might support your position. I know you care about our son just as much as I do, but I think I tend to be more protective than you are. You might even think I am overprotective at times. However, I have read some articles about the risks of head injury to children riding bikes, and even though it does not happen often, when it does, it can be devastating. For me, this is a major concern."

Which opening assertion is more likely to invite a response that resolves the concern? As with solving problems, a key to successfully resolving a major concern is taking personal responsibility for having the concern. Blaming and criticizing rarely works.

The second important emotional issue is a willingness to help resolve each other's major concerns. The commitment is to having a co-parenting relationship in which both parents trust that the child is safe in the care of the other parent. This is a necessary condition for the co-parenting relationship to work well. There is a temptation to resist this and to take a stand that might be described in these terms: "I control what goes on in my house, and you can control what goes on in your house." The feeling undergirding this natural, but immature, stand is one of feeling criticized and controlled by the ex-spouse. This strident stand causes ongoing conflict, because unless some control is shared, the children will be put in the middle of unresolved concerns and the distrust and fear that this causes.

Summary

Major concerns occur on an emotional level and on a rational level. On the emotional level, there are two key standards: first, the parent with the concern takes responsibility for the concern—not see it as a point of criticism for or blame of the other parent; and second, the parents accept that when it comes to major concerns, control of the child's life is shared, independent of the residential placement schedule.

The rational level of solving major parenting concerns is presented in the following Six-Step Procedure:

Six-Step Procedure for Solving Major Parenting Concerns

Step One: Make an Appointment
It is a courtesy to ask the other parent when he or she can spend time

helping you resolve a concern. The *person with the concern* should make the appointment and describe about how long it will take. It could be that the other parent will respond, "Now is a good time." This then could be the appointment, but only after asking and receiving permission.

Step Two: Describe the Concern

Avoid making accusations; instead use "I messages." State the concern in observable terms (e.g., "Amanda has not been turning in her schoolwork, and when I discussed this with her, she told me that she does not do homework at your house."), not in vague criticisms. State in very concrete terms the manner in which you believe this is a safety issue or one that will negatively affect the long-term outcome for the child.

"If Amanda does not do all of her homework, her grades will ultimately suffer, and her choices in the future will not be more limited. Plus, she is likely to lose interest in school if she is not working to her full potential. More than either of these concerns, I am worried that she will grow up thinking that she does not have to be conscientious in what she does, that she will have poor work habits, and that she will fail at whatever she tries."

Step Three: The Other Parent Responds

This is a tricky step because the other parent is likely to feel blamed or criticized. Also, it is important that the other parent not make the mistake of *stealing the concern* (see "Solving Problems"). If you are the parent with the concern, do not let the other parent steal it.

The response should be an effort to give the other parent some information with which to work.

"I do not supervise the homework for several reasons. I get home from work at 6:00 p.m., and the entire evening is taken up with dinner, showers, and a little fun time. Amanda is supposed to get her homework done before I get home. Plus, I do not think it is my responsibility to check it, and she knows that. School is her responsibility, and she needs to learn that if she wants to succeed, she needs to take responsibility for doing her work."

By giving the other parent information without stealing the concern away from him or her, you are helping the parent with his or her concern. The more information the parent has about this concern, the easier he or she can come up with potential solutions.

If you are the parent with the concern and need some more information in order to come up with a proposal, ask questions. It is *your responsibility* to get enough information about the concern to be able to propose solutions that will work.

Step Four: The Person with the Concern Proposes a Solution
Now that the person with the concern has information, a solution is proposed. Remember, if it is *your concern*, the solution is *your responsibility.*

"I had no idea evenings are so stressed. I see your point. I also agree with you that Amanda should be taking responsibility for how she does in school. However, right now she is not doing that; she is simply not doing her work. I propose that you continue with your expectations that she do her own work before you get home and that you do not have to check up on her. I will work with the school to find out daily whether or not she is turning in her homework. I will set up a reward system for her for doing and turning in her homework every day. If she is not turning it in every day, I propose that we both support grounding her the following weekend for her to do makeup work, no matter which house she will be at that weekend. That way, you do not have to change your schedule, she learns better work habits, and is still being taught to take responsibility for her own work."

Step Five: Discussion
In this step, the other parent either agrees or disagrees with the proposed solution, or with parts of the solution.

"I am fine with your proposal, except for one thing. What if we have already made plans for the weekend that we really do not want to change? I won't agree to give up our plans and punish everyone for what Amanda does."

If there is disagreement, the person with the concern must make other proposals.

"Good point. Let me modify my proposal. I propose that she is grounded from her activities, like with her friends, but that if we have plans, we can

decide either to do them or not do them. If the whole weekend immediately following the day she does not turn in her work is planned, like when you guys go camping, I propose that the next weekend is the one when she is grounded. Or if you prefer, she can miss the activity and spend the weekend at my house doing makeup work. That would really teach her a lesson."

Do not let the other parent steal your concern by making proposals. It is your job to make proposals. If you get stuck, or run out of ideas consider these options:

- Sleep on it.
- Make another appointment.
- Ask some friends for ideas (though this should be done with discretion and care).
- Ask the other parent for some ideas, but be careful of this, because you may fall into a bad pattern of relying on the other parent to solve your problems.
- If you start to argue, stop and make another appointment.
- If there is doubt about a solution, try an experiment and set a review date (e.g., "Will you at least try this for one month? If it is not working, you can stop, and I'll try to think of something else").
- Stay on task. If other concerns come up, make other appointments. Only resolve one concern at a time. Especially avoid tit-for-tat discussions (e.g., "I will be happy to do what you are asking me to do, if you will do something that I want.").

These tit-for-tat approaches hardly ever work and almost always escalate into power struggles and unresolved conflict. Work on one concern at a time.

A commitment is a commitment. This only works if people do what they say. Only agree to something if you will do it. If you make an agreement and you don't like the way it is going, you now have a "problem"; make an appointment with the other parent and use the Six-Step Procedure for Solving Parenting Problems.

For the parent without the concern, don't be childish. Don't only agree with proposals that reflect your ideas of what the other person should do. Don't criticize the other person's ideas (e.g., "Okay, but I don't think it will work."). Use as a standard that you will agree with a proposal *if you can do it*, not just that you think it is a good idea.

Remember, mature people let others learn from their experiences. If it was a bad idea, let the other person find that out on his or her own. If the proposed solution doesn't resolve the concern, the other person can always make another appointment with you.

Step Six: Recap

Once the other parent has accepted a solution, the person with the concern should recap the discussion, especially the solution. Without this, parents might remember the outcome differently, especially if many ideas were discussed. Also, the person with the concern might want to write out the solution to make it clear when memories wane. Recapping might also include direct action with the child.

"I propose that we both sit down with Amanda and tell her that we are concerned that she is developing some bad work habits in school. I will take responsibility for explaining why we are concerned, since I brought it up. I will then explain what we are going to do to get her back on track. Can we do that Saturday, when I bring her over to your house? It should only take five minutes or so."

Solving Minor Parenting Concerns

The steps to resolve a minor concern are very different from resolving a major concern. After the parent who has the concern has decided that it is minor, that parent needs to express the concern to the other parent, but because it is minor, that is all that needs to be done. All parents need some independence to make their decisions on minor issues (concerns). Input from the other parent is extremely helpful, but it is a mistake to try to control the way the other parent deals with the children on minor issues. Children must come to terms with differences between their parents.

The rational level of solving minor parenting concerns is presented in the following Six-Step Procedure.

Six-Step Procedure for Solving Minor Parenting Concerns

Step One: Make an Appointment

The parent with the concern asks the other parent for an appointment to deal with a minor concern.

Step Two: Express the Concern

The parent with the concern expresses the concern in very concrete and understandable terms. It is of little use to the other parent to use vague impressionistic language. Telling the other parent that you are concerned about "the emotional climate" in the home is meaningless. Translating that into a concern that there is a high level of activity in the other home and that the child finds this exhausting is much clearer.

Step Three: Express Why It Is of Concern

Parents do well to assume that the other parent has the same goals. Thus, the concern is best expressed in terms of those goals. For example, if one assumes that both parents want to teach the child useful skills, a concern might be expressed in the form of that goal. Using our example above, the parent might say something like, "If the child is always busy with organized activities, she will not learn how to balance her life, including having relaxing time or time to explore personal interests."

Step Four: Persuade the Other Parent to Do Things Differently

At this point, the parent with the concern simply tries to make persuasive arguments that will hopefully convince the other parent to do things differently. We often confuse constructive arguing with destructive conflict. A good argument is accomplished by clearly defining a position and then offering proofs that gain the *voluntary* agreement of the other party. We rarely obtain voluntary agreement from people when we use destructive tactics, such as criticism or assaults on character.

Step Five: Other Parent Listens

Because the issue was described as a minor concern, the other parent should listen, give genuine consideration to what the other parent is saying, but know that it is his or her decision. A responsible parent will listen to the asserted concern, ask questions to be sure that he or she understands the concern, and listen to the "proofs" offered by the other parent before making a decision.

Step Six: Feedback

Decide if when the parent hearing the concern makes a decision, the other parent wants to know the decision. If the parent listening to the concern needs some time to think about what was said before making a decision, set a time for feedback (e.g., "I want to think about this. I will let you know what I have decided before the weekend.").

Even when one parent decides to do things differently than the other parent might wish, this open communication process lowers the pressure for distrust and conflict. The independence of both parents is respected, but both parents are also afforded a feedback loop that helps them reflect on their parenting choices.

Solving Parenting Conflicts

Like problem solving and solving parenting concerns, conflict resolution occurs on an emotional level and on a rational level.

On the *emotional level,* assuming equal power is a key to success. Parents can rely on court orders to resolve conflicts (e.g., "Gee, that's tough, but the order says I have the child that weekend"), but this takes control out of the hands of the parents, making a piece of paper the decision-maker rather than having parents be the decision-makers in each situation. One parent might *win* one conflict using this strategy, but this sets a precedent, and the other parent will *win* on another day in this negative tit-for-tat game. The result is that neither parent is really resolving conflicts in a way that serves everyone's best interests, especially the child. Parents can get into this kind of negative tit-for-tat battle relying solely on court orders, but in the long run, everyone loses out. The flexibility that families need is lost in this rigid approach. Additionally, the child does not learn how to resolve conflicts.

This might be a big pill for some parents to swallow-- that is, giving both parents equal power over conflicts, especially when one parent has the legal advantage in a particular situation. It might be difficult to give up that power and start with a level playing field, but for parents to be successful, learning to resolve conflicts with each other has an enormous payoff. First of all, a good conflict resolution process teaches the art of getting solutions, when it appears that there are none to be had. All people need to learn strategies for finding solutions to problems that appear to have none. If people were not able to do this, almost all marriages would fail, almost all political issues would end in war, and almost all disputes in the world would end in murder.

Assuming equal power and developing a conflict resolution strategy also establishes a *positive* tit-for-tat game, which in Game Theory is the most successful type of game two people, with interests at odds with one another, can play. Finally, and not least important, by learning to do this, through modeling and instruction, parents can teach their child these skills—skills that will positively affect the rest of their child's lives. Imagine having a child who knows how to resolve win-lose conflicts with people.

Another key emotional ingredient is to accept that many conflicts cannot be resolved until parents get to impasse. "Impasse" is the point where there seems to be no solution. It is a tense emotional time when it becomes clear that one of the parents must *give in*. It is a dangerous point with separated parents who have had control problems, because usually in those situations, each parent might feel like he or she was the one who always gave in during the marriage. The point of impasse can become an ego battle in which each parent tries one more time to win the control battle. However, social scientists who have studied successful conflict resolvers have found that if the parties, in our case the parents, stick with it and do not start fighting dirty, they will often get through impasse by having new ideas dawn on them that resolve the conflict. In order to be successful at resolving conflicts, therefore, parents must accept that there will be some tense emotional times, points at which there seems to be no solution.

Next, parents who feel like they have gotten the short end of the stick in a separation and divorce may be tempted to take advantage and to turn everything they do not like about the residential placement schedule into a *conflict*. This is an abuse of the process, really having more to do with revenge than real conflicts, and it will lead to failure. Conflicts should only be very special situations that have a *major effect* on the parent or on the child. Wanting the children for an unscheduled weekend because the parent misses them is probably not a conflict. Wanting the children because there is a once-in-a-lifetime family reunion probably is. Wanting the children because a parent misses them falls more under access (see "Establish Parent-Child Access Arrangements" in Chapter 4).

Finally, conflict resolution is one of the most difficult types of communication between parents, and not all parents can successfully learn how to equalize power and resolve real conflicts. If, after a number of attempts, perhaps even with the assistance of a counselor or a mediator, parents only end up in regular destructive arguing, then they might do better to just follow the court order. Everyone loses this way in the long run, but the gains of avoiding regular destructive arguments might outweigh these losses. We do suggest that if parents are having difficulty with this type of taking action, then they should meet with a skilled co-parenting counselor to practice this complex procedure.

On a *rational level,* solving conflicts is presented in the following Six-Step Procedure. This procedure has been proven effective through research. Parents should examine these steps and see if this approach might work in their circumstances. If they agree to try it, they should do so religiously for a while, until the steps become second nature. Because conflict resolution requires "giving in" and reaching impasses, it is an emotional experience. Strictly following the structure of a procedure enhances the likelihood of success.

Six-Step Procedure for Solving Parenting Conflicts

Step One: Make an Appointment
The parent who first becomes aware of a conflict makes the appointment. Do not make this a more complicated step than it is. Call the other parent up and announce that there appears to be a conflict, or if the conflict becomes apparent during a discussion with the other parent, ask to schedule a special time to focus on just this one conflict.

Step Two: Describe the Conflict
It is important that the conflict be described in concrete, observable terms. Avoid accusations. Instead, use "I messages" and focus on goals for the children, not the wants of the parents. Let us return to our examples. If it is a choice of school, describe the conflict as, "I want Joey to go to St. Catherine's, and you want him to go to Westside Elementary. He cannot go to both, so we have a conflict." In our example of weekends, the dad might say, "I want Sharon for the weekend of August 11 and 12 for a family reunion, and you want her to go to the cabin with your sister and her family." These simple

descriptions identify the scope of the conflict without provoking more emotion than is inherent in the conflict.

Step Three: Limit the Conflict

This is a critical step because by the end of this step, the parents will have a clear definition of the conflict and will have certainly determined whether or not one really exists. A thorough discussion by both parents ensues, with real listening to each other's point of view. Do not argue with the other person's feelings. Limit the conflict to the parts that are really in conflict. For example, the dad wants the child for the family reunion and the mom wants to go camping with family. However, after a detailed discussion, the parents might determine that neither really needs to have the child for the whole weekend. What started out as a conflict over a weekend might get narrowed down to overlapping hours on Saturday. It is a lot easier to give in on three hours than on a whole weekend. Only negotiate on the part that is really mutually incompatible. As another example, one parent might want to change the placement schedule to get Wednesday evenings with the kids to take a parent-child piano class. Through a discussion, it might be revealed that the class is only for eight Wednesdays. The eight days are the conflict and perhaps only a few hours on Wednesday are at stake, not the entire residential placement schedule.

In this step, parents might also discover that there is no conflict. For example, an issue about choice of school might resolve without having to treat it as a conflict. After discussing the reasons that the mom wants the child to go to parochial school and the dad wants the child to go to public school, the parents might discover that there is a way for both of them to get what they want for the child. For example, the mom explains that she believes that academic training is very important to the life of the child and that the academic success of the parochial school is proven, relative to the public school system. The dad might explain that the main reason he wants the child in public school is for the wide variety of extracurricular activities available. While academics are important to the dad, he also believes that exposure to extracurricular activities, including music and athletics, are very important. At this point, the parents might realize that they can ensure that the child gets good academic training *and* extracurricular activities in either school. If it is the parochial school, the parents might make a point of enrolling the child in non-school-connected extracurricular activities, or if it is the public school, they might make a point of exposing the child to special academic training opportunities. This is a win-win situation in which no real conflict may exist. In our weekend example, the mom might be able to change the camping weekend.

Step Four: Determine What Is at Stake for the Child

Parents will have their own investment in the incompatible differences that cause the conflict, but it is important to have a clear definition of what parts of the conflict affect the child. Knowing that a child has a lot at stake will hopefully shift the motives and determination of the parents in the negotiations away from a situation where there is little at stake for the child. Both parents will tend to exaggerate the effects on a child in a way that supports their *winning* the conflict. This is unavoidable, but by listening to each other, both parents will learn what is really at stake for the child. A once-in-a-lifetime reunion with family members whom the child would otherwise never meet might compare easily to a camping weekend with relatives the child sees regularly. Since the solution to a conflict involves someone giving in, different weights given to the child-related interests might prepare the parties for that step.

Step Five: Negotiation

Conflicts are resolved through negotiations. A different and more accurate way to describe the resolution of a conflict is that it is the *art of giving in.* Here are some keys to successful negotiating:

- Keep discussions on the level of *concrete issues.* Keep it clean, and if you slip, apologize and go on.

- If stuck, ask the other parent to *restate* his or her interests (e.g., "This is obviously more important to you than I thought, and I didn't really get why. Can you say why again?").

- Only work on *one conflict* at a time. Don't fall into the trap of reminding each other of all the times you gave in before. If this occurs, try to move past this distraction.

- Separate short-term consequences from *long-term* ones. If one parent's interests are short term and the other's are long term (e.g., one parent wants to take the children to see a dying grandparent, and the other person is worried about the effect of staying up so late on a school day), lean in the direction of the long-term goal.

Think in terms of *twos*. Children will have a better holiday if they have two relaxed Christmas celebrations on different days compared to their running back and forth on one Christmas. Children can have two birthdays too. In fact, this is the one benefit children report liking about divorce—they get two of everything. Two great birthdays are better than one rushed and tense birthday.

Use *trade-offs* rather than compromising whenever possible. Trade-offs allow both parents to get something important to them. Compromise usually means neither parent gets all of what they want. If something is important to you, try this: "What would it take for you to give me what I want on this?" There is usually an answer to this. At least it opens up more negotiating. Parents can start offers with, "I will give in to you on this conflict if . . ." and then list some conditions under which they will give in.

If really stuck, bring in a *third person*. A third person can sometimes be more objective about what is at stake for everyone and can offer creative ideas that the parents cannot think of because they are emotionally involved. If the issue concerns the residential placement schedule, a professional mediator can be very helpful. The mediator might have seen similar situations resolved in other families to everyone's satisfaction. Even if not a residential placement schedule issue, facilitative mediation can sometimes help, because mediators are trained in the art of trade-offs.

Take markers. If there seems to be no way through a particular conflict, one parent can give in and take a *marker* (e.g., "I'll give in this time, but only if you promise that the next time we have a conflict and we can't solve it, I can ask to call in my marker and you have to give in."). This is a form of trade-off.

Remember, conflicts are only resolved when one of the parties ultimately gives in. Ideally, your job is not to win all of the time. It is to either find a way to make it okay for the other person to give in, and to find a way for it to be okay for you to give in. Ideally, both parents will walk away from a conflict feeling good about the outcome. For example, if you really want the children on Christmas Day but the court order says it is the other parent's day with the children, you have to come up with an offer that makes the other parent feel like, even though he or she gave in, it was an *equal or better deal*.

Step Six: Recap

One or both parents need to recap, especially stating the final agreement. Again, it may be important in some situations to memorialize the final agreement in writing. It is also important when recapping in conflict resolutions to "equalize." By this, we mean that parents need to stop and think and make certain that *both are satisfied* with the outcome, at least enough to accept and commit to it.

The Six-Step Procedures previously described can be used to make financial decisions and solve financial problems when those are part of the post-divorce Financial Planning Game.

CHAPTER 8

Checklists

Game Theory Checklist:
Putting A New Way Of Thinking Into Practice

CHECKLIST SUMMARY

"… Game theory is not just another way to win…!
"… If you change the rules, you change the game…!

1. PRINCIPLES: Game Theory Bargaining Principles

a. **Parties to a divorce play multiple games.** Parties play two major games: the child game and the financial game. Within each of those games, they play the legal game and the planning game. Each of these games has subgames. The Game Theory principle causes you to think of divorce as a process, where the parties are playing a series of subgames.

b. **Game Theory bargaining is an inductive process.** Begin with the smallest games (simple and single) and build a solution to the major games. Balance simple single games that favor one party with other games that favor the other party. Consider having the parties rate the solution to each simple single game and share the ratings so each knows where he and she "stands" in the process.

c. **Reaching optimal solutions requires exploring the objective and subjective family life-goals of the parties for each game played**. Rather than start by playing the legal games (asking about desired outcomes), especially in the initial meeting with a party or even during the bargaining process, following the Game Theory principle, you inquire about their long-term life goals for themselves and for their children. If a party begins by stating a legal outcome (e.g., "I want 50/50" or "I have to end up with my pension intact" or "I don't want to divide a certain asset"), redirect to life goals by asking, "Why do you want that?" or "What are you trying to accomplish in the long run by getting that?" Reframe their answers into objective and subjective goals. For example, "I want to be an equal part of my children's lives" is translated into, "What I hear you saying is that you want to spend as much time with your children as you can, participate in their lives at school and in their activities, and know their friends so that when they grow up, you will have a strong relationship with them and will have been an important part of their lives." The client might then add to this. What you are doing is turning a legal position into multiple payoffs for future games.

d. **When a point of dispute arises, back step and explore the subjective family life-goals of the parties.** Find out what they are trying to accomplish with their positions. This will usually identify simple single games to be played.

e. **There are two axiomatic standards for agreements (the Marital Settlement Agreement):** (1) content standards, based on the objective and subjective family life-goals of the parties, and (2) process standards based on the 5-E's—educated, effective, equitable, equilibrant, and envy free. These standards should be agreed upon at the beginning of the bargaining process. By exploring the payoffs for each decision, when proposals are made or received, they can be measured against how well they accomplish the payoffs—meaning, whether they meet the axiomatic standards established at the outset of the case.

f. **On each issue, bargain through the three stages of bargaining in sequence:** cooperative bargaining, compromise bargaining, and win-win-plus bargaining. The cooperative bargaining phase focuses not only on the objective and subjective family life-goals of one's client, but also on those of the other party. If receiving a proposal for which the objective and subjective family life-goals and values of the party making the proposal are not clear, ask for them.

g. **Determine if the game is a normal form game, a repeated form game, or both.** If normal form, emphasize the content of the issue; if a repeated form game, emphasize the procedures needed; if both, focus on content but also introduce procedures for dealing with future decision nodes. If possible, establish axiomatic standards to apply to future nodes.

h. **Manage information, making it public, verifiable, perfect, and complete**.

2. SKILLS: Game Theory Bargaining Tools

a. **Focus on maintaining non-zero-sum games**. Do not turn non-zero-sum games into zero-sum games.

b. **Separate mixed games with multiple payoffs into simple games with one payoff or a closely related set of payoffs that cannot be separated.** Playing simple games accomplishes two tasks: the solutions are easier to find, and the solutions can be more creative and accomplish more of the parties' subjective family life-goals.

c. **Separate multiple games into single games.** Solve the multiple game by solving each of the single games.

d. **Use Bayes rule, by taking turns with proposals and identifying the objective and subjective family life- goals of the parties undergirding each proposal, to create a convergence of expectations and reach creative solutions**. Each proposal should include objective and subjective family life-goals. If a proposal received does not do this, before responding to it, ask what the other party is trying to accomplish with the proposal. Let this new information update beliefs and inform the cooperative bargaining phase.

e. **Resolve true conflicts by playing multiple games and creating trade-offs in order to facilitate reciprocity in the bargaining process**. An effective trade-off is when the party "giving in" gets something in return of equal or higher value.

f. **Use BATNA (best alternative to a negotiated agreement) to establish *status quo* positions.** By establishing an expected range of outcomes if litigated and by adding transaction costs, the parties establish the safety of a floor and ceiling, and create an incentive to try to improve the agreement through cooperative bargaining.

g. **Continue with cooperative bargaining on each issue until the agreement cannot be improved for one or both of the parties without reducing the payoff value to the other party**. Resist the temptation to leave the cooperative bargaining phase prematurely, merely because the parties reach an agreement.

h. **When there are planning games with future nodes, first develop axioms for future decisions and introduce procedures for those nodes.** (Refer to Chapter 7 regarding these procedures.) Emphasize the importance of establishing a positive tit-for-tat game at those future nodes. Consider asking the parties to assign ordinal values to those nodes, share them, and see where they "stand" in the game.

i. **When the agreement can no longer be improved but the game is not solved, shift to compromise bargaining.** Equitable agreements are best resolved by splitting the difference and/or offering trade-offs for "giving in." The parties should look for a trade-off that is of equal or better value than the issue "lost."

j. **When an issue appears to be a conflict, follow the recommended Conflict Resolution Steps.** (Refer to Chapter 7 regarding these Steps.) Most importantly, examine the conflict to see if it meets the axiomatic standards for a true conflict. Look for solutions that allow both parties to accomplish what is subjectively important to them, and narrow the conflict as much as possible to the incompatible issue.

k. **When the payoff structure is complete, and the Marital Settlement Agreement appears to be finished, explore the possibility of bringing in an expert to try to improve the value to one or both parties without reducing the value to the other.** This is the win-win-plus bargaining phase. Consider asking the parties to think about improving the agreement for at least one of them without diminishing the payoff value for the other. Bring in an accountant/financial planner (financial) or child specialist (parenting) to see if the solution can be improved.

l. **Before signing the Marital Settlement Agreement, assuming it meets the parties' content standards (i.e., their objective and subjective family life-goals), determine whether it meets their process standards (i.e., the 5-E's.)** If it does not, consider returning to the bargaining process. If you continue bargaining, keep the focus on the total package, not any individual part of the agreement. Only return to an individual part if bargaining can improve the payoff value for one party without reducing the payoff value to the other party. For example, if a parent says, "I just cannot go five days without seeing the children," suggest that the family start a new tradition-- that on the third day of the five, each of the parents has breakfast out with the children, unless the other parent is gone with the children (e.g., on a camping trip), etc. If a party says, "I just cannot afford to pay the monthly support," suggest that they increase the payment slightly but tax-effect it, so it is tax-deductible to the paying party, etc.

m. **Divorce is one mega-game, with four major subgames.** Within each major subgame, there are numerous simple and single games with different forms (normal form versus repeated form) and with different points of focus (content versus procedures). By understanding how to play the game, and how to modify it, attorneys and mediators can help parties plan their futures, increase the chances of resolving disputes should they have them, and prevent escalation of the divorce conflict.

n. **By redefining the rules and payoff structure, the professional can create a game in which the most rational strategy is cooperative behavior.** Most of these changes in the game can be accomplished in the context of existing laws and local rules in most jurisdictions. To transform the practice of family law, only one thing is needed: the professionals need to learn and apply the game theory bargaining skills discussed in this book.

Child Planning Game Checklist

1. Divorcing spouses play two parallel games simultaneously relative to the child-related aspects of their divorce—the Legal Game and the Child Planning Game.

2. There are major child-related tasks in the Legal Game: (1) custody/decision-making, (2) physical custody/residential placement schedule and (3) relocation of the children to another state.

3. The Legal Game is not the goal. It is the means by which parties try to accomplish long-term family life-goals.

4. In the Legal Game, attention is mainly on *content*. For custody/decision-making, physical custody and relocation issues, these issues involve playing only the legal game, because once the issue is resolved, the agreements become part of the final Marital Settlement Agreement and Judgment of Divorce, where the issue might be final. These are the Normal Form Games played as a goal-based planning process rather than a strictly competitive normal form game.

5. There are some child-related issues that may call for the divorcing spouses to play the Child Planning Game. These issues, while settled at the time of the divorce, involve repeated form games. In the Child Planning Game, attention is on *procedures,* such as conditions for modifications of the residential schedule, co-parenting issues (see Chapter 4), or meeting with experts.

6. It is important to remember that parties who have continuing repeated form games to play should begin to play the Child Planning Game at the time of separation. Developing cooperative bargaining habits early often has the positive effect of supporting a cooperative relationship with regard to the children later. While it is difficult to play the Child Planning Game well shortly after a separation, parties will be grateful down the road if and when they at least start the process.

7. Assume that the parties' child-related interests are more in concert than in dispute.

8. Recognize that the parties are playing multiple games in the divorce process and that the demands of each game might conflict. The legal game and the child planning game are two of the important games played, but individual legal and planning games might conflict.

9. A determination must be made in each game as to whether it is a normal form game (focusing on content), a repeated form game (focusing on procedures), or both (focusing first on content and next on procedures).

10. Manage information by making it public, verifiable, perfect, and complete. Managing the disclosure of information will optimize the likelihood of and quality of the settlement. Take advantage of Bayes rule by taking turns making proposals and include the subjective family life-goals of the parties in those proposals.

11. Spend time learning about the objective and subjective family life-goals of the parties for every major child-related issue. This might seem cumbersome (which is true), but doing so is at the heart of getting an optimal settlement and having the parties experience satisfaction with the process.

12. Set axiomatic standards for every agreement based on the objective and subjective family life-goals of the parties for that issue. Measure every agreement against those standards, and either revisit an item

if it does not or balance that issue with another issue. Measure the entire settlement against the Five E's: educated, equitable, effective, equilibrant, and envy free.

13. Identify the parties' shared interests and, on every issue, bargain through the three bargaining phases in sequence: cooperative bargaining, compromise bargaining, and win-win-plus bargaining.

14. During bargaining, separate multiple games into single games and mixed games into simple games. Play a subgame for each game and payoff.

15. Game Theory principles also apply to the extensive repeated form game of child planning that will last for the rest of the parents' lives.

16. When designing the settlement of the child-related issues, and in designing procedures for any repeated form games facing the parties, a final step is to measure the payoff packages against the Five E's axiomatic standards.

    a. Is the package educated, equitable, effective, equilibrant, and envy free?

    b. If the package does not meet these standards, it will (in most cases) be worth revisiting issues and bargaining again.

    c. Sometimes attorneys see a settlement as "fragile" and are frightened of the whole settlement coming apart if revisited. However, if the settlement is fragile, perhaps it should come apart.

    d. Only when both spouses can look at a settlement and agree that it meets the Five E's standards is it no longer fragile.

    e. The parties can then walk away from the settlement feeling the losses involved, but knowing that their payoff package is as good as could be accomplished within the limits of the fact situation.

17. **EXAMPLE:** Regarding the Residential Schedule:

    a. Break the residential schedule into simple and single games by playing separate games for each part of the game and by separating out the payoffs for each game into separate games.

    b. Analyze the positions of the parties by determining their objective and subjective family life-goals and payoffs for which they are playing the games- not only what each of them wants, but also why they want it or what they hope to accomplish in the long run for the children with those payoffs.

c.   Subjective payoffs are determined in two ways: First, by setting axioms, where the parties disclose their outcome goals. Second, when the parties run into a dispute, they shift (on their own or with the assistance of an attorney or mediator) to what they are trying to accomplish with their positions.

d.   By revealing the objective and subjective family life-goals of the parties, we create conditions of perfect, complete, public, and, to the degree possible, verifiable information, which facilitates best possible outcomes for both parties.

e.   This goal-based planning process accomplishes two important outcomes: First, it focuses the parties on the design of a residential schedule that works best for everyone involved, and it moves the entire process in the direction of win-win-win (a win for the mother, for the father and for the children). Second, it models and practices an axiomatic, procedurally based approach to decision-making in an extensive repeated form game format, which can be used in the future by the parties to adjust the residential schedule to fit the facts of the family and the needs of the children.

Financial Planning Game Checklist

1.   Divorcing spouses play two parallel games simultaneously relative to the financial aspects of their divorce—the Legal Game and the Financial Planning Game.

2.   There are three major financial tasks in the Legal Game: (1) property division; (2) allocation of debt and (3) establishment of support.

3.   The Legal Game is not the goal. It is the means by which parties try to accomplish long-term family life-goals.

4.   In the Legal Game, attention is mainly on *content*. Most of the financial issues involve playing only the legal game, because once the issue is resolved, the agreements become part of the final Marital Settlement Agreement and Judgment of Divorce, where the issue is final and generally not modifiable in the future. These

are the Normal Form Games played as a goal-based planning process rather than a strictly competitive normal form game.

5. There are some financial issues that may call for the divorcing spouses to play the Financial Planning Game. These issues, while settled at the time of the divorce, involve repeated form games. In the Financial Planning Game, attention is on *procedures,* such as conditions for modifications, exchanges of tax returns, or meeting with experts.

6. The Financial Planning Game primarily applies to support determinations- child support, maintenance, Section 71 payments, possible long-term property settlement and the like.

7. It is important to remember that parties who have continuing repeated form games to play should begin to play the Financial Planning Game at the time of separation. Often, people with repeated form games have children involved, and developing cooperative bargaining habits with regard to money often has the positive effect of supporting a cooperative relationship with regard to the children.

8. Assume that the parties' financial interests are more in concert than in dispute. They might have similar long-term family life-goals for themselves and for each other.

9. Recognize that the parties are playing multiple games in the divorce process and that the demands of each game might conflict. The legal game and the financial planning game are two of the important games played, but individual financial games might conflict. For example, owning real estate might conflict with retirement security. Thus, optimal solutions to one game might adversely affect the solution to a different game.

10. A determination must be made in each game as to whether it is a normal form game (focusing on content), a repeated form game (focusing on procedures), or both (focusing first on content and next on procedures).

11. Manage information by making it public, verifiable, perfect, and complete. Managing the disclosure of information will optimize the likelihood of and quality of the settlement. Take advantage of Bayes rule by taking turns making proposals and include the subjective family life-goals of the parties in those proposals.

12. Spend time learning about the objective and subjective family

life-goals of the parties for every major financial issue. This might seem cumbersome (which is true), but doing so is at the heart of getting an optimal settlement and having the parties experience satisfaction with the process.

13. Set axiomatic standards for every agreement based on the objective and subjective family life-goals of the parties for that issue. Measure every agreement against those standards, and either revisit an item if it does not or balance that issue with another issue. Measure the entire settlement of all of the financial issues, including the payoff structure, against the Five E's: educated, equitable, effective, equilibrant, and envy free.

14. Identify the parties' shared interests and, on every issue, bargain through the three bargaining phases in sequence: cooperative bargaining, compromise bargaining, and win-win-plus bargaining.

15. During bargaining, separate multiple games into single games and mixed games into simple games. Play a subgame for each game and payoff.

16. Game Theory principles also apply to the extensive repeated form game of financial planning that will last for the rest of the parties' lives.

17. When designing the settlement of the financial issues, and in designing procedures for any repeated form games facing the parties, a final step is to measure the payoff packages against the Five E's axiomatic standards.

    a. Is the package educated, equitable, effective, equilibrant, and envy free?

    b. If the package does not meet these standards, it will (in most cases) be worth revisiting issues and bargaining again.

    c. Sometimes attorneys see a settlement as "fragile" and are frightened of the whole settlement coming apart if revisited. However, if the settlement is fragile, perhaps it should come apart.

    d. Only when both spouses can look at a settlement and agree that it meets the Five E's standards is it no longer fragile.

    e. The parties can then walk away from the settlement feeling the losses involved, but knowing that their payoff package is as good as could be accomplished within the limits of the fact situation.

18. **EXAMPLE:** Regarding the Support Proposal:

    a. Break the support alternatives into simple and single games by playing separate games for each part of the game and by separating out the payoffs for each game into separate games.

    b. Analyze the positions of the parties by determining their objective and subjective goals and payoffs for which they are playing the games- not only what each of them wants, but also why they want it or what they hope to accomplish with those payoffs.

    c. Subjective payoffs are determined in two ways: First, by setting axioms, where the parties disclose their outcome goals. Second, when the parties run into a dispute, they shift (on their own or with the assistance of an attorney or mediator) to what they are trying to accomplish with their positions.

    d. By revealing the objective and subjective goals of the parties, we create conditions of perfect, complete, public, and, to the degree possible, verifiable information, which facilitates best possible outcomes for both parties.

    e. This goal-based planning process accomplishes two important outcomes: First, it focuses the parties on the design of a support proposal that works best for everyone involved, and it moves the entire process in the direction of win-win-win (a win for the wife, for the husband and for the children). Second, it models and practices an axiomatic, procedurally based approach to decision-making in an extensive repeated form game format, which can be used in the future by the parties to adjust the residential schedule to fit the facts of the family and the needs of the children.

Glossary of Game Theory Terms

Axiom – standards, agreed upon before bargaining, by which outcomes are measured. Those can be content standards, which are the family life-goals and values of the players; or, they can be process standards, such as the Five E's.

Bayes rule – the concept that people change their expectations and beliefs with new information. In bargaining, as players receive new information about the other player's type and goals, beliefs about the objective and subjective family life-goals of the other player are updated and there is a convergence of expectations on solutions.

Boulwareism bargaining – making a fair and reasonable but final offer.

Chicken – two cars are driven directly at one another and the driver who pulls out first loses. In bargaining, the players play chicken when they hold to their positions to the "courthouse steps" and one of the players gives in.

Compatibility of interests – when the preferred outcomes of both parties are the same or compatible.

Compromise bargaining – bargaining when the gains of one or both of the players are at the expense of one or both of the players. In game theory, this is called non-cooperative bargaining but because this has pejorative implications, we have renamed this compromise bargaining.

Cooperative bargaining – bargaining when the gains of one or both of the players do not diminish the value of the payoffs to the other player.

Deductive bargaining – starting with a position and making arguments to support that position.

Dominant strategy – the strategy is strictly dominant when the player will win, independent of the choices of the other player; the strategy is weakly dominant when the player will likely win but is somewhat dependent on chance or the choices of the other player.

Dominated strategy – the strategy is strictly dominated when the player will lose, independent of the choices of the other player; the strategy is weakly dominant when the player will likely lose but is somewhat dependent on chance of the choices of the other player.

Extensive repeated form game – a game is played more than one time with no predetermined end point. Because an extensive repeated form game anticipates future choices and game nodes, the focus is on deciding on axioms and procedures for those future nodes.

Five E's – axiomatic process standards by which to judge a payoff or payoff structure. The axioms are that the outcome of the game is: Educated; Effective; Equitable; Equilibrant; and Envy free.

Game – the strategic interaction between two or more people (players) with rules and choices available to the players that affect the outcome (payoffs) for each of them.

Game node – in a repeated form and an extensive repeated form game, a point at which players play a sub-game and one or both of the players receive a payoff.

Inductive bargaining – bargaining from the goals of the players and building a payoff structure absent initial positions.

Information management – qualities of the information in the bargaining process. The four qualities are: public – known to all of the players; verifiable – either by proof or by reputation; complete – players know the complete history of the game; and perfect – players know all of the rules and the potential payoffs.

Legal game – the legal tasks that must be accomplished.

Mixed game – one game is played for multiple payoffs.

Multiple game – more than one game is played as though it is a single game.

Nash equilibrium – John Nash's solution concept. The solution to a game will be a combination of enhancing the payoffs for both players (cooperative) and compromising on payoffs that remain unsolved after the cooperative phase is complete.

Node – See Game node.

Non-zero-sum game – the gains in payoffs of one or both of the players are additive and do not lower the payoffs to the other player.

Normal form game – a game played one time for one set of payoffs and is then complete. Because the game is played only one time, the focus is on the facts (content) at the time of the game.

Optimal solutions – payoffs are efficient/equilibrant. The payoffs cannot be improved for either player without reducing the value of the payoff for the other player.

Optimism model – the irrational belief in a positive outcome when the outcome is ambiguous.

Payoff – the perceived value of an outcome by a player. The value might be objective, such as a dollar amount, or subjective, such as status.

Payoff structure – the group of payoffs received by both players when multiple and mixed games are played and resolved. In divorce, the MSA is a document listing the payoff structure for both players in the divorce.

Planning game – the extensive form game in which future choices and nodes are anticipated. In divorce, there is the child planning game, the future co-parenting relationship, and in some cases a financial planning game, when future decisions are to be made about the financial relationship.

Psychological importance of prevailing – in conflict, players have an inherent desire to prevail. The desire to prevail can make the player irrational and make choices or engage in strategies that are self-defeating.

Rational player – players are rational when they make choices that are in their self-interest. Because choices reflect both objective and subjective values and goals, the definition is probabilistic, that is, the players are rational in that on average they will make choices in their self-interest.

Repeated form game – a game that is repeated in nodes to a predetermined end point.

Reputation – what other players believe about the type of one player. In bargaining, when information is unverifiable, it can be verified if the person asserting the information has a reputation of being honest.

Simple game – a game being played for one payoff or a closely related set of payoffs that cannot be separated.

Single game – a game that cannot be separated into subgames.

Solution concept – the choices or strategies that are likely to be employed by players once the rules, payoffs and choices available are known.

Zero-sum game – the payoffs are limited and any gain by one player is at the loss of the other player.

Word Index

Access to Activities Outside of the Homes 167
Alternatives to the Traditional Divorce Model 119
Auction Example 2
Auctions 44
Axiomatic Standards 74
Axioms 53, 98, 147
BATNA 267, 299
Bargaining Basics 182, 232
Bargaining: Three Phases 266
Bargaining to Optimal Solutions 184, 193, 255
Battle of the Sexes Game Example 33
Bayes, Thomas 45
Bayes Rule 45, 60, 95, 189, 299, 309
Brain Stem Thinking 226
Checklist–Game Theory: Putting A New Way
    Of Thinking Into Practice 297
Child-Initiated Off-Schedule Access 165, 166
Child Game 65, 173, 255
Child Planning Game Checklist 301
Child Planning Game (Co-parenting Tasks) 148
Child Planning Tasks 148
Co-parenting 65, 81, 121, 211
Coin Flip Game Example 61
Communication 14, 123, 150, 163, 271
Complete Information 37, 96
Compromise Bargaining 46, 53, 55, 266
Conflicts 271, 290
Cooperative Bargaining 46, 53, 226, 266, 309
Content Standards 255, 298, 309
Convergence of Expectations 46, 61, 189

Cooperative Bargaining 46, 53, 225,255, 266, 309
Cooperative Parties 211
Coordinate Parenting.. 149, 170
Custody... 38, 64,121, 127
Decision- Making Phases 199
Decisions and Strategies... 23, 28
Discovery and Disclosure 181
Dividing Cash and Auction Bidding Example 33
Divorce Case Study Using Game Theory Principles................... 112
Divorce Lawyers Have a Reputation Problem 15
Dominant and Dominated Strategies 247
Enhanced Settlement Solutions... 242
Examples: Playing Normal Form Games 66, 194, 209
Expanding the Pie 184
Extended Family Access 166
Extensive Form Game...................................... 37, 109, 303, 310
Extensive Repeated Form Game.................................. 310
Family Law Attorney Challenge 21
Family Law System- Undergirding Principles 28
Family Life-goals.. 297, 309
Five- E's.. 100
Financial Games 176, 271
Financial Planning Game Checklist................................... 304
Financial Planning Games.. 208
Game Changer 71
Game Definition.. 27
Game Theory 146 Percent Pot... 42
Game Theory Bargaining 91,140, 175, 297
Game Theory Chance 37
Game Theory Preferences.. 221
Game Theory Principles 27
Glossary of Game Theory Terms 309
Goal-Based Planning 125, 147
Goals and Priorities.. 260
High-Conflict Families 60
Holiday Schedule Game 138
Incomplete Information.. 32, 95
Imperfect Information 90, 96, 238
Information Management 30, 91, 183, 237, 310

Joint Decision List 150

Joint Decision-Making 271

Joint Decision-Making Tasks 271

Law of Unintended Consequences 3

Legal Custody/Major Decisions 128

Legal Games 232

Legal Game: Custody/Decision Making and
    Residential Placement Schedule 127

Making Decisions 81, 154

Major Concern 158, 283

Major Decisions 123, 128, 134

Managing Information 91

Minor Concern 158, 161, 283, 288

Mixed Games 39, 48, 90, 186

Multiple Games 38, 65, 83, 187, 215, 255, 297

Multiple Players 215

Narcissism versus Altruism 228

Nash, John 22, 45, 180, 310

Nash Equilibrium 55, 180, 263, 267, 310

Nodes 37, 217

Non-Cooperative Parties 211

Non-Verifiable Information 91, 94, 238

Non-Zero-Sum Games 51, 74, 117, 245

Normal Form Games 66, 79, 116, 194

Objective Payoffs 33, 256

Objective and Subjective Goals 36, 191, 260

Optimism Model 254, 311

Parent Mistakes 274

Parent-Child Access Arrangements 148, 164

Parent-Initiated Off-Schedule Access 166

Parenting Concerns 158, 271, 283, 288

Perfect Information 37, 96, 238

Players Definition 27

Payoffs 10, 23, 27, 32, 260, 310

Payoffs Definition 27

Perfect Information 36, 96

Players 27, 29

Players Definition 27

Prisoner's Dilemma Example 1

Private Information.. 91, 237
Procedure-Based Planning.................................... 211
Procedure Standards 158
Process Axioms 192
Public Information 91
Remaining Dispute Game...................................... 145
Repeated Form Games.. 38, 66
Residential Placement Schedules 114, 121, 135, 137
Rules 27, 31
Rules Definition 31, 63
Rules of Conduct.. 149
School Days Off Game 144
School Year Weekend Game................................... 143
Separating the Games 56
Shapley, Lloyd 45
Sharing Information 150, 271
Similarizing Homes 131, 132
Simple Games... 47, 59, 186, 256
Single Games... 38, 83, 187
Six-Step Procedure: Joint Decision-Making............. 275
Six-Step Procedure: Solving Major Parenting Concerns 284
Six-Step Procedure: Solving Minor Parenting Concerns............. 288
Six-Step Procedure: Solving Parenting Conflicts 290
Six-Step Procedure: Solving Parenting Problems......................... 279
Solving Major Parenting Concerns... 283
Solving Minor Parenting Concerns 288
Solving Parenting Conflicts.. 278
Solving Problems 154, 271, 278
Split the Dollar Game Example................................ 54
Standards for Settlement... 191
Subgames 65, 217, 297
Subjective Payoffs 10, 33, 39, 244
Subjective Values 40
Summer Schedule Game... 142
Taking Action... 153
Taking Turns 80
Telephone Access 165
Transition Management.. 169
Traditional Divorce.. 107, 177